Unforgettable

The Biography of Capt. Thomas J. Flynn

**World War II Veteran
28th Infantry Division, 110th Infantry Regiment, K Company**

By Alice M. Flynn

Cover photo taken by Ed Esbeck:
1st Lt. Thomas Flynn with Biff on September 6, 1944,
the day he left for combat duty in Europe.

www.UnforgettableVeteran.com

ISBN: 1452814961
ISBN-13: 9781452814964

Dedication

I dedicate this book in loving memory to my father, Thomas Joseph Flynn; my dad, my hero, and my best friend. He truly is unforgettable to me and those who knew and loved him.

Table of Contents

PART II

ADDITIONAL MATERIALS

Acknowledgments

Two key sources for Part I of this book, which covers the years from 1920 to 1950, are interviews and recollections of Amelia Flynn Graue (Tom Flynn's youngest sister) and Anna Bennedsen Flynn (Tom Flynn's wife of 51 years).

In addition, two in-depth interviews with 1st Lt. Thomas J. Flynn that were conducted on May 1 and 2, 1945, by Army Field Historian Capt. William Dunkerly at the Moosburg, Germany, prisoner of war (POW) camp where Tom was held, formed the basis for chapters 4, 5, and 6. The Allied Forces liberated the camp on April 29, 1945. These interviews are part of the National Archives WWII Records Group 407. Tom Flynn also wrote fourteen pages of additional details on his combat and POW experience on an application for VA medical benefits in 1983.

An additional source for this book was an interview with Col. George H. Rumbaugh, Tom's 3rd Battalion commanding officer during the Battle of Hürtgen Forest. Capt. John S. Howe, Army historian with Corp V, conducted the interview Dec. 15-16, 1944. This interview was obtained through the National Archives in College Park, MD, and is archived in WWII Records Group 407.

Last but not least, through the Freedom of Information Act, I obtained a copy of Tom Flynn's military file through two additional sources, the Regional Veteran's Administration Office in Portland, Oregon, and the National Personnel Center in St. Louis, Missouri. These files provide specific details of Tom's military service record, in addition to all personal correspondence with the Veteran's Administration.

I have tried to confirm all the facts provided by each source. Where there were contradictions in dates or details, I have used what I believed to be the best-documented, most accurate historical information. Some of the story details provided by Tom Flynn were inconsistent between his original interviews in 1945 and his VA medical benefits application in 1983. I chose to use the original interviews as the foundation for this book because I believe it to be the most accurate version, while supplementing the story with some details from the application written almost forty years later.

Two other veterans of the 28th Division, 110th Infantry Regiment deserve special mention, not only for their dedicated service to our country during WWII but for their willingness to help our family understand what Tom Flynn's experience was from November 1944 through the end of WWII: Private Robert Phillips (medic for the 110th), historian, and author of *To Save Bastogne*; and Joe Reed, who was technical sergeant with K Company of the 110th and under Lt. Tom Flynn's command for a brief period during the Battle of the Hürtgen Forest, before being wounded.

Stories and remembrances for Part II, covering Tom's life after WWII, are provided primarily by Anna Bennedsen Flynn and her eight children; the Kimballton, Iowa, Centennial Book 1882-1982; and Tom's friends, who provided heartwarming stories of the Tom Flynn they knew, loved, and respected from June 1950 until his death on November 19, 1993.

Typical Unit Structure in the World War II US Army[1]

(This page may be helpful for reference when reading chapters 4 & 5.)

These are approximations, as strength levels, attached units, and command structure often varied.

Army Group: Between 250,000 and 600,000 soldiers; commanded by a four-star general

Army: Between 60,000 and 120,000 soldiers; commanded by a lieutenant (three-star) general

Corps: Between 30,000 and 60,000 soldiers; commanded by a senior-level major general

Division: 14,000 soldiers, commanded by a major (two-star) general; two or more divisions per corps

Regiment: 3,500 soldiers, commanded by a colonel; three regiments per division

Battalion: 900 soldiers, commanded by a major or a lieutenant colonel, three battalions per regiment

Company: 190 soldiers, commanded by a 1st lieutenant or a captain; four companies per battalion

Platoon: Forty soldiers, commanded by a 2nd lieutenant; four platoons per company

Squad: Twelve soldiers, commanded by a buck sergeant; three squads per platoon

---

1 John C. McManus, Alamo in the Ardennes: The Untold Story of the American Soldiers Who Made the Defense of Bastogne Possible (New York: NAL Caliber, 2008), p xx.

Executive Officer 1st Lt. Thomas J. Flynn's Chain of Command
European Theater Campaign

Twelfth Army Group: Commanded by General Omar Bradley

1st Army: Commanded by Lt. Gen. Courtney Hodges
V Corps during the Battle of Hürtgen Forest
Commanded by Maj. Gen. L. T. Gerow
Composed of the 8th, **28th** and 112th **Infantry Divisions**

VIII Corps during the Battle of the Bulge
Commanded by Maj. Gen. Troy Middleton
Composed of the **28th**, 109th, and 112th **Infantry Divisions**

- **28th Infantry Division**
- Commanded by Maj. Gen. Norman D. Cota; Gen. George A. Davis, assistant commander
- Composed of the 109th, **110th**, and 112th **Infantry Regiments**
- 107th, 108th, 109th, and 229th Field Artillery Battalions
- 103rd Engineer Battalion (road and bridge maintenance, set and clear mine fields, etcetera)
- 707th Tank Battalion
- 630th Tank Destroyer Battalion
- 447th Anti-Aircraft Artillery Battalion

  - **110th Infantry Regiment**
  - Commanded by Col. Theodore Seely (during the Battle of Hürtgen Forest, wounded Nov. 24, 1944) and then Col. Hurley Fuller, Nov. 24-Dec. 18, 1944 (Battle of the Bulge)
  - Composed of the 1st, 2nd and **3rd Battalions**

- **3ʳᵈ Battalion**
- Commanded by Col. William S. Tait (Nov. 2-7, 1944) and Lt. Col. George "Howdy" Rumbaugh (Nov. 7-16, 1944) in Hürtgen Forest and then Lt. Col. Harold F. Milton, Nov. 16-Dec. 18, 1944 (Battle of the Bulge)
- Composed of the I, L, **K,** and M **companies**

  - **K Company**
  - Commanded by Executive Officer **1ˢᵗ Lt. Thomas J. Flynn** during the Battle of Hürtgen Forest (Nov. 8, 1944-Dec. 5, 1944), at which time Capt. Frederick Feiker returned to duty after having been wounded in an earlier battle. Capt. Feiker assumed command of the unit from Dec. 5-18, 1944, and 1ˢᵗ Lt. Flynn reverted to second in command of K Company.

CHAPTER 1

1920-1940: Growing up on East End Avenue

Thomas Joseph Flynn was born August 21, 1920, the fourth child of Richard E. (age twenty-eight) and Josephine Engfer Flynn (age thirty). The 1920 U.S. Census records show Richard and Josephine Flynn and their three children, William (four), Richard (three) and Agnes (one), lived at 307 West 147th Street, New York, at the time the census was taken. By August, when their fourth child was due to be born, they had moved their growing family to the Upper East Side of Manhattan to an area called "Yorkville." Their new apartment at 64 East End Avenue in Manhattan had five rooms, one bathroom with no sink, and coin-operated gas lighting.

The buildings on their even-numbered side of the street had no street-level shops, only residential apartments. Across the street, the buildings mainly consisted of five stories of apartments above the ground-floor retail stores. There were only two apartments on each floor in Richard and Josephine's building, one on each side of the central stairwell and running the length of the building. These "railroad" type apartments were designed so one had to walk through every room to get from the front to the back of the apartment, just like walking through the cars on a train. During the 1920s and '30s, the building across the street from the Flynn apartment had a grocery store, a butcher shop, a drug store, and an antique shop, which worked out well for the growing family.

Josephine didn't work outside the home after the children were born but she had her work cut out for her with no washing machine, clothes dryer, or electric iron. She heated a heavy iron on the stove to iron their clothes, making sure she kept all the children clean and neat, especially for school. Josephine was a loving mother and a devout Catholic, having converted to Catholicism when she married. The Flynn family attended mass at the Church of Saint Monica at 413 E. 79th Street every Sunday and on holy days.

Photo: Josephine Engfer Flynn

Tom's father, Richard, was a delivery truck driver in New York's garment district and worked long hours to support his family. Richard was a likeable man and loved to go fishing. Sometimes he would even join his boss on fishing trips. However, like many Irish men, Richard drank frequently and often had a bad temper when he came home. Tom learned very early in life to stay out of his father's way when his temper flared. Tom's younger brothers and sisters looked up to Tom as they grew up, and he looked out for and protected them.

Photo: Richard E. Flynn

By 1927, Tom had three younger brothers, Chuck (five), Joe (two) and newborn Eddie, as well as a sister, Amelia (four). All ten of them now shared the same five-room apartment and sleeping quarters were cramped. With only one bathroom that contained no sink, getting ready for school was definitely a challenge. The gas heat in each apartment in the building was regulated by a coin-operated system and it would get very cold in the winter if one ran out of change. Sometimes it would get cold enough in the outer rooms that the family could see their breath when they talked. On those days, changing their clothes for bed was done as fast as possible and then they would leap into bed and huddle together to get warm.

Photos: (l-r) Tom's first communion; Tom at approximately age ten

Tom's younger sister, Mel, reflected that Manhattan was a great place to live when they were growing up. Yorkville was like a little town within the city. Picturesque East End Avenue was only ten blocks long and the neighborhood streets were made of cobblestone. The family never felt hemmed in, as the view of the East River from their apartment and the street was spacious and wide. They were also just two blocks from Carl Schurz Park, which ran for five blocks along the East River, ending at the official home of New York's mayor. Gracie Mansion was already a historic landmark at the time, having been rebuilt in 1799 after the British destroyed it in September 1776, during the Revolutionary War.

While Yorkville in this period was typically considered a middle- to working-class neighborhood, it was also home to many affluent and famous people. Within just a few blocks on either side of the Flynn apartment lived movie stars, theater stars, and opera stars, including Helen Hayes, Joan Crawford, James Cagney, Lawrence Tibbett, James Melton, and, later, Don Ameche and Arthur Godfrey, to name a few. Nobody in the neighborhood bothered the rich and famous as they walked by. Around the corner from their apartment was also Brearley School, an exclusive girl's school attended by many girls of New York's high society, including Gloria Vanderbilt and Dianna Barrymore. Everyone in the neighborhood felt safe in the area and thought nothing of walking around late at night.

Even though the Flynn family was surrounded by rich and famous people, they never thought of themselves as poor. They never went hungry, unlike many families during the Depression, and their parents always managed to provide what they needed. East End Avenue was the Flynn children's playground for skating, playing kickball, sleigh riding, and enjoying games of all sorts. The East River was wonderful in the summer when it was hot and it was where all the kids in the neighborhood learned to swim. Typically, the children would stay outside playing until nine or ten o'clock at night, only returning to the apartment to eat. The Flynn children were always very busy. Despite the fact that they each had their own friends, they spent a great deal of the time together. Their mother, Josephine, was always glad to get them out of the house when the weather was nice, as being cooped up in a five-room apartment with eight active children nearly drove her crazy some days. If a passing rainstorm wasn't too bad, she would often let them go outside and they would play cards or jacks in the street doorways to stay dry.

During the early 1930s, construction of the 9.5-mile long Franklin D. Roosevelt East River Drive began along the East River, including a promenade near the park. The Flynn children watched the construction with amazement and wonder, and being typical silly kids, they thought it was great fun to throw candy down the manhole where the workers were drilling. Later, when the work was completed, they would sit for hours on the promenade by the East River and read or watch the boats sail by. They also loved it when the cobblestones of East End Avenue were paved over, as the paving made a much better surface for skating and playing kickball.

Tom's paternal grandmother, Mary French Flynn, was widowed early in life and was able to spend a great deal of time with the grandchildren, helping Josephine care for them. Her Irish family had already lived in the country for two generations and her father had been a drummer for the Union Army during the Civil War. Grandmother Mary had a great sense of humor and the family loved her dearly. Tom and his siblings had a lot of fun when she was with them and they would entertain her for hours. A favorite pastime was playing the *Carmen* recording on the record player with one of them acting as the bullfighter, causing Grandmother Mary to laugh hysterically.

Looking back, Tom's sister reflected that they had a great family and a lot of fun together. Sunday afternoons after dinner were particularly special for all of them, as the family would sit around the table singing in harmony, with their mother Josephine, a great alto, holding them all together.

Photo: Josephine Engfer Flynn and Mary French Flynn

Fortunately, both Richard and Josephine had learned to read and write and they agreed that education was very important for their children. With their parents' influence, all the Flynn children learned to love reading and they took full advantage of the fact that they had three New York City public libraries nearby. The libraries served as a great source of pleasure and entertainment for all of them and the children spent many hours there. Tom developed speed-reading skills at a young age, often reading an entire book at the library before going home after school.

Tom grew from a cute little boy to a very handsome young man. By the time he was in high school, he stood 5' 10" tall and had a slim, muscular build; wavy, light-brown hair; amazing sky-blue eyes; and a thin upper lip.

Mel remembers the young girls in the neighborhood turning their heads to watch Tom walk down the street. She loved to go on walks with her big brother and found it very entertaining that she would be the subject of their gossip. She could often hear the other girls whisper to each other, "Who's THAT with Tommy?" Mel also remembers that even when Tom would walk into her sewing classroom to see her during the school day, all activity would stop so her high school sewing teacher could talk to him. Her teacher even gave Tom a sheepskin coat one year as a Christmas gift, a gesture that would seem inappropriate to many people nowadays.

Needless to say, Tom was always a favorite with the ladies. Although he dated frequently, he never had a serious relationship with anyone until later on, after he left home.

The Flynn family lived within walking distance of the Museum of Natural History, where Tom spent many hours exploring the exhibits. Both the Museum of Art and Central Park were also just a short walk away, and the family never missed one of the grand New York City parades. There were eight different movie houses close by and they all loved to go to the movies when they could spare the nickel admission charge. On summer weekends, there was often a band playing in the bandstand in Carl Schurz Park. All the families in the neighborhood would attend the concerts, while the children ran around playing with their friends. Everyone had fun. One summer, Tom attended a nature camp outside the city—perhaps an early indication of his interest in animals and the great outdoors.

Photo: Tom Flynn's high school graduation photo, 1937

One of Tom's favorite activities was listening to and/or watching the Yankee's play baseball. Yankee Stadium, also known as "the House that Ruth Built," was just five miles from the Flynn apartment and with a steady stream of championship teams and exceptional ball players (Babe Ruth, Lou Gehrig, Joe DiMaggio, Phil Rizzuto, Yogi Berra, Mickey Mantle, and Roger Maris, to name just a few), Tom always felt he had plenty to brag about. Tom would go to their games as often as he could and during his lifetime, the Yankees would play in thirty-one World Series contests, winning twenty-two championships.

Many immigrant families lived in Yorkville—Irish, German, Austrian, Czechoslovakian, and Hungarian—with German families dominating the area between East 84th and East 90th Streets. East 86th Street was nicknamed "German Boulevard" and the area was called "Little Germany," as the street was filled with German *brauhauses* and other German-owned businesses. Josephine's parents had been among the many German and Austrians immigrating to the United States in the late 1800s in search of a better life, although her family did not live in this part of New York.

During the 1930s, Little Germany became the home base of the most notorious pro-Nazi group in America, which resulted in many violent street battles between pro- and anti-Nazi Germans and German-Americans. The leader of the group, Fritz Kuhn, was considered the country's leading Nazi sympathizer at the time and while his group proclaimed its anti-Semitic philosophy, it failed to attract much support, even within the German-American community where he lived. These Pro-Nazi supporters proudly held parades on East End Avenue, marching down the street in the signature Nazi goose-step style while chanting "Sieg Heil." The Flynn family witnessed many pro-Nazi events during this period, when these parades passed right by their apartment.

As Tom became a teenager, he was already developing traits that would define him for the rest of his life. Tom's youngest brother, Eddie, recalled one story that epitomizes Tom's love and care for his family. Being the youngest of eight, Eddie typically got only hand-me-downs for clothes. When he was five or six years old, he remembered sitting on the curb outside their building playing in the dirt, his sneakers old and torn. As he played, Eddie looked up and saw his big brother Tom walking toward him. Tom bent down to talk to him and then took him by the hand. Together they walked to the shoe store, where Tom bought him a brand new pair of sneakers. They were the first new thing that Eddie could remember ever being given. Eddie treasured that moment of kindness, generosity, and brotherly love, enough so that he shared it with his wife, Mary, many years later. Tom would have been a young teenager at that point, with Eddie just seven years younger.

Tom excelled in school and high test scores enabled him to skip the equivalent of two grades prior to completing high school. He was extremely intelligent and won many academic awards as well as scoring 140 on an IQ test. His exceptional test scores qualified him to attend a special academic high school in New York. Unfortunately, Tom would have had a lengthy commute each day, so the family decided it would be best for him to attend the local public high school, instead. Tom took advantage of the foreign language classes offered in school and became fluent in German, having already learned some Latin as part of his catechism classes at church. At some point, Tom also learned French, although it is not clear whether he took classes in high school or just picked it up while in the Army in Europe several years later.

Tom graduated from Benjamin Franklin High School on June 25, 1937, at the age of sixteen, having completed high school in just three years. Tom was recognized for academic excellence (one of the top nineteen of 234 graduating seniors) and even though he was the fourth oldest in the family, he was the first to earn a high school diploma. By the time Tom graduated, his three older brothers and sisters had moved out of the apartment and all were married.

At the time of Tom's graduation, however, the country was in the middle of the Great Depression. The poverty and unemployment levels remained extremely high in the late 1930s and breadlines were very long. It seems likely that these economic factors, along with his personal exposure to local pro-Nazi, German-American demonstrations, contributed significantly to Tom's decision to lie about his age and join the New York National Guard on October 21, 1937—just two months after he turned seventeen. Tom became a corporal with Company L, 165th Infantry (Rifle), New York National Guard, and was required to participate in regular training at Camp Dixon, New Jersey.

At some point during the late 1930s, the family moved to an apartment across the street, at 69 East End Avenue, which had electricity; they were all excited about this great improvement in their lives.

Tom continued to live at home after high school, landing a job at a nearby bank during the day. He became interested in the wide variety of stamps that he saw on the incoming mail and started a stamp collection. At night, he took classes at the College of the City of New York, eventually completing half a year of business administration courses. Tom also worked during the holiday season wrapping presents at Macy's.

In 1938, Tom decided to take a break from school after being hired on full time at the *New York Post*, which is still located at 75 West Street in New York, where Tom worked. He spent a year as a stock clerk earning $19 a week and a year as a cost accounting clerk for $21 a week. Tom was well liked by the staff at the *Post*, and the secretaries in each department saved all the foreign stamps from the incoming mail to add to his stamp collection.

Another special story Tom's sister, Mel, remembers from this time took place one day while she and her brothers were in the park playing. From out of nowhere, a cute little puppy with long white hair came running up to them, wagging his tail with much enthusiasm, wanting to play. They instantly fell in love with the puppy and were having a great deal of fun playing with him when they noticed he had no dog collar. Together they debated taking him home but decided there was no way their mom would consent to keeping him. Reluctantly, they let the puppy go on his way, hoping he would be okay and that his owner would find him. When the children returned home, though, there was the puppy! It was a miracle. Tom had also seen the cute little puppy wandering the neighborhood on its own and had brought him home. Now that he had a job and could pay for what the puppy needed, he knew that his mom would let him keep him. They named him Scrappy and he made himself right at home. Scrappy was a very special part of the family for the next thirteen years.

The Developing War Overseas

During the late 1930s, while the United States was in the midst of what later became known as the Great Depression, Adolf Hitler had begun to exert power over Europe. On March 13, 1938, Great Britain and France allowed Hitler to take control of Austria. In September of that year, Hitler gained control of a portion of Czechoslovakia at the Munich Conference, taking the rest of the country by force within six months. Neither Britain nor France immediately grasped Hitler's goal of dominating the continent, and later regretted the foothold they had conceded simply to avoid a repeat of the devastation suffered during World War I, less than twenty years earlier.

On September 1, 1939, when Germany attacked Poland, the other European countries finally had to act. Both Great Britain and France demanded that Hitler withdraw German forces from Poland. Hitler ignored their demands and instead sent his troops deeper into Poland. Feeling there was no alternative, Great Britain and France declared war on Germany on September 3, 1939. Hitler's reign of terror had begun. His troops began to round up, arrest, detain, and execute perceived enemies, including political activists, former officers, actors, and the intelligentsia.

On Germany's eastern front, Hitler planned to overtake the Soviet Union. He viewed it as militarily weak and an easy conquest, eventually making the decision to invade in the spring of 1940. In addition, he planned to wipe out the large Jewish population of Eastern Europe as part of the Holocaust and the area became the site of many of the extermination camps, death marches, and ghettos.

On March 18, 1940, Benito Mussolini aligned himself with Hitler, and Italy joined the war with Germany.

In April 1940, Hitler began to aggressively move west, where his forces easily took control of Finland, Norway, and Denmark. Sweden maintained a policy of neutrality, yet would supply Hitler's forces with most of the iron ore used in manufacturing during the war, as well as with strategic military bases. In May 1940, the

Netherlands, Belgium, and Luxembourg also fell under German rule, leaving Hitler free to begin an assault on France along the border with Germany.

In June 1940, Mussolini's Fascist Italy formally declared war on both Great Britain and France, and the premiere of France broadcast an appeal for American intervention. France soon fell under German rule, and Germany quickly began its assault on Great Britain while Mussolini continued his assault on Northern Africa.

Facing strong pressure from western European countries to join the war, US President Franklin D. Roosevelt signed the Selective Service Bill on September 16, 1940, which began America's first peacetime draft. By October 16, 1940, 16 million men had already registered for the draft and Tom's New York National Guard unit (also known as "The Fighting Irish") became the first unit to be activated in the US prior to the attack on Pearl Harbor on December 7, 1941.

Photo: Tom Flynn in uniform was taken 1940.

Tom's Good-bye to New York

With orders for Tom's unit to begin training at Fort McClellan, Alabama, the *New York Post* staff gave Tom a going-away party following his last day of work on October 10, 1940. Stan MacGovern, creator of the popular "Silly Milly" cartoon, head of the Art Department, and one of the *New York Post's* most popular cartoonists over several decades, created the cartoon shown on the next page for Tom's going-away party. The 20-x-24-inch poster was signed by many of the staff and contains 110 signatures, including that of a famous columnist, Franklin Pierce Adams, whose name appears as the second one down in the second column.

The Flynn family sadly watched Tom leave with his unit for Fort McClellan, Alabama, and as Tom paraded up the avenue with the other soldiers in his unit, his dad ran out to embrace him one last time.

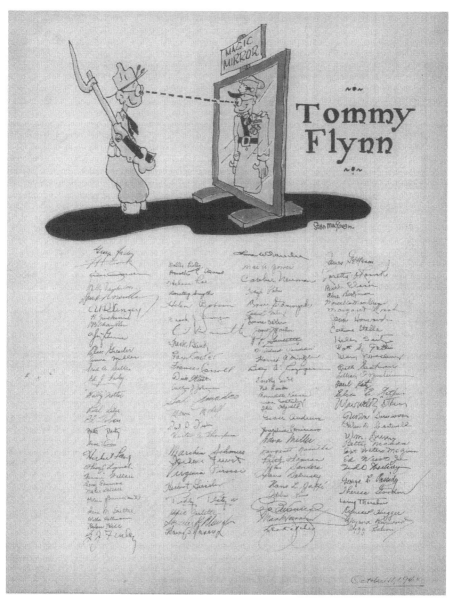

Photo: New York Post going-away gift to Tom,
created by Stan MacGovern, October 10, 1940.

CHAPTER 2

1940-August 1942: Early Military Life

Following the activation of Tom's National Guard unit, Tom quickly earned a promotion to weapons platoon sergeant, 165th Infantry Regiment, 27th Infantry Division, on November 9, 1940.

On December 2, 1940, just over a month after Tom left New York, he received word that his dad had died of a massive heart attack. Richard Flynn and Tom's older brother, Richie, who were working together, had just had lunch and as they left the restaurant, their father collapsed to the sidewalk. Richie tried to help his dad, but Richard died in his arms. The next day, Tom was given a four-day leave to go home to attend the funeral. Tom thought back about the last time he saw his dad and how he had run out to hug him in the street one last time as he left New York with his army unit.

Since Tom's mother hadn't worked outside the home since the children were born, she was able to arrange for Social Security payments for herself and the four children still at home under age eighteen: Chuck, Mel, Joe, and Eddie. It was going to be difficult supporting the five of them, so Tom arranged to have $35 per month sent home from his paycheck to help his family. While Tom was home, he also noticed Mel's winter coat was looking very old and worn and before he left, he took her shopping for a new one, as he knew that his mom wasn't going to have any extra money to spare that winter.

As soon as Tom returned to Fort McClellan, the 165th Infantry Regiment received flu inoculations and the entire unit became violently ill with intestinal influenza. He later attributed the illness to a bad batch of vaccine. Feeling miserable, Tom took a buddy's suggestion to smoke a cigarette as he swore it would help him feel less nauseous. That was the beginning of Tom's lifelong addiction to cigarettes.

Over the next sixteen months, Tom and his regiment underwent infantry training at the base in Alabama. Daily maneuvers that utilized the full area around camp made for long and tiring days for the men. Tom quickly decided he didn't care much for the heat and humidity of the South but he enjoyed playing baseball, softball, and football with the other men when they had time off. He also enjoyed target shooting and became an excellent marksman.

Several times when Tom accumulated a week or more of furlough days, he went home to New York to visit. Tom's sister, Mel, remembers his visits home, but emphasized that he wasn't actually "home" much, and as she put it, "What independent young man would be?"

Photos: Weapons Platoon Sgt. Thomas J. Flynn at Fort McClellan, Alabama, 1941

Japan Joins the War

During this time, the Japanese emperor decided to join what was now truly a "world war." Japan sided with Germany and Italy, and the Japanese military and naval forces moved into strategic positions to control China and Southeast Asia. Japan clearly understood that to be successful in a war with Western nations, it would need a steady supply of oil. To this end, it seized Indochina in June 1941. The United States and other Western governments reacted to Japan's aggressive actions against Indochina by freezing Japanese assets. In addition, the US issued a complete oil embargo on Japanese imports at a time when the US supplied close to 80 percent of Japan's oil supply. Japan considered this a declaration of war and secretly made plans to retaliate.

On December 7, 1941, Japan simultaneously attacked British, Dutch, and American positions in Southeast Asia and the Central Pacific. This included the dawn attack on the American fleet at Pearl Harbor, where over 3,600 American servicemen were killed or wounded in less than an hour. These attacks prompted the

United States, England, other Western Allies, and China to declare war on Japan. Germany and the other members of the Tripartite Pact responded by declaring war on the United States. Stalin and the Soviet Union felt it was in their best interest to maintain a neutrality agreement with Japan and did not join the Western Allies in their declaration of war against Japan.

Infantry Officer Candidate School

Twelve days after the Japanese attacked Pearl Harbor, Tom's unit, the 27th Infantry Division, received orders to report for duty in the South Pacific. They would be one of the first units to depart for combat in WWII. On January 7, 1942, Tom, along with the rest of his regiment, received a vaccination against yellow fever, which was required for all troops assigned to combat duty in the South Pacific.

However, Tom would not be going with his unit overseas, as he had been accepted for Infantry Officer Candidate School (O.C.S) at Fort Benning, Georgia. While his friends shipped off for Hawaii and beyond, he was granted a week's leave before classes began and took the train home to New York to visit his family from March 1-7. As usual, when Tom came home, Scrappy was the first one to greet him, wagging his tail in excitement and demanding his full attention. The rest of the family would be completely ignored by the two, at least temporarily.

It was obvious how much Tom's family loved each other and they all did what they could to help their mom keep a roof over their heads. During the 2½ years that Tom had been in the armed forces, Tom's brother, Chuck, and his sister Mel, had both graduated from high school and gotten jobs. Both gave most of their paychecks to their mom to compensate for the decrease in Social Security income she received as each had turned eighteen. Joe and Eddie were still in high school. Despite the hardships Tom's mother Josephine had experienced, she had done a wonderful job raising eight loving and giving children, and together they always managed to make ends meet somehow.

Photos (top): Tom and his sister, Amelia (Mel); (bottom) Tom and his younger brothers and sister (l-r) Joe, Mel, and Eddie in the back row, Tom holding Scrappy, and Chuck

When Tom arrived at Fort Benning, southeast of Columbus, Georgia, for Infantry Officer Candidate School (O.C.S), he became sick with jaundice almost immediately, exhibiting all the typical symptoms—yellow eyes, skin, and urine, and an upset stomach. Tom went to the base hospital twice for medical treatment but never got in to see a doctor. The only person there was a medical administrative officer, who sent him back to duty each time. Much to his frustration, he discovered that once again, the batch of vaccine given to the troops in January had been contaminated, as Tom and many of his fellow soldiers from the 27th who had shipped out to Hawaii had contracted infectious hepatitis. This was the second time he had been inoculated with contaminated medicine.

Officer's Candidate School was going to be tough, even without being ill, as only the top candidates were accepted into the program. The Army described the school as an intense program that involved both classroom and field training to develop leadership skills considered unmatched by any other program. The goal was to develop a candidate's potential mentally, physically, and emotionally by teaching leadership development, military skills, and adventure training.

Despite being very sick, Tom did well at Infantry O.C.S. He graduated on June 8, 1942, accepting an appointment as 2nd lieutenant in the United States Army. Tom's transfer, effective June 9, 1942, sent him to the newly established Camp Carson near Colorado Springs, Colorado, to help open the new camp as part of the 89th Infantry Division.

Now that Tom was a commissioned officer in the United States Army, his payroll deduction sent home to support his family ended on May 30, 1942, after 2½ years.

Tom tracked the movement of his friends in the 27th Infantry Division when he could, as he had known many of the men since 1937. The 27th went on to see action against Japan in the Marshall and Gilbert Islands, Saipan, Guam, and the Philippines, and was among the forces that eventually occupied Japan.

Summer of '42

In June of 1942, when Tom arrived at Camp Carson in Colorado, he was assigned as the 2nd Platoon Leader with the Anti-Tank Company, 353rd Infantry, 89th Infantry Division and began training with his new unit.

During the same month, Japan began bombing the American installations in the Aleutian Islands off the southern coast of Alaska.

The war in Europe continued on, and following the Soviet victory at the Battle of Stalingrad in the summer of 1942, the tone of Nazi propaganda changed to proclaim the Nazis were defending Western civilization against the destruction by the Eastern Europeans who were pouring into Europe. Advancing Soviet troops, under Stalin's orders, showed no mercy and committed numerous atrocities against enemy soldiers and civilians alike, including the murder of prisoners of war and Polish citizens.

CHAPTER 3

August 1942-September 1944: Anna and Early Married Life

Tom & Anna

On August 12, 1942, 2nd Lt. Anna Bennedsen, a twenty-two-year-old registered nurse in the Army Nurses Corps, arrived at Camp Carson with her friend, Helen Gehling, a fellow nurse from Omaha, Nebraska. Helen and Anna became friends when they attended nursing school and together they had enlisted in the Army Nurses Corps. Anna and Helen both received notice they had passed their Iowa Nursing Boards on December 8, 1941, the day after the Pearl Harbor attack. Shortly thereafter, they each received a letter from the Army requesting their services. Neither had any reservations about joining the Army and both accepted immediately. It took almost six months before they heard back from the Army but they finally receive their orders in August 1942 requiring them to report to the Camp Carson Base Hospital for duty. Once there, they would receive additional training and work at the base hospital until further orders came through.

On the first day in camp, at the urging of the other nurses whom Anna had met that day, she and Helen agreed to join five other nurses for a fun night out. All dressed up in their pretty skirts and dresses, the beautiful entourage of young nurses set out on foot down the dirt road from their barracks to the Bing Crosby and Phil Silvers USO show on base that night.

It didn't take long for a couple of handsome young officers in a jeep to spot the young nurses, and the two stopped to offer them a ride. The driver was John Kiley, a young doctor from the base hospital, and in the passenger seat was, of course, 2nd Lt. Tom Flynn.

While the other nurses gladly accepted the offer and piled in, Anna was somewhat reluctant. Waiting until last to climb into the jeep, the only place left to sit was on Tom's lap in the front passenger seat. To this day, Anna will not confirm or deny that she sat on Tom's lap on the way to the show, so it is up to the reader to decide what to believe; however, Anna does confirm that she sat next to Tom at the USO show. It was love at first sight for Tom and he and Anna started dating right away. It is not hard to believe that Tom fell quickly for Anna, as she was a beautiful, blonde, Danish girl with hazel eyes and lovely full lips. The only makeup Anna ever wore was red lipstick. That was all she needed. She was a natural beauty.

Anna had grown up as a first-generation American born to Danish immigrants in the small Danish community of Kimballton, in southwest Iowa. Anna had many relatives still living in Nazi occupied Denmark. She was shy, quiet, and quite naïve, and so very different from all the big-city girls whom Tom had known growing up in New York.

Photo: Anna Bennedsen at her Nursing School graduation in 1941.

After that night at the USO show, Tom and Anna saw or talked to each other every day and enjoyed going to the movies when their schedules allowed. Anna liked spending time with Tom, as he always made her feel very special. Anna's boss, the head nurse at the base hospital, quickly became concerned with the sudden seriousness of Tom and Anna's relationship. Within two weeks, she issued transfer orders for Anna that would send her to an Army base in the Aleutian Islands, off the southern coast of Alaska. Anna was unaware of the pending danger and the continued Japanese attacks on the islands. Still adjusting to life in the Army and only beginning to learn her new routines, Anna was very frightened at the prospect of being shipped off to such a remote outpost. She did not want to go to Alaska, but most of all, she did not want to leave Tom.

When Anna talked to Tom later that day, she told him about her pending transfer. It didn't take Tom long to decide what needed to be done, as he realized he had already fallen in love with Anna. How could he risk losing her? So while on their date at the movies that night, Tom took Anna by the hands, looked her in the eyes and said, "Anna, what if we got married? Then you wouldn't have to go." Anna was surprised and shocked by the proposal. At twenty-two, Anna had never even dated before. She wondered to herself how she could marry someone she had only known for two weeks. Anna declined to give Tom an answer that night in order to consider her options: Should she go to the Aleutian Islands or marry someone she had only known for two weeks? Which was the lesser of two evils? If she married Tom, the marriage clause would allow her to leave the service. Time was short, however, because the Army was allowing the marriage clause to expire. It was losing too many female recruits because of this loophole.

Anna wrote home to her parents in Iowa the next day and told them about the decision she needed to make. Her mother immediately wrote back to say that they would give their blessing for the marriage if that is what she wanted to do. Anna was surprised at their response and decided to accept Tom's proposal of marriage.

Anna and Tom had to plan their wedding around Anna's work schedule as the head nurse refused to give Anna any time off. So after working until noon, Anna ran home to clean up and change, and then she and Tom were married at 2 p.m. on Sunday, September 13, 1942, in the Camp Carson Chapel just one month after they met. Camp Carson's Chaplain, Father Kenneth A. Hans, performed the ceremony. Anna's maid of honor was her nurse friend from Omaha, Helen E. Gehling; and John W. Kiley, Tom's doctor friend who was driving the jeep on the night they met, was the best man. Six other officers from Tom's unit attended their wedding, but since Anna had spent most of the last month with Tom when she wasn't working, she really didn't have any girlfriends to invite other than Helen. After the wedding, Tom and Anna drove to Colorado Springs and Tom splurged on his beautiful bride, staying at the luxurious Broadmoor Hotel for the night. Anna had to return to work by the start of the 7 a.m. morning shift the next day.

Photo: Father Hans and newlyweds 2nd Lts. Anna and Thomas Flynn.

As retribution for Anna's marriage to Tom in defiance of the transfer, the head nurse scheduled Anna to work twelve-hour shifts for thirty-one days straight, from 7 p.m. to 7 a.m. Anna's discharge papers were signed in mid-November after she had served just ninety-four days in the Army Nurses Corps. For the first time since Anna was a young girl, she didn't have to work outside the home to help support the family. She was now an officer's wife and Tom's salary could support both of them. Tom and Anna lived in Colorado Springs while he was stationed at Camp Carson.

In October 1942, just a month into their marriage, the home of Anna's parents in Kimballton, Iowa, burned down. The fire appeared to have started in the chimney near the roof. Anna's nineteen-year-old brother, Magnus, went up on the roof to try to put the fire out but had no luck. Because the fire started at the top of the two-story brick house, it took longer to spread to the main level. Everyone in Kimballton knew Anna's family, as her father was the rural mail carrier, and neighbors immediately came from all around to help. They managed to carry almost everything out of the house before the house burned to the ground, even the baskets of fresh fruit in the basement that the Bennedsens had harvested from the fruit trees on the farm. The men had so carefully carried the china hutch, loaded with fragile items, out of the house that miraculously nothing was broken. The biggest blessing of all was that no one was injured in the fire.

Anna's parents stored everything they could in the barns and storage buildings on the farm and temporarily moved into the small hotel in Kimballton while her father rebuilt the brick and stone house. He had built the house for Anna's mother in 1915 before they had married. Tom and Anna went to visit her parents for Christmas while they were still living at the hotel, and that is where Tom and Anna spent their first Christmas together. Bing Crosby's newly released "White Christmas" was number one on the radio that winter and it would prove to be a special song for Tom and Anna for many years to come as they looked back on their life together.

Nineteen forty-two was definitely a year of changes for Anna's family. Anna's older sister Eva was married on June 3 before Anna left for Colorado, and her husband was also in the Army, stationed in Nashville, Tennessee. Anna's oldest brother, Ole, who had been training in Connecticut as a Boeing B-17 bomber pilot, received transfer orders in mid-June for Minneapolis, Minnesota. On the spur of the moment, Ole asked his eighteen-year-old girlfriend, Elizabeth Wihart of Thompsonville, Connecticut, to marry him so that she could go with him. They were married on June 26. Anna's sister, Helga, had also moved to Minneapolis, where she now worked in a factory painting lettering on military equipment. Magnus, the only sibling still at home, was a mechanic in a local garage in town and was considering enlisting in the Army, too.

Photo: Chuck Flynn with Anna and Tom Flynn, spring 1943.

When Tom and Anna returned to Colorado Springs after Christmas, Tom's brother, Chuck, was now stationed nearby at Buckley Air Force Base near Denver, Colorado. Tom and Chuck were still very close and Tom made sure Anna got to know his little brother before Chuck left with his flight crew for duty in Europe in early 1943.

Chuck was tail gunner on "The Golden Goose," a Boeing B-17 bomber with the 8th Air Force, 551 Bomb Squadron, 385th Bomb Group and would be flying missions over Germany, a very dangerous and nerve-wracking job. In his position in the gun turret atop the plane, he would be staring directly at all the enemy aircraft as they fired at him and his plane. If the plane were to get shot down, Chuck would be the only one of the crew who could not wear a parachute during flight due to the small space in which he was confined. If the order came to abandon the plane, he would have to climb down from the turret and strap on a parachute before jumping.

On duty, Tom worked hard and excelled as platoon leader. On March 3, 1943, he was promoted to 1st lieutenant, Company Executive Officer of the Anti-Tank Company, 353rd Infantry, 89th Infantry Division.

While Tom and Anna lived in Colorado Springs, Tom got a collie he named Biff. Tom enjoyed playing with and training the dog in his free time.

Tom took Anna to meet his family in New York in June 1943, during their first summer together. His family was still living in the same neighborhood so Anna was able to see where Tom had grown up. Everyone loved Anna, finding her to be very sweet and loving, and very much in love with their Tommy. Tom's family recalls that Anna was tall, blonde, and beautiful. During their visit, a nephew was asked to go with Anna to run an errand and he was more than happy to be escort for Uncle Tommy's gorgeous wife. It was a warm day and Anna was wearing shorts. Anna quickly realized that her short shorts were not what the girls in the neighborhood were wearing and became somewhat embarrassed. She didn't realize that the fashions in New York

City would be so different. Tom's nephew didn't mind at all though and happily recalled the story more than sixty years later at a Flynn family reunion.

Photos: (l) Tom, friend's child (Tommy), and Biff, 1943; (r) Anna and Tom's sister, Mel, in New York, June 1943

While they were in New York, Tom treated Anna to a show at Radio City Music Hall. The chief attractions were a floor show by the Rockettes and a performance of the Broadway play, *The Dragon Seed*, starring Katharine Hepburn.

On July 10, 1943, after Tom and Anna returned to Camp Carson, Tom was admitted to Camp Carson Station Hospital with moderately severe pain in his right shoulder, anterior thorax, and abdomen. No specific cause was determined and Tom was released on July 12.

In August 1943, Tom was assigned company commander of a newly formed division, Company E, 85th Infantry Regiment (Mountain), 10th Infantry Division out of Camp Hale near Leadville, Colorado, where he prepared himself and his troops to join the Army ski troops in Europe. To prepare for this duty, the company was required to learn the technical skills needed for rock climbing while carrying ninety-pound rucksacks on their backs. The soldiers "liked" it so much they had a song about "Ninety Pounds of Rucksack." Anna stayed in Colorado Springs while Tom was at Camp Hale training each week, since the men were allowed to go home on the weekends.

On October 10, 1943, during a rock climbing exercise with his ninety-pound rucksack, Tom's right arm suddenly became numb, causing him to lose his grip on the rocks. Unfortunately, the troops were training that day without safety ropes and he fell thirty to forty feet to the ground from the rock face. Tom's fall further injured his right shoulder, causing significant nerve damage and leaving him unable to raise his right arm. Remarkably, no other major injuries were sustained.

Tom spent two weeks at Station Hospital, Camp Hale, where he recuperated from the fall and started physical therapy. Tom was transferred to a position as the Regiment Police & Prisons Officer within his unit while he recovered; however, his shoulder condition continued to deteriorate and Tom's arm soon became totally paralyzed.

Tom was admitted to Fitzsimmons General Hospital in Denver, Colorado, on December 29, where he spent the next two months. After extensive physical therapy, Tom was assigned to Limited Service Status in March 1944, as the Company Executive and Training Officer of Company B, 58th Battalion, Infantry Replacement & Training Center at Camp Wolters, Texas. Continuing physical therapy at Ashburn General Hospital in McKinney, Texas, over the next three months, Tom trained infantry troops until he recovered and was restored to full service on June 24, 1944.

Photo: Tom and a friend at Camp Hale, 1943.

The War

Since late 1942, the Germans had been forced into a slow retreat in both Italy and North Africa, and German industrial cities had been under frequent attack by American and British bombers, disrupting their much-needed supplies of raw material and finished goods. The Allied naval forces had also contained the threat of German submarine attacks, thus allowing the massive buildup in England of the military personnel, weaponry, and supplies that would be needed to mount a major offensive against Germany. France and its neighboring countries had been under German control for four long years, and the Allies were determined to finally drive the Germans from Western Europe and ultimately destroy the Nazi regime.

On June 6, 1944, the Western Allies, commanded by US Army Gen. Dwight D. Eisenhower, landed on the beaches of

Normandy in northern France, beginning a massive assault against Hitler's Germany. Dozens of minesweepers led the way for the enormous warships across the English Channel followed by hundreds of ships and watercraft, while three divisions of paratroopers (two American, one British) were dropped behind enemy lines.

They arrived at their strike zones just before daybreak. Guns from the warships bombarded German positions inland and six divisions (three American, two British, and one Canadian) stormed ashore on five main beaches, nicknamed "Utah," "Omaha," "Gold," "Juno," and "Sword." After two months of bloody battles, the Allies' continual assaults forced the Germans to retreat, enabling the Allies to secure the Normandy positions in late July and move deeper into northern France. In August, another landing in southern France was the final thrust needed to get the German army to retreat totally from France and secure the country's liberation. With the Soviet Union pressing Hitler's armies back from the East, Germany was being forced back toward its homeland.

It was at this point that Tom was assigned to combat duty as part of the Allied Ground Forces Replacement System in the European Theater Operation (ETO). Heavy fighting across northern France and throughout Luxembourg had claimed the lives of many soldiers and left others severely wounded in several infantry divisions. Replacement troops and officers were badly needed.

Tom was ordered to report for duty in early September and was given personal leave on August 24 before leaving for Europe. He took Anna and Biff to her parents' home in Kimballton. Tom left by train on September 6 from the nearby town of Harlan, Iowa, and made a brief stop in New York to see his family on the way to Camp Kilmer, New Jersey (New York Point of Entry).

Photo: Tom and Anna in Kimballton, September 6, 1944, before Tom left for Europe.

The Bloody Buckets

The unit that Tom would soon join as a replacement officer was the 28th Infantry Division (aka the Pennsylvania National Guard). This unit was working its way across France into Central Europe, earning a fierce reputation among the German troops along the way. The Germans mistakenly interpreted the red Keystone emblem on the left shoulder of each soldier's jacket as a "Bloody Bucket," believing the insignia reflected the toughness of the unit's fighting ability, and the name stuck.

The 28th Infantry Division, composed of the 109th, 110th and 112th Infantry Regiments, had been in the middle of intense combat since late July. Parent headquarters, not seeing the results it had counted on, perceived a lack of leadership and notified Major Gen. Norman D. Cota on August 13 that he was to take command of the 28th Infantry Division. Under General Cota, the 28th began to move briskly through France and the number of German prisoners increased significantly. After completing these missions, the 28th was reassigned under Major Gen. Leonard Gerow's V Corps.

The successful landing in southern France in August had finally forced the German army to retreat toward its homeland and on August 29, the 28th Infantry Division entered Paris, parading through the Arc de Triumph down the Champs-Elysées to a cheering Parisian crowd. However, there was no time for rest, and the 28th quickly swept through Belgium, averaging seventeen miles a day against heavy German resistance. The 109th and 110th Infantry Regiments then continued on to liberate the northern part of Luxembourg.

On September 11, the 28th Infantry Division entered Germany, where it destroyed or captured 153 pillboxes and bunkers, becoming the first Allied unit to reach the German border. Along the West Wall, better known to Allied soldiers as "the Siegfried Line," were approximately 150 miles of anti-tank, steel-reinforced, concrete pyramids standing over four feet tall, called for obvious reasons the "dragon's teeth."

By now, the morale of the American soldiers was very high, having pushed the German army back across France, Luxembourg, and the German border in just a few months. It was during the first weeks of September, while Tom was preparing to leave Camp Kilmer, New Jersey, that the European Allied commanders began to believe that the German army was exhausted, dispirited, and disorganized and that the war might be over by Christmas. It was also widely believed that the next breakthrough would lead to certain victory for the Allies. Tom had every reason to be optimistic when he boarded the Queen Elizabeth on September 23, 1944, and arrived in England just one week later on October 1. Tom would spend the first two weeks of October in England learning about his possible new assignments on the Western Front before crossing the English Channel.

Anna & Family

After Tom left for Europe, Anna went to visit Tom's brother, Chuck, and her sister Eva and brother-in-law George, as both men were now stationed in Nashville. Chuck had just returned from his tour of duty in Europe, where he had been stationed at Great Ashfield Air Base. His crew had been flying bombing missions from England in support of the Infantry Divisions' advancement on the ground. Chuck had earned the rank of staff sergeant, flying in twenty-five missions on the "Golden Goose" between March 1944 and July 1944. For his service, he received the Air Medal with four stars and the Distinguished Flying Cross, and was credited with shooting down one enemy plane. Everyone was glad he had returned home safely and without any injuries.

Anna's brother, 2nd Lt. Ole B. Bennedsen, also left for England in September 1944 with the 839th Squadron, 487th Bomb Group and was stationed in Lavenham, Suffolk. Ole and crew would also be flying bombing missions from England deep into Germany in support of the Infantry Divisions, just as Chuck and his crew had done. Ole had affectionately named their plane the "Bonnie Lassie" in honor of his little girl at home with his wife, Betty.

CHAPTER 4

October & November 1944 in the European Theater: The Battle of Hürtgen Forest

About this chapter: The 28th *Infantry Division (composed of the 109*[th]*, 110*[th]*, and 112*[th] *Infantry Regiments) fought in the Battle of Hürtgen Forest from Nov. 2-16, 1944. Tom did not join the 28*[th] *Infantry Division as a replacement officer until Nov 8, 1944. Because there is very little documented information about the second week his unit fought in this battle, the information here is primarily based on accounts of the first week in battle, and I believe it is consistent with what Tom experienced after he joined the 28*[th] *and was engaged in battle.*

Anna returned to her parents' home in Kimballton in October 1944 and planned to stay there until she could find a nursing job. There was no reason not to work while Tom was gone overseas. This was the first time that Anna and Tom had been separated for any length of time since they met and Anna wrote to him frequently as she had promised, praying for his safe return. A month had already gone by with no word from Tom.

The War in Europe

During September and October of 1944, General Cota, commander of the 28th Infantry Division, had to deal not only with the exhaustion of the troops, some of whom had been fighting for several months, but also the training and incorporation of thousands of replacement troops the division received during this period. Finally, on October 1, the unit was sent to the rear for rest and recovery. Many soldiers went on leave to Paris while others stayed behind to train the new soldiers who were being added to the unit. Most of the replacements arrived as individuals and the majority of the enlisted men had little or no infantry training. The battle-weary veterans were leery of the new men, concerned that their severe lack of combat training might put them at risk during intense fighting—like the fighting they had just experienced.

By mid-October, the German army had retreated far inland and the 150-mile western border of Germany, nicknamed the Siegfried Line, became the primary objective of the American army. At the southern end, the Battle of the Hürtgen Forest had begun on September 12, 1944, when the 9th Infantry Division was sent to seize control of the crossroads village of Schmidt and, thus, secure the right flank of VII Corps before a larger offensive was to begin. The Army experienced major communications problems within the chain of command and had entered the Hürtgen Forest before proper intelligence had been gathered on German strength in the area. As a result, the 9th Infantry Division was suffering a much higher casualty rate than expected and the Army began moving thousands more replacement troops into the area for quick deployment, when and where they were needed.

Tom was part of this group being positioned to join the Battle of the Hürtgen Forest, if needed. From England, replacement troops were transported by ship across the English Channel onto the beaches of Normandy, where the Allied forces had landed just a few short months ago, and then transported by truck inland. Tom arrived in France on October 18, 1944, almost seven years to the day after he joined the New York National Guard.

The Hürtgen Forest

The Hürtgen Forest was one of the largest forests in Germany, covering an area of approximately fifty square miles between Aachen, Monschau, and Duren on the Belgian-German border. At its widest points, the forest was twenty miles in length from north to south and ten miles wide from west to east. The forest was part of the northern portion of the Ardennes region of Belgium and Luxembourg and the Eifel region of Germany. The area contains some of the most rugged terrain in Europe, characterized by steep, wooded slopes reaching 1,000 feet in elevation, with numerous, deep valleys and ravines and very few roads or trails.

The Siegfried Line ran right through the middle of the forest whose 75- to 100-foot tall fir trees were so dense they impeded both foot and motor traffic, preventing the sun from reaching the forest floor. Even at high noon, the sunlight barely reached the spongy bed of pine needles and decaying logs at the base of the forest.

The enemy soldiers who awaited the American soldiers in this sector were certainly not Germany's finest; for the most part, they were the very young and the very old. However, they were mixed in with combat veterans, who provided the backbone for the units in the area.

The Germans had turned the forest into a labyrinth of well-camouflaged earth and log bunkers and concrete pillboxes, many still intact from WWI. These structures provided excellent interlocking fields of fire and were augmented with booby-trapped concertina wire and minefields designed to restrict all enemy movement. Throughout the forest, the Germans also had laid dense belts of barbed wire and planted thousands of mines and booby traps; many designed to maim rather than kill. One mine was notorious for amputating legs and the male genitals. The numerous bunkers in the area were the Germans' key centers of resistance. They defended the few roads and trails that bisected the forest with intense machine gun and artillery fire. The rough terrain complicated the situation, as advancing soldiers easily became confused and disoriented in the dense forest and large groups could easily become separated, lost, and disorganized.

The Germans knew well how to use the terrain to their advantage. They turned even the thick forest of evergreens into weapons as artillery blasts were frequently aimed to explode at the treetops, spraying the American soldiers below with both wood and steel splinters. Soldiers learned quickly that lying prone on the ground while receiving artillery fire was the worst possible thing to do. Instead, soldiers learned to crouch or stand close against a tree, minimizing the bodily surface area they exposed to the blast. Still, there was no safe place to hide from the tree bursts.

The Battle of the Hürtgen Forest

After stubborn fighting by the German army in the Hürtgen Forest throughout September and early October, the Americans reevaluated the situation and decided there was no way the war would be over by Christmas, as previously expected. The 9th Infantry Division had done its best but had little in the way of positive results to show after almost six weeks of heavy fighting and suffering more than 4,500 casualties. The division desperately needed a break to rest and rebuild, and on October 26, the 28th Infantry Division moved forward to replace the 9th.

Further attacks were postponed until the 28th Infantry Division was able to move northward to the Hürtgen Forest. Much to the frustration of General Cota, Major General Gerow of V Corp ordered the three regiments of the 28th Infantry Division, the 109th, 110th and 112th, to split up, giving each a different strategic objective. General Cota was concerned that each regiment in his division had to attack a different location, each moving out in opposite directions across the most difficult terrain in the western part of Europe. The specific mission of the 110th Infantry Regiment was to clear the woods next to the River Kall, capture Simonskall, and maintain a supply route for the advance on Schmidt—an objective the 9th Infantry Division had failed to achieve.

In hindsight, it seems clear that General Cota failed to demand detailed intelligence on the area before making the decision on the plan of attack. As a result, the main supply route he chose for the 28th was the Kall Trail, which was just that, a trail. In good weather, the dirt trail was barely adequate for vehicle travel. In bad weather, it was practically impassable, even for tracked vehicles, yet this route was chosen to be the main supply route for the entire division of over 6,000 men, vehicles, and pieces of equipment. By early November, the rain and snow had turned the Kall Trail into a muddy lane with the mud six to ten inches deep in some places.

November 2

The 28th began its attack on November 2, 1944, after an intense hour of shelling by tactical air support. Each regiment moved out from the woods west of Germeter towards the assigned targets of Vossenack, Simonskall, and Schmidt, amid savage fighting. The weather had taken a turn for the worse over the previous week. It started to rain a cold and relentless drizzle, and with the Hürtgen Forest now covered in fog and mist, further air support was suspended until November 5.

Tom was still waiting not far away in France and had been assigned to the 3rd Replacement Depot, awaiting further orders. Tom was taking this time to get to know the non-commissioned officers (NCOs) who also had been assigned to the Replacement Depot, and from which he would possibly need to select his men when he was assigned a combat unit.

The 110th Infantry Regiment's 2nd (E, F, G, and H companies) and 3rd battalions (I, K, L, and M companies), moved south out of Germeter—directly into the heart of the Siegfried Line pillboxes— toward the town of Simonskall and a fortified strongpoint called Raffelsbrand. The 1st Battalion (A, B, C, and D companies) remained in the rear as a small divisional reserve.

Moving into the sector just vacated by 9th Infantry Division was a horrifying experience for the soldiers of the 28th, particularly for the large number of replacement soldiers with no combat experience. As the black, shattered trees swallowed up the 28th, the soldiers were shocked by what they saw and the morale of the men plummeted from the moment they entered the tangled fir forest. The forest bore the scars of war: the record of the bitter contest waged by the 9th was apparent as abandoned helmets, gas masks, blood-soaked field jackets, and loose mines lay all about. Water-filled shell holes were everywhere. Even worse, the bodies of German and American soldiers, some of which had been booby trapped by the Germans overnight, lay entangled in the sucking troughs of mud, lying unclaimed by Graves Registration units. It was a grotesque and gloomy landscape. The somber-faced men of the Graves Registration units quietly moved among the bloated, mutilated corpses that now stank, unceremoniously slinging them on the backs of their trucks. Soldiers who had expected an easy victory were shocked by the hard reality that severe fighting lay ahead.

The enemy was not the only source of casualties with which the 28th would have to contend. Cold and wet November weather, with temperatures hovering around freezing, would take a terrible toll on the soldiers. Many were still wearing the summer clothing they had been issued when they first went into battle. Without proper cold-weather gear—items such as over boots, field jackets, woolen caps, and long underwear—trench foot and respiratory infection cases skyrocketed. K and C rations, the standard combat issue for each soldier, were intended to provide three nutritional and satisfying meals a day, whether served hot or cold. However, given the conditions under which the soldiers were fighting, many men lost their appetites and ceased eating altogether. Battle conditions were much too dangerous to risk bringing hot meals or drinks forward. The soldiers also were unable to build fires to warm up, dry off, or to heat their food to make it more palatable, since their proximity to the enemy was sure to draw automatic rifle and mortar fire. All too often, enemy soldiers lay hidden just a stone's throw away. The continual lack of hot rations and constant cold and wet conditions contributed significantly to the declining health and morale of many of the soldiers.

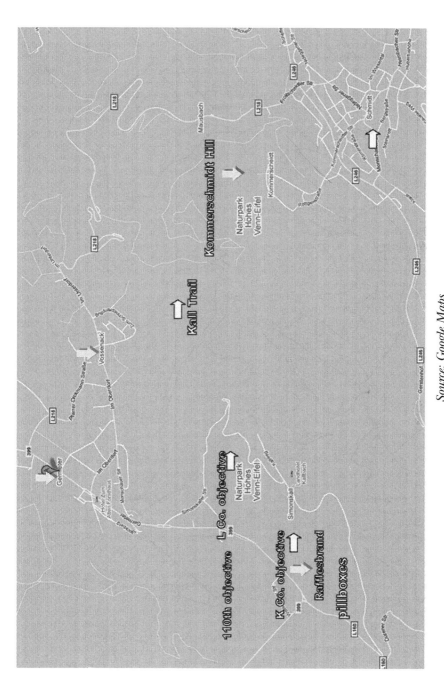

Source: Google Maps

Map: 28th Infantry Regiment's strategic objectives in the Hürtgen Forest

Within the 3rd Battalion, K Company was to move to the right and capture Simonskall. L Company was to move to the left, penetrate enemy defenses, and capture the horseshoe bend in the road east of Simonskall. Only two hours prior to departure, patrols in the area had reported a German defensive line south of Germeter made from concertina wire, which is a razor type barbed wire that is can be rolled out in large coils. Two rolls stretched side by side through the trees, with a third placed on top of them, creating a six-foot tall barrier. In front of the wire, German troops had hand dug a shallow ditch that varied in width from four to six feet and strategically positioned several machine-guns to saturate the defensive perimeter in-between the well-concealed bunkers and pillboxes. Unfortunately, this report did not make it down to the men on the line and they were unaware that this obstacle lay ahead.

L Company came under immediate fire after leaving the woods west of Germeter but continued to fight until they reached the ditch. K Company made it to the ditch, but heavy German machine-gun fire immediately wounded or killed twelve men, with most injuries occurring from the waist down because of the low position from which the enemy fired. The soldiers were suddenly living out their worst nightmares, learning quickly what tree bursts were. The men prayed even as they searched for ways to protect themselves. Some even tried to cut the fallen trees, arranging them for protection over a dugout.

Third Battalion commander Lt. Col. William Tait called the battalion back to the line of departure late in the afternoon, as no progress toward their objective had been made.

November 3

At 0700 on November 3, K and L companies set out again and tried twice to capture their objectives. Both times, they suffered so many casualties that they had to fall back and regroup. Unbeknownst to them, the Germans had strengthened their defensive position overnight by over 200 riflemen and K Company experienced much heavier losses than the day before. Once again, at 1600 hours, Lt. Colonel Tait ordered those who were able to move back to their line of departure. Some of the men had to remain in position as they were pinned down by enemy fire.

November 4

At 0430 on November 4, the 1st Battalion was added to the attack plan and set off to approach the objective from the north, from Vossenack. The 2nd and 3rd battalions were to hold their defensive positions and exert pressure on the Germans to cover the attack. Using this strategy, the 1st Battalion met little enemy resistance and captured both the bend in the road and Simonskall, but it was now surrounded and in danger. The men dug into position for the night.

The 109th and 112th regiments were experiencing similar results throughout the forest, as the men of the 28th tried their best to do as they had been ordered. But advance after advance was halted as the American soldiers had been ordered to advance through heavily mined areas. Constant German machine-gun fire and mortars kept engineers from clearing the minefields or evacuating the dead. And all too often, wounded soldiers who lay helpless and stranded on the cold, wet ground would freeze or bleed to death during the night.

After only two days under these conditions, the 110th was no longer an effective fighting unit. Despite its weakened condition, however, it continued to attack when ordered. With each passing hour, the number of casualties grew, yet it made no measureable progress toward taking its assigned objectives.

Due to the heavy casualties taken by the 110th, particularly by the 3rd Battalion, Tom and the 41st Replacement Battalion left France on November 5, en route to the Germeter and Vossenack area to join the 28th Infantry Division in the battle in the Hürtgen Forest.

November 5

Around 1030 on November 5, General Gerow, the V Corps commander, arrived at General Cota's command post, where General Cota assured him that despite the failed attack on Schmidt, a plan was being drafted to take the town the following day. Of great concern to General Cota, though, was the fact that for the past four days his division had been the only allied division attacking into Germany along the 150-mile front. Worse still was the fact that the VII Corps attack had been postponed indefinitely until the weather improved. General Cota perceived that the Germans would now be able to concentrate their forces on the lone enemy division trying to take Schmidt.

To appease his commanding officer, General Cota created Task Force Ripple on November 5, under the leadership of Lt. Col. Richard W. Ripple, commander of the 707th Tank Battalion. Task Force Ripple was to consist of the already weakened 3rd Battalion (I, K, L, and M companies), 110th Infantry Regiment, (now numbering only 316 men of the original 871 and of which only 200 were infantrymen), eight tanks, and nine tank destroyers. The plan was to moved out through Vossenack, pass through the Kall Valley, and join forces with the depleted and exhausted 112th Infantry Regiment that was pinned down on Kommerscheidt Hill, and then combine forces to retake Schmidt.

November 6

Task Force Ripple left the line of departure near Germeter at 0245 hours on November 6. As it moved through Vossenack, it once again encountered a barrage of artillery fire. Waiting for the bombardment to end, the tank destroyer crewmen asked for infantry support to accompany their guns down the Kall Trail. Colonel Ripple refused the request. The four supply jeeps for the task force left on their own, without cover, and headed south along the Kall Trail. They were soon ambushed, and half the men in the party were killed or wounded. It now became apparent that the

Kall Trail was completely controlled by the Germans, so Colonel Ripple ordered the remaining vehicles to return to Germeter. Because his infantry force was already too depleted, Ripple tried to avoid a fight along the trail by taking a firebreak paralleling the trail 200 yards to the west instead. The change in tactics made no difference, though, and almost from the moment the infantry entered the woods at the firebreak, they came under small arms fire that lasted all the way to the Kall River. It was mid-day before they reached Colonel Peterson's troops on Kommerscheidt Hill. Colonels Tait and Ripple reported they had lost another fifteen men and two officers on the fire trail.

The scene that Task Force Ripple found upon arrival on Kommerscheidt Hill was one of misery and desolation. The American tanks and tank destroyers in Kommerscheidt had prevented German infantry from forming to attack. However, enemy tanks were positioned on the higher ground around Schmidt, and poured round after round into Kommerscheidt and positions held by the 112th. Maneuvering on the lower ground around Kommerscheidt, American tanks and tank destroyers were no match for the German Mark IVs and Vs. It was apparent that even the combined forces would be no match for a continued attack on Schmidt.

Colonel Ripple and Colonel Peterson, commander of the 112th, C Company in Kommerscheidt, postponed the joint attack on Schmidt as they assessed their situation. As the officers discussed their options, the situation quickly worsened. In a matter of minutes, German snipers concealed in the woods wounded or killed the 3rd battalion commander, Colonel Tait, the executive officer, S-2 officer, and a company commander. Colonels Ripple and Peterson finally decided that without supplies or armor, outnumbered by enemy forces, and with their men shattered by exhaustion, cold, and unrelenting fear, that the suicide mission of Task Force Ripple was out of the question. They judged it would be impossible to mount a successful attack under these conditions. Canceling the proposed attempt to retake Schmidt, Colonel Peterson told the men of Task Force Ripple to dig in along the woods line north of Kommerscheidt instead, to strengthen their defensive position.

While Task Force Ripple and the 112th waited for reinforcements on Kommerscheidt Hill, the Germans counterattacked. Some of the exhausted men simply fled in panic, as they just couldn't take the fighting anymore. The soldiers who stayed on Kommerscheidt Hill as ordered endured another night of freezing cold and rain.

Also on Monday, November 6, General Cota left his division command post in his jeep and made his only recorded visit to the forward positions of his divisional units during the Vossenack-Kommerscheidt-Schmidt battle. He was finally face to face with the reality of the conditions under which his men operated and the true condition of the Kall Trail he had designated as the 28th's main supply route. General Cota finally admitted to himself that this was an impossible battle to win, and he sought and received approval for his units to fall back behind the Kall River. Unfortunately for the 28th, the retreat was to be temporary, as once his units had regrouped and replacement troops were added, General Cota's commanding officers forced him to renew the attack. Cota reluctantly committed to being ready in three days if sufficient replacements arrived as General Hodges of the 1st Army would only approve the withdrawal of his troops from beyond the Kall River under those conditions.

November 7

News that Colonel Tait had been injured reached Lt. Colonel Seely at the 110th command post but it was uncertain whether he had been injured or killed. Capt. George "Howdy" Rumbaugh had just arrived at the regimental command post and was anxious for a position along the front line. He was ordered to take several Weasels and four jeeps with supplies to the men in Kommerscheidt, find out Colonel Tait's condition, and take command of 3rd Battalion, if needed. Through many close calls, with much effort, and despite the loss of most of his supplies, Captain Rumbaugh arrived in Kommerscheidt at 0500 on November 7. Upon discovering that Colonel Tait had been evacuated, he assumed command of the 3rd Battalion.

November 8

On Wednesday, November 8, during a drenching rainstorm, the battle-worn survivors began their withdrawal to the rear, disabling and abandoning any equipment as quietly as possible so the Germans would not know they were retreating. The men carried as many wounded as they could, but the men were physically exhausted and retreating units were forced to leave behind scattered groups of soldiers, some badly wounded, and others who had not received the notice to withdraw. On the way out of the woods, the men met up with Task Force Davis, which had been established to help guide them out of the woods. When they reached the task force, however, they were told to dig in for the night and that they would resume their march out in the morning. The men escaping from Kommerscheidt were forced to spend yet another miserable night in the nearly freezing temperatures, most of them soaked from the waist down after crossing the Kall River.

While Task Force Ripple and the 112th were retreating, Tom and the 41st Replacement Battalion had begun to arrive at the rear assembly area near Germeter to fill out Colonel Seely's depleted troops. Maj. Harold M. Milton, who was also part of the Replacement Forces, had taken command of the 3rd Battalion until Captain Rumbaugh could return to the rear assembly area, and he assigned Tom as Executive Officer of K Company, 110th Infantry Regiment. Over the next two days, 500 reinforcements were added to the 110th, 200 of whom went to the 3rd Battalion and one hundred of whom were specifically assigned to K Company. Tom handpicked his NCOs while enlisted men were assigned in groups of tens and twenties to platoons and companies. But even the 500 new bodies barely qualified the 110th to be considered ready for combat duty, as the regiment was still far from being considered full strength and most of the new soldiers had only the minimum basic training and no combat experience.

Tom assumed command of K Company and began to evaluate the situation. As an infantry unit commander, Tom was responsible for the unit's training and would direct and control the unit's tactical deployment in combat. Tom would also evaluate intelligence, make estimates of tactical situations, and decide to commit his troops to combat, coordinating and directing the fire of his unit in combat so as to take advantage of terrain and cover, while at the same time bringing maximum fire on the enemy opposing his sector.

November 9

By 0530 on November 9, it had begun to snow. Captain Rumbaugh was anxious to get his men out of the woods and so he told the 3rd Battalion to fall in behind him. He led the survivors the rest of the way back to Germeter (approximately 200 of the 316 who had set out in Task Force Ripple). Stragglers continued to arrive throughout the day. The men were given quick but thorough medical checks and those suffering from trench foot, battle fatigue, or other injuries or ailments were evacuated to the rear for rest or hospitalization. Out of the original 871 men in the 110th's 3rd Battalion that had entered the forest on November 2, only seventy-five men were still capable of fighting. The battalion had lost its commanding officer, executive officer, S-2 intelligence officer, S-3 operations officers, executive surgeon, and its medical assistance officer. There was only one officer left with K Company, and since Tom had already selected his NCOs, he was reassigned as the transportation officer for the 110th.

Men from other units stationed in the area made temporary shelters with heat, blankets, and straw for bedding for the men escaping from Kommerscheidt Hill. They even arranged for the replacement of lost equipment. Officers donated their liquor so that those who returned might each get a small drink. As soldiers arrived, aid men met them to tend their wounds and issue them their small ration of liquor. Vehicles were serviced or replaced and mess kits and new clothing provided. Tom and the other replacement officers made a point to talk to the survivors about the battlefield conditions they had experienced in preparation for their next assignments. The weather was not letting up and the snow continued to fall.

Men who were wounded at Kommerscheidt but couldn't escape were scattered all along the trail back to Germeter and several medical officers located at the aid station in the Kall Gorge negotiated a temporary cease-fire on their own for both sides to evacuate their wounded. Oddly enough, despite the intense fighting, German soldiers helped evacuate some of the wounded American soldiers and gave up their coats to help keep them warm while they awaited evacuation.

The few veteran enlisted men who were able to return to battle were allowed only one day to rest. Tom and the other company officers were notified at 2200 hours on November 9 that at 0700 the next day, the 110th was to move out to assault the enemy stronghold at Rafflesbrand, capture it, and continue the attack toward Monschau in the southwest. This left minimal time for all the new officers to gain satisfactory ground reconnaissance or work out company-level assault plans, so they were not happy with the decision. By now, almost a foot of snow had fallen.

From what they had seen and heard in the two days since arriving in the area, it was clear they were up against what appeared to be insurmountable odds. The sheer number of casualties to the unit in just a week could hardly be dismissed or give the new officers much hope that their efforts would result in any better outcome. Many of the men of the 28th began referring to the forest as the "Green Hell" and the "Death Factory" and the soldiers believed the commanding officers were simply unwillingly to admit defeat.

November 10-13

As 0700 approached, the rest of the 3rd Battalion—armed only with rifles—including Tom, the few remaining veteran enlisted men in K Company, and the one hundred replacement enlisted men and NCOs, left the Germeter assembly area still short of automatic weapons, mortars, and appropriate clothing for the winter weather. In addition to his rifle, Tom carried his own personal weapons, a .45-caliber Smith and Wesson revolver and a Thompson submachine gun. The men slogged through snowdrifts as the guns rumbled and thundered and as machine guns rattled not far away. The main objective for K Company that day was the line of pillboxes outside the village of Rafflesbrand…again.

En route to Rafflesbrand, Tom and the new replacements soon witnessed the carnage, giving them a glimpse of what the veterans of this battle had already experienced. The men moved cautiously through a recent battlefield scattered with wounded and dead. Out of the corner of his eye, Tom caught the movement of a German medic attending to a wounded German soldier. As Tom's unit passed by, the medic raised his gun to shoot at Tom's men and Tom responded without hesitation. Tom's aim was good and the medic fell dead in the snow.

Based on the information he had been able to gather while still in Germeter, as well as from reports by the veterans in his unit, Tom believed that the main roads in the area were filled with anti-tank and anti-personnel mines. Tom tried to avoid having his men needlessly injured by skirting areas of concentrated minefields. At some point along the route, Tom and his unit were stopped by a West Point officer in a jeep, who ordered Tom to take his men down the road, rather than avoiding it. Tom refused and tried to explain that the road was heavily mined. The officer disagreed with Tom, becoming angry and threatening to write Tom up for insubordination. As the officer drove off down the road, he passed over a buried mine. The explosion killed the officer. After that incident, Tom concluded that being a graduate of West Point didn't necessarily mean that one was smart.

K Company encountered heavy fighting all morning as the soldiers worked their way toward Rafflesbrand but by 1230, Tom was ordered to have K Company instead replace Task Force Lacy, a special composite unit under the command of 1st Lt. Virgil Lacy. Their mission for the next several days would be to move to the northeast to protect the left flank of the regiment, coordinating their movement with that of the 109th Infantry Division to their north.

On the night of November 10, after the men of K Company had dug in for the night, Tom went to check on his men in the forward positions and came under intense enemy fire. Tom dove to the ground to avoid the gunfire, and unable to see the unfamiliar terrain in the dark, went over the edge of a drop-off into a small quarry. Tom injured both his knees, the right one more severely, but managed to make it back to the company command post. The next day, in the command post dugout, Tom's right knee was so swollen he couldn't bend it. Nevertheless, he remained with his unit at the request of his men and managed to get by with some assistance from the company aid man.

The weather was still extremely cold and wet, and Tom suffered along with his men. Their foxholes filled with water and ice as the foot of snow partially melted then froze again when temperatures dropped below freezing, making it difficult to keep themselves and their weapons dry. Tom sent several of the enlisted men back to the hospitals to get treatment for frozen feet. Their combat boots had gotten soaking wet in the snow and mud, and in the cold temperatures, their feet had frozen. When the soldiers removed their shoes at night, their feet would often swell up so much that it was difficult to put their boots back on in the morning. During this period, both of Tom's big toes froze.

There are no other records of the intense fighting that Tom and his unit experienced over these first three days in combat. But when interviewed sixty-five years later, in November 2009, Joe Reed of K Company remembered that he was injured by shrapnel as they initially attempted to attack the line of pillboxes near Rafflesbrand, just as they had been ordered to do. Army historians interviewing surviving personnel from this battle had not had time to complete company-level interviews with 3rd Battalion officers, such as Tom, prior to the Battle of the Bulge.

With that said, Tom saw almost all of his men—more than one hundred—killed, wounded, or otherwise disabled before his unit was withdrawn from the Hürtgen Forest. In an interview concerning the Battle of the Bulge six months later, Tom said the unit of 160 men he commanded several weeks later in Hosingen was almost

100 percent replacement forces, except for twenty returning to duty from previous injuries and his NCOs, which seems to support this assumption.

Even though the attack on Rafflesbrand was called off at 2300 on November 11, all battalions continued to receive heavy mortar and artillery fire for two more days, making it impossible to organize into platoons and companies, although there were clearly leaders within each group providing direction. The 110th had done its best but the exhausted and dispirited troops were in no shape for any attack to be a success. "Visiting the 110th regiment on November 13, the assistant division commander, General Davis, caught a glimpse of the depressing situation firsthand. What he discovered prompted him to call off all offensive action by the regiment."[2]

November 14-16

Beginning November 14, the U.S. 8th Infantry Division, which had been resting in Hosingen, Luxembourg, moved forward and relieved the 28th, under continued artillery and mortar fire.

"At 1300 on November 15, officers and guides from the 3rd Battalion, 13th Infantry Regiment, 8th Infantry Division arrived at the 110th command post. They were met by officers of the 110th, oriented on the positions they would occupy and the mechanics of the relief worked out. During the afternoon and night, the 110th was relieved and moved into a rear assembly area in preparation to moving to the vicinity of Wiltz, Luxembourg. The relief was completed by 2300."[3]

On November 16, 1944, Tom was finally able to have his knee injuries and frostbite treated at the 42nd Evac Hospital. Tom's injuries were considered serious enough that they sent him to the

---

2   Scorpio's Web site, The Battle of the Hürtgen Forest, http://www.Hürtgenforest.be/ (Dec. 29, 2009).

3   Col. Hurley E. Fuller, Unit Report No. 5–110th Infantry Regiment, 28th Infantry Division; 01Nov44-30Nov44, (Consthum, Luxembourg), 4.

3rd Battalion, 110th Infantry Aid Station, where they had additional medical equipment and medicine to aid in Tom's recovery.

Battle Summary

During the first eight days of the attack in the Hürtgen Forest, the 28th Infantry Division reported 2,631 casualties with an additional 2,328 casualties over the five subsequent days of attack, for a total of 4,939. Of these casualties, the great majority (4,238) were infantrymen.

Half of those casualties can be attributed to the 110th Infantry Regiment, whose original strength was 3,202 men. The regiment saw sixty-five men killed in action, 1,624 wounded in action, 253 taken as prisoners of war, 288 missing in action, and eighty-six men with non-battle related casualties, totaling 2,316 casualties. As mentioned before, 3rd Battalion and specifically K Company's casualty rates were among the highest within the regiment.

Nine thousand overshoes arrived for the 28th Infantry Division just as it withdrew from the Hürtgen fighting.

CHAPTER 5

December 16-18, 1944 in the European Theater: The Battle of the Bulge

After four days at the 3rd Battalion, 110th Infantry Aid Station, Tom rejoined the men of K Company on November 20 in Hosingen, Luxembourg, about sixty miles south of Hürtgen Forest. The company's new assignment was to rest and recuperate in the "quiet sector" of the Ardennes Forest. The 8th Infantry Division, which had previously rested in the town, was now taking its turn in the Hürtgen Forest battle from hell.

K Company's commanding officer, Capt. Frederick Feiker, who was injured prior to the Hürtgen Forest action, was not yet able to return to active duty, and therefore rebuilding the unit and preparing the company for its next combat assignment fell on Tom's shoulders as the executive officer. Tom was well prepared and knew what to do, having been in charge of training infantry units in the states for several years. His original training at Fort Benning as a Weapons Platoon Sergeant and commanding officer of the anti-tank unit at Camp Carson in Colorado Springs would also prove invaluable, given his expertise with all the equipment and weapons available.

Upon entering Hosingen, Tom was very pleased to discover that the town had sustained little damage during the war and that the civilian water and electrical systems were still intact. The Americans had liberated Luxembourg on September 19 after four long years under German control, and the locals still living in the area were supportive and friendly.

Defensive Positioning and Strategy

Along with K Company, the entire 28th Infantry Division had been repositioned along a twenty-five-mile stretch of the Our River. Even though this vicinity was considered the quiet sector, it still bordered Germany and was a critical frontline position. It was also more than three times the area an infantry division was typically expected to defend. The 112th Infantry Regiment protected five miles of the northern section, the 109th covered nine miles on the southern end, and the 110th Infantry Regiment was responsible for more than a ten and a half mile section in the middle.

The 1st and 3rd battalions of the 110th were spread along one of the best-paved highways in the Ardennes, nicknamed "Skyline Drive" by the 28th Division. This north-south highway ran parallel to the Luxembourg-German border, along the ridge top between the Our and Clerf rivers, reminding the men from Pennsylvania of Skyline Drive in the Blue Ridge Mountains back home. The road was also a supply route referred to as the "Red Ball Highway" and known to locals as Highway N16.

General Cota's 28th Division command post was located in Wiltz, halfway between the frontline and Bastogne.

Even though the ten and a half mile area defended by the 110th comprised more than twice the territory that a regiment would normally be expected to control, General Cota made the decision to maintain the 2nd Battalion as the division's only infantry reserve. This left the 1st and 3rd battalions spread so thinly along the sector that they were only able to maintain five company-sized strong points in critical towns along Skyline Drive. The strong points primarily provided coverage for the four main east-west roads that crossed the 110th's sector, along which any German attack would have to pass.

The five strong points, along main east-west routes, and the company and commanders that held them, were as follows in November 1944, starting from the north and moving south (see map):

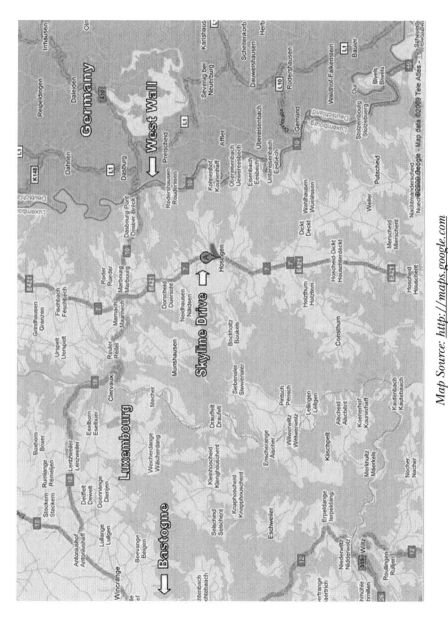

Map Source: http://maps.google.com

Map: Bastogne corridor held by 110th Infantry Regiment's during Battle of the Bulge.

- A Company held Heinerscheid and Col. Donald Paul's 1st Battalion command post at Urspelt;
- **Dasbürg-Clervaux-Bastogne route**; B Company and a platoon from the 630th Tank Destroyer Battalion held Marnach and Colonel Fuller's 110th command post was in Clervaux;
- **Ober Eisenbach- Hosingen-Drauffelt route**; K Company and two platoons of M Company held Hosingen (M Company was the heavy weapons company for the battalion);
- **Gemund-Holzthum-Wilwerwiltz route**; Company L & M (remaining platoons not at Hosingen) held Holzthum and Maj. Harold F. Milton's 3rd Battalion command post was located in Consthum;
- **Stolzembourg-Hoscheid-Kautenbach route**; I Company held Weiler.

Components of the 28th Infantry Division during the Battle of the Bulge are provided in the table below.

Components of the 28th Infantry Division During Battle of the Bulge*
<ul><li>Commanded by Maj. Gen. Norman D. Cota; Gen. George A. Davis, assistant commander</li><li>Composed of the 109th, 110th, and 112th **Infantry Regiments**</li><li>109th and 687th Field Artillery Battalions</li><li>103rd Combat Engineer Battalion (road and bridge maintenance, set and clear mine fields, etc)</li><li>707th Tank Battalion</li><li>630th Tank Destroyer Battalion</li><li>447th Anti-Aircraft Artillery Battalion</li><li>103rd Medical Battalion</li></ul>*Action Report, Col. Daniel B. Strickler[4]

---

4 Col. Daniel B. Strickler, 110th Infantry Action Report of the German Ardennes Breakthrough, As I Saw It from 16 Dec. 1944 -2 Jan. 1945, http://history.amedd.army.mil/booksdocs/wwii/bulge/110thInfRegt/Strickler%20AAR%20Bulge.html (Dec. 29, 2009).

110ᵗʰ Infantry Regiment's Defensive Positioning Summary

110th Infantry Regiment, Col. Hurley Fuller's command post was in Clervaux; executive officer was Col. Daniel B. Strickler

1ˢᵗ Battalion held the northern section with Col. Donald Paul's command post at Urspelt:
- Company A held Heinerscheid.
- Company B held Marnach.
- Company C was in "reserve" in Munshausen.
- Company D held Grindhausen and three machine-gun crews from Company D held Reuler.

2ⁿᵈ Battalion was in reserve:
- Companies E, F, G, and H were held behind the lines at Donnange and Wiltz, where they served as the division's only infantry reserve.
- General Cota's 28ᵗʰ Infantry Division command post was in Wiltz.

3ʳᵈ Battalion held the southern section with Maj. Harold Milton's command post at Consthum:
- Company I held Weiler-les-Putscheid.
- Company K held Hosingen (Company K had approximately 160 men, twenty of whom were just returning to duty.) Also in the town were Company B, 103ʳᵈ Engineers Battalion (125 men), 2ⁿᵈ and 3ʳᵈ platoons of M Company and twenty men from a "Raider" unit (organization unknown) who had come in for specialized training in scouting and patrolling. Only K Company was originally involved in the defensive organization of the town.
- Company L & M (remaining platoons not at Hosingen) held Holzthum (just south of Hosingen).
- Companies M and A of the 447ᵗʰ Anti-Aircraft Artillery were in Consthum.
- Companies C and L, 110ᵗʰ, were the "reserve" company for each battalion.
- Companies D and M, 110ᵗʰ, were the heavy weapons companies for their battalions and each had spread their men and weaponry between the strong points of each battalion.

Also operating in the area of the 110ᵗʰ Infantry Regiment:
- 707ᵗʰ Tank Battalion was at Wilwerwiltz.
- 630ᵗʰ Tank Destroyer Battalion (57-mm guns) and 447ᵗʰ Anti-Aircraft Artillery Battalion had also spread their men and weaponry between the strong points of each battalion.

Hosingen was at the midpoint of the 110th's ten and a half mile section, along the Ober Eisenbach-Hosingen-Drauffelt route and directly on the crucial road to Bastogne to the west. The "road" from Ober Eisenbach to Hosingen was a four-mile, unpaved trail through terrain cut by ridges and a draw running east-west, making direct observation of the Our River impossible from the town's observation posts. The banks of the Our River were extremely steep, and the access road wound steeply upward with sharp, hairpin turns. From Hosingen, the road continued down the west side of the ridge to the town of Bockholtz, where the path then split to cross the bridges over the Clerf River at Drauffelt and Wilwerwiltz. The town of Hosingen, therefore, controlled the main approach from Luxembourg to both critical bridges.

Maj. Harold F. Milton, who had appointed Tom as executive officer of K Company on November 8 during the Hürtgen Forest battle, was now commanding officer of the 3rd Battalion, 110th Infantry Regiment, having relieved Capt. Howdy Rumbaugh.

With the relocation to Hosingen, the 28th Infantry Division was transferred to VIII Corp, which was commanded by Gen. Troy Middleton. Following the Hürtgen Forest action, many of the officers of the division were replacements and each regiment of the 28th once again began to take in thousands of replacement troops. With so few combat veterans still able to fight, the 28th Infantry Division no longer looked like the Pennsylvania National Guard unit that had once made up its ranks.

At the suggestion of Gen. Troy Middleton, on November 24, General Cota named Col. Hurley Fuller as commanding officer of the 110th Infantry Regiment after Major Seely was wounded by shrapnel in the Hürtgen Forest. Colonel Fuller set up his command post in Clervaux.

Given the strained resources of the Army in late November, General Middleton and his commanding officers realized it would be impossible to effectively cover the eighty-mile section of the frontline to the south of the Hürtgen Forest now occupied by the 106th, 28th, and the 4th infantry divisions, the 14th cavalry group, and 9th armored division without adding additional units. They knew it was a calculated risk and justified their decision to leave this area more thinly defended than other areas based on the belief that the Germans were not capable of putting together a substantive counterattack. Even if they did attack, they believed it was unlikely the Germans would come through the Ardennes Forest. Middleton also believed that if the 28th was attacked, it could easily fall back into rear positions while reinforcements were moved into place.

As Tom and K Company made defensive preparation in and around Hosingen, they took into consideration that General Cota favored a defensive pattern of dug-in positions extending well outside each strong point. However, given the less than optimal number of men available in each location now defended by the 110th and the distance between each strong point, that simply was not possible. Instead, each battalion was to establish five squad-strength outposts along the west bank of the Our River across from the enemy's main positions along the Siegfried line on its east side. These outposts were only maintained during the day, as General Cota allowed the troops to withdraw to the villages and warm sleeping quarters at night.

During the hours of darkness, night patrols worked between company strong points and east to the Our River. German patrols typically made their river crossings at night and operated from small towns on the west bank of the river during the day. During the night, the area between the ridge and the river became a no man's land, with German and American patrols stalking each other.

During late November and the first half of December, the Americans had many warnings of a pending German attack in the Ardennes from German POWs, deserters, and locals who were firsthand witnesses to the massive German buildup of men and equipment across the Our River. Unfortunately, most of these reports were not deemed reliable, and the farther up the chain of command each report went, the less seriously it was taken.

The foggy weather, mixed with rain and snow, typical of the Ardennes Forest in winter, helped conceal the buildup of German forces on the east side of the Our River from American pilots.

American intelligence reports also indicated that the German units on the east side of the river were recovering from extensive combat fighting and were too battered to launch an attack of their own. Due to these factors, the 28th Infantry Division did not rate German forces in the area very highly for their fighting capabilities. One of the last S-2 intelligence reports that K Company read in mid-December rated the enemy's capabilities closest to Hosingen as that of strong patrolling only.

Preparing Hosingen

The Men

When Tom arrived in Hosingen, he immediately began to assess the situation. Most of the NCOs of K Company were men who had also been a part of the 41st Replacement Battalion and seen action in the Hürtgen Forest along with Tom. For the most part, he had selected them on the basis of their visible abilities and the fact that he was already familiar with their qualifications. About twenty of the men in Hosingen had just returned to duty (RTD) from prior injuries. Due to the heavy losses in the Hürtgen Forest, the balance of K Company's strength of about 160 men now based in Hosingen was almost 100 percent replacement. There were still a few mild cases of frozen feet that were healing, including Tom's, but on the whole, the men were in good physical condition.

The 2nd and 3rd platoons of M Company, the battalion's heavy weapons company, had been moved into Hosingen for support of K Company. For additional support, the 2nd platoon (thirty men) of the division's 630th Tank Destroyer Battalion was located here as well, with three 57-mms and three .50-caliber machine guns guarding the crossroads south of Hosingen from Steinmauer Hill.

Also in the town were 125 men with Capt. William Jarrett's Company B, 103rd Engineers Battalion. These engineers were responsible for the maintenance of about fifteen miles of Skyline

Drive, the secondary road to the west and the muddy road that led east to Eisenbach. In the first two weeks of December it had snowed or rained almost every day and the engineers' primary task was keeping the roads clear of snow and icy slush. Lastly, there was a group of twenty men from a "Raider" unit (possibly Army Rangers but their organization was unknown), who had come in for specialized training in scouting and patrolling. Neither of the latter two units was originally involved in the defensive strategy employed to protect the town, although the engineers had eight to ten .50-caliber machine guns mounted on their trucks that were utilized after the early stages of battle.

The Setting

The village had suffered little damage from the war thus far, and the houses, shops, and hotels still had electricity and running water. This made the town a comfortable place to rest and train new troops, although Tom got the impression that the 8th Infantry Division had considered the town a rest center rather than a defensive position. Given that their prior action in the Hürtgen Forest was only sixty miles away, Tom and his officers deemed the 8th Infantry Division's defensive preparations unsatisfactory and set about improving them.

In Tom's opinion, overall, the defensive pattern established by the 8th Infantry Division seemed to have been designed and executed to meet the approval of inspecting officers rather than for a tactical defensive situation. Foxholes had been dug around the town and the approaches had been mined and booby-trapped. However, the minefields and booby-traps seemed to present more danger to friendly troops than to the enemy. Tom worked with the engineers to establish a better defensive plan, relocating potentially dangerous mines, building additional minefields along potential lines of attack, and planting a minefield on the Eisenbach road.

Ammunition and Supplies

Ammunition was of great concern to Tom and K Company officers, as only one day's supply was available from day to day. Although K Company advocated having on hand a three-day supply, just a single daily issue was brought up from the rear each afternoon to cover the following day's needs, leaving little in reserve should the daily supply run be disrupted. The supply sergeant picked up extra ammunition and other supplies when he could, but only in small amounts. Some quartermaster supplies (general supplies, clothing, equipment, food, and rations), ordnance supplies (mortars, rifles, machine guns, and replacement parts) and signal equipment also had slowly been coming in. On occasion, a patrol had to borrow the battalion compass to continue its training, as the forest in the area was dense and the men needed to be able to successfully perform their training exercises and return to Hosingen as ordered.

Communications

Tom coordinated with Major Milton's 3rd Battalion command post in Consthum to make sure reliable primary and backup communication systems were in place through the battalion switchboard at Bockholtz. As a result, K Company believed its communications systems to be in excellent condition. There were twenty-four lines from the company switchboard that established wire contact with the engineers, each platoon command post, north and south observation posts, the flanking cavalry run units, artillery forward observers, and 3rd Battalion headquarters. Through the 3rd Battalion switchboard, they could also reach other companies as well as Colonel Fuller's 110th Regiment headquarters in Clervaux.

There were two SCR-300 Backpack Radios in the K Company command post, one used solely for 3rd Battalion contact and the other radio tied in with SCR-300 radios in the 1st and 2nd platoon command posts. Since K Company had only four SCR-300 radios, the 3rd Platoon command post south of Hosingen had to rely solely on wired communications through the battalion switchboard.

The Motorola SCR-300 was a portable, waterproof, battery-powered FM voice receiver/transmitter intended for field use by infantry units. It weighed thirty-five pounds so a soldier could carry it on his back. It had a reliable range of three miles.

Training the Replacement Troops

K Company was responsible for guarding a two-mile section of Skyline Drive around Hosingen and the area just south of it, blocking the Ober Eisenbach-Hosingen-Drauffelt road, which was one of the four main roads across the ridge. At Hosingen, the Our River was four miles to the east of Skyline Drive. The Germans patrolled along the east side of the river and maintained several outposts overlooking K Company's positions. They also frequently crossed the river at night so they could operate from outposts in the small towns on the west bank of the river during the day.

Tom followed the strict regimental and divisional directives for training the replacement troops in scouting and patrolling, sniping, and observation. A prescribed number of hours was required for each soldier in "on the spot" practical work. The usual method was to send out run patrols with an officer and six or seven men, using routes selected by Battalion Headquarters. The men were alternated and the patrols were gradually extended to the Our River; however, no patrols were allowed to cross the river.

These patrol missions offered the only opportunities for replacement troops to test-fire their mortars and new A-6 light machine guns (LMGs). Because no shooting was allowed on the west side of the river, the weapons had to be hand carried close enough that when fired, the mortar rounds and bullets would land on the east bank. There were several clashes with the enemy west of the river and in one instance, a patrol ran into a German outpost. One German was killed and one was wounded in the skirmish.

The following night, the 3rd Battalion command post directed that one patrol was to go out and destroy the German outpost using a 60-mm mortar. As the officers of K Company feared, the patrol was ambushed. Although there were no casualties, the mortar was abandoned. A third patrol sent to retrieve the weapon the next day, found that it, as well as the Germans, were gone. The mortar was never replaced.

S-2 intelligence reports were made to 3rd Battalion headquarters in Consthum every two hours during the day and every hour after dark. Positive reports were written and negative reports were phoned in.

Defensive Strategy

Tom carefully studied and implemented a defensive strategy in and around the town to protect Hosingen should the Germans attack. He established K Company's command post at Hotel Schmitz, a two-story building in the middle of Hosingen. As mentioned before, General Cota's defensive plan favored a defensive pattern of dug-in positions extending well outside the town; however, K Company estimated that a unit of battalion strength would be required to defend properly its entire zone in this manner. Instead, K Company planned a defense within the town. Because no armored units were available to K Company when making the initial plans, the defense was established considering only the defensive capabilities of K Company. Because there was snow on the ground for most of the month, Tom used white sheets from villagers to camouflage their defensive positions; with luck, they would blend in with the snow.

The 2nd Platoon of M Company and its three .50-caliber machine guns reinforced K Company's 3rd Platoon position south of Hosingen on Steinmauer Hill. In addition, the 2nd Platoon (thirty men) and three 57-mm antitank guns from the division's 630th Tank Destroyer Battalion guarded the actual intersection of Skyline Drive with the east-west road to Bockholtz. This intersection was located about 200 meters to the south of the village's edge.

Map Source: http://maps.google.com

Map: Defensive positioning of K Company, 110th Infantry Regiment in Hosingen during Battle of the Bulge.

The rest of the 2nd Platoon of M Company and its .50-caliber machine guns supported the 2nd Platoon of K Company in the south part of town, also covering the south and southeast approaches. One section of 81-mm mortars was set up behind a building in the center of town.

The weapons platoon of K Company was in the north end of town, with LMGs covering Skyline Drive to the north and 60-mm mortars set up in a courtyard (minus the one that had been lost during the patrol to the river). The 1st Platoon of K Company originally was positioned at the north end of town on the main road when Tom first arrived, but on about December 12, this unit was relieved by a cavalry unit and Captain Feiker directed them to withdraw to the northern edge of town, as well.

Single-squad observation posts were maintained on high ground both to the south of town on the crown of Steinmauer Hill (about 250 meters southeast of the village), and in the water tower in the northeast corner of town. Unfortunately, the Our River (and German front line) could not be seen from either observation post due to intervening high ground.

To the north, a platoon of Company B, the 32 Cavalry Squad, maintained a run screen between K Company's 1st Platoon on the north edge of Hosingen and an unknown unit further north. Another cavalry unit maintained similar contact between the K Company's 3rd Platoon, located south of the road junction, and elements of Company I, 110th Infantry Regiment, whose command post was in Weiler, south of Hosingen on the main road. This pattern of alternating cavalry units and infantry companies had been followed up and down the line.

The artillery forward observer had laid out defensive fire plans on the draws and approaches to Hosingen. However, a Division order prohibited actual adjustment of these fire plans. This same order forbade the firing of any other weapons, except at enemy observed west of the river. All other firing had to be done across the Our River. Because of how spread out K Company's defensive positions were, they relied heavily on Browning automatic rifles (BAR) and M1 rifle fire to cover draws and high ground, adjusting the company's mortars to cover the low spots that the riflemen could not see. The .30-caliber model M1 Garand rifle is a semi-automatic rifle, fed by a clip of eight cartridges. Gas-operated and self-loading, the M1 is a shoulder weapon that has a maximum range of 500 yards. The Browning automatic rifle is also a .30-caliber weapon that is a gas-operated, air-cooled automatic rifle fed by a clip holding twenty cartridges. The BAR can fire 450 shots per minute and may be fired from shoulder or hip, or mounted on a bipod. When used automatically, it is fired in short bursts.

Letters from Home

Thanksgiving Day was November 23 in 1944 and Tom and his men were fed a nice Thanksgiving meal. Tom was thankful just to be alive and that his knee and foot injuries had not been worse than they were.

Tom kept himself busy with all the work that needed to be done, also thankful to have the distractions that his position demanded. Tom missed his wife, Anna, and his family in New York, and anytime he was alone, his mind would wander back to favorite memories of them. Fortunately, mail from home finally started to catch up to him, and once Captain Feiker arrived on December 5 and resumed command of K Company, Tom had a brief reprieve from duty and was able to catch up on some correspondence.

Over the next week, a few more letters from his mom and his siblings arrived, but there was nothing from Anna. This was odd because she was always so good about keeping in touch and she had promised to write him frequently. Tom wrote his mom a couple of short letters, knowing she would make sure that Anna got word that he was okay and let her know where he was. Regardless of how Tom actually felt, he did not want his family to worry about him, and like many soldiers writing home during the war, he downplayed the Hürtgen Forest action.

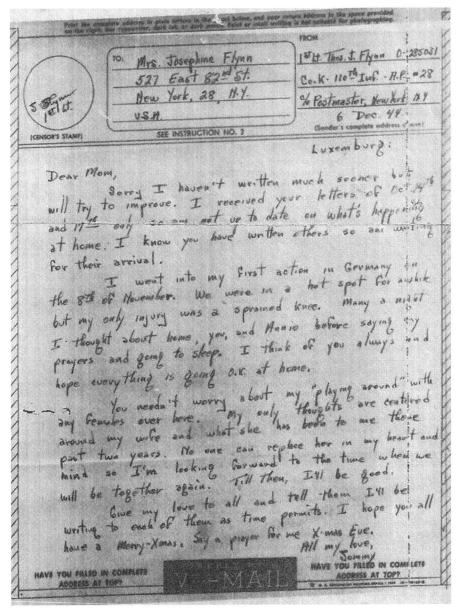

Photo: *Tom's letter home on Dec. 6, 1944*

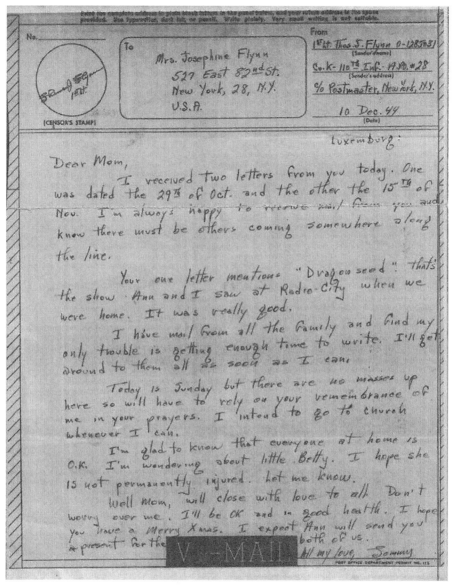

Photo: Tom's letter home on Dec. 10, 1944

Anna had returned to her parents' home in Kimballton in October after her trip to Nashville. She had planned to stay there through the New Year's holiday but she was getting restless. She had been helping her parents around the house and on their small farm but she really wanted to go back to work as a nurse. With Tom in Europe indefinitely, there was no reason not to work. It did not take Anna long to get a job as a registered nurse at Northwestern Hospital in Minneapolis and she had already made plans to move there to begin work in early January 1945. Anna would be able to stay with her sister, Helga, who had lived there for several years and still worked in a factory painting military equipment.

Anna was very concerned that she hadn't heard from Tom yet, as it had been three months since he had boarded the train in Harlan to leave. She had done as she'd promised Tom and written him at least once a week, unaware that none of her letters had reached him yet. She had no idea where he was or even whether he was still alive.

Something's Not Right

In general, the mood of many of the men and officers of the 28th Infantry Division was all too relaxed going into the month of December. Hollywood movie star Marlene Dietrich and her USO troupe were making the rounds throughout the Ardennes, entertaining the American troops. Those lucky enough to get at least a two-day pass often went to Clervaux, where Colonel Fuller's 110th command post was located. Clervaux was a picturesque resort town boasting hot-spring spas, mud baths, German *brauhauses*, theaters, and best of all, women. Some men, with enough days off to allow it, headed to Paris.

Those who stayed behind, however, observed many signs that something was going on east of the Our River. K Company patrols saw increased German patrols on the west bank of the Our River and increasingly heard sounds of moving vehicles and equipment. K Company even heard a report from a German deserter, who walked out of the woods one day with his hands in the air to surrender. The soldier, a twenty-five- or thirty-year-old teacher, had had enough fighting and warned the K Company riflemen in their foxhole that there was going to be a big push before Christmas. The riflemen had him taken to Captain Feiker for interrogation, but even though K Company officers reported everything they observed, there is no record that this warning was taken seriously by those further up the chain of command.

K Company officers did their best to prepare the town and men for an attack. They knew it was likely that something would happen; they just didn't know when. With every new piece of evidence, they became more convinced that the Germans were not going to sit quietly across the Our River for the winter, regardless of whether their superiors agreed with this belief. Much to Tom's frustration, even Major Milton at 3rd Battalion headquarters in Consthum didn't think the topic worth discussing when Captain Feiker and Tom visited his command post in December.

Unfortunately, official scouting reports did not relay the detailed information that company-level troops were observing in the area. Those in command, therefore, were skeptical that the German army would consider or be capable of pulling off the large-scale invasion that was rumored. Both Gen. Omar Bradley and Gen. Dwight Eisenhower knew that the Allies could not be strong everywhere and called the weakly held Ardennes sector a calculated risk, as some portions of the 200-mile front had to be deemphasized. Not remembering or considering what had happened during WWI and 1940, they felt the Ardennes was the safest place to take that risk. This also meant that they saw no reason to order reconnaissance into the German sector in the area, either by ground or by air. Even the weather helped to hide what was going on, as the cloudy, foggy conditions remained bad enough to ground the planes that would have flown routine surveillance missions.

Eventually though, by mid-December, persistent compelling evidence of the pending danger finally convinced Colonel Fuller at the 110th's headquarters in Clervaux of a pending attack. General Cota, however, was unimpressed and disregarded Fuller's concerns. Even if General Cota had agreed, it was already too late at that point, as the German attack was poised to come right through the middle of his division.

Hitler's Last Offensive

On the other side of the Our River, preparations were indeed well advanced. Hitler's forces had put together an amazingly detailed plan to launch a massive counter-offensive against the Allied army in an attempt to split their forces in two, isolate the British 21st Army Group, retake the ocean port of Antwerp, and thereby force the Allies into a negotiated peace. Hitler knew he had to lay it all on the line; his empire had steadily crumbled before his eyes since the Allies' initial assault on D-Day. General Hasso von Manteuffel was appointed commander of the 5th Panzer Army, the unit that ultimately led the assault on the 110th through the Ardennes.

All that fall, Hitler had been busy moving his scattered armies into the Ardennes region, rebuilding battered units with replacements troops, pulling soldiers from other military branches, and refitting them all with new equipment. By winter, Hitler had accumulated "an army of 250,000 men, hundreds of tanks, hundreds of self-propelled weapons, thousands of trucks, half-tracks, armored cars, and other vehicles. The Luftwaffe had even assembled one thousand planes for this operation."[5]

In late November, just after the 28th Division arrived in the Ardennes to recover and rebuild from the Hürtgen Forest action, General Hasso von Manteuffel visited the area and saw for himself just how thinly held the Ardennes' border with Germany was. His intelligence reports gave him a clear picture of the status of the battered 28th Infantry Division and he personally observed the Americans withdrawing their patrols to their fortified villages at night.

With this knowledge, Manteuffel was able to persuade Hitler to modify his plans to permit him to infiltrate infantry assault teams across the Our River under the cover of darkness, and maneuver into positions around the American-held garrisons. The plan

---

5   McManus, 29.

would get underway just before dawn, with a surprise artillery bombardment against the American-held towns. Manteuffel's engineers would then begin to build a series of bridges over the Our River to allow the mechanized units to cross. Once the sleepy towns were seized and the bridges were built, the tanks would roll through to Bastogne and on to Antwerp. This attack would hit three American infantry divisions across an 80-mile front: the 106th at the north end in the Schnee Eifel region, the 28th in the Bastogne corridor and the 4th to the south. If all went according to plan, the armored battalions would be across the Clerf River by the end of the first day and on their way to Bastogne.

Bastogne was the critical point of this attack and speed was of the essence. Hitler and Manteuffel agreed that Bastogne had to fall on the second day of the assault, before the Americans had time to send reinforcements to defend it. Bastogne, with seven major roads running through it, provided critical access for the supplies that Hitler would need to finalize his assault on Antwerp. Without it, the entire offensive would be in jeopardy and any delay or deviation from their precise timetable would certainly put the success of the assault in jeopardy.

The primary unit of Manteuffel's 5th Panzer Army that would attack through the Ardennes region assigned to the 110th Infantry Regiment, 28th Infantry Division, was General Heinrich von Lüttwitz's XLVII Panzer Corps. The unit was made up entirely of army divisions; the 2nd Panzer, Panzer Lehr and 26th Volksgrenadier Divisions (VGD), which included 27,000 infantrymen and 216 tanks, assault guns or tank destroyers, compared with the 5,000 men of the 110th Infantry Regiment.

Hitler considered Von Lüttwitz's 26th VGD to be the best infantry division of Manteuffel's 5th Army. Twelve thousand men strong and under the command of Maj. Gen. Heinz Kokott, they were to capture the towns held by the 110th from Marnach to Weiler, seize control of the bridges over the Clerf River and then swiftly move into Bastogne by the end of the second day. Lüttwitz was specific about how many men he needed in order to capture each town—ordering squads, platoons, or company-size units to surround each town. But in Hosingens' case, Lüttwitz committed an entire battalion to the assault. As the German command would soon find out, it would take much more than that to get Hosingen to fall. Before the men in Hosingen would fire their last shots, the battle would involve the 304th Panzergrenadier Regiment from the 2nd Panzer Division and the 39th and 77th Volksgrenadiers from the 26th VGD, in addition to the 78th Panzergrenadiers initially held in reserve.

Friday, December 15, 1944

At 1800 on December 15, after the daily patrol had returned to Hosingen, activity was heard along the Our River and Tom quickly went to the southern observation post to see if he could help identify or pinpoint any specific noise. Due to the distance between Hosingen and the river (approximately four miles) and the winding, wooded draws in between, the sounds were quite distorted, making identification or location by compass bearings impossible. However, Tom believed that it was probably German motorcycles used by couriers. Eventually, the noises ended and the area was quiet once again. No patrols were due to go out until 0530 the next morning and so the customary 50 percent alert was maintained with men in buildings that had observation posts on the top floors or on high ground.

As a precautionary measure, the officers of K Company also decided to change the location of their mortars, which would prove to be an extremely important, tactical decision.

Shortly thereafter, between 2200 and 2300 hours, Tom and the men in Hosingen observed the Germans shining searchlights, the reflections from which bounced off the low winter clouds, lighting up the entire area almost as brightly as daylight. This was not the first time the Germans had done this at night during the past month, so American officers did not immediately sound an alarm. No further enemy activities were reported. The men of the 110th were unaware that the reflection of the lights off the low clouds was bright enough to help Manteuffel's army cross the Our River and find its way through the woods on the American-occupied side of the river.

In retrospect, we now know that what Tom had heard was the German troops beginning to cross the Our River and move into position around the towns occupied by the 110th.

Saturday, December 16, 1944

The Predawn Hours

Around 0300 on December 16, elements of the 304th Panzergrenadier Regiment from the 2nd Panzer Division and the 39th and 77th Volksgrenadiers from the 26th VGD began quietly crossing the twenty-yard span of the Our River in small rubber boats, their movements hidden by a thick fog blanketing the river. As each group disembarked on the west bank, it quickly moved up the wooded hills through the snow-covered forest into position. The 77th Grenadier Regiment, 26th VGD, assembled in the woods just 300 yards from Hosingen. Their mission was to bypass Hosingen to the north and head straight towards Drauffelt in order to seize the bridges over the Clerf River for the Panzerlehrdivision.

Throughout the area, all the American defenses were quietly being surrounded as the Germans skillfully approached to within striking distance of the towns of Marnach, Hosingen, Holzthum, Consthum, Weiler, and Munshausen. Once in place, some of the impatient German infantry began quietly attacking foxholes and outposts surrounding each position along the frontline. However, most of the German units waited for the first shots of the artillery bombardment that would signal the beginning of the attack as they had been ordered.

Even as Lüttwitz's 77th Regiment was still crossing the Our River for the initial assault, the regiment's engineers had begun working on bridges at Gemünd and Ober Eisenbach, with a third bridge under construction farther north at Dasbürg. At these crossings, the river was usually narrow and not very deep, although extremely steep banks made bridges a necessity to enable the tanks to cross. Lüttwitz had hoped to have the three bridges operational by noon so his tanks could follow closely behind his 26th VGD in case his infantry ran into heavy resistance moving through the Bastogne corridor. This would also help Lüttwitz meet the strict timetable Manteuffel required to satisfy Hitler. Lüttwitz's panzers needed to reach the Clerf River by nightfall on Dec 16 if they were to take Bastogne the following day. He could not afford any major delays.

At 0530 on December 16, a cold Saturday morning, the two young GIs who had been stationed all night in the observation post atop the water tower in northeast corner of Hosingen had just called to report into Captain Feiker at the K Company command post, when the entire German line across the Our River suddenly became filled with "pinpoints of light." Before the young GI who was describing what he saw could finish his sentence, German artillery began to land in Hosingen and all around, severing all wire communications. What they had just witnessed were the muzzle flashes of over 2,000 German artillery pieces aimed at Hosingen and the surrounding area.

An artillery shell made a direct hit on a three-story building just down the street from the water tower where Medic Robert Tucker was working with his unit, starting a fire. They all gathered what medical supplies they could carry and made it across the small town square to a former hotel, noticing along the way that their jeep had also been hit and destroyed. The medics set up a new aid station in the basement.

During the artillery barrage, every man in K Company was sent into his prepared defensive positions. The war had suddenly become very personal and their hearts pounded with the sudden adrenaline rush. Tom immediately went to the north end of town to monitor the 1st Platoon situation and Lt. Bernie Porter went to the south end with the 2nd Platoon. Tom jumped into the foxhole with two of his machine gunners, standing behind their LMGs and kept a watchful eye on Skyline Drive. By now, five buildings were on fire and the artillery shells kept coming down. "The town was pretty well lit up," Tom recalled, illuminating the whole ridge top, but fortunately, there had been no casualties. He and Captain Feiker had no idea of the scope of the attack that was taking place but they knew they should be prepared for a full-scale enemy assault.

Captain Jarrett, Company B Engineers, called Captain Feiker over the radio, and they agreed upon a radio channel over which they would all keep in contact since the shelling had cut all their phone lines. At this point, the men in Hosingen were unaware that artillery shells were also hitting every American-held position of the division—including Colonel Fuller's 110th regimental command post in Clervaux. It was obvious that the Germans were well prepared as their artillery barrages hit their marks, taking down all phone lines within the entire division. Even the radio reception from each company to its battalion headquarters and to regimental headquarters was intermittent at best, as the Germans also jammed reception to prevent communication between and within units.

The heavy artillery barrage lasted forty-five minutes. When the shelling ended, the men of K Company observed the German artillery shells had fallen on every position in town where the mortars had been located just a few hours before. They would have all been destroyed if Captain Feiker had not paid attention to the signs of a pending attack and had his men move them.

Here Comes the Sun

Between 0615 and 0715, K Company could hear the enemy moving up a draw and crossing the road to bypass the town to the north. But it was still too dark for K Company to see the Germans. When the sun finally rose, around 0730, the intensity of the fighting quickly escalated. Through the smoke, morning fog, and low-hanging clouds, K Company could begin to make out shadows moving in the distance and Tom ordered his riflemen to open fire with their BAR and M1 rifles on the Germans crossing Skyline Drive. The LMGs knocked out quite a few Germans and interfered with their westward movement. Tom had trained his men well over the past month and they were well disciplined; they didn't fire unless they were sure of their target. They all knew that with only a day's ammunition on hand, they didn't have any to waste.

At the same time, Sgt. James Arbella, a 60-mm mortar section leader from M Company, quickly climbed into the water tower with the two GIs from Tom's 1st Platoon stationed as lookouts and gave his mortar crew directions as to where to aim their mortars along the Skyline Drive. One of their 60-mm mortars had a damaged bipod from a direct artillery hit but was still functional, so Arbella's men carried it up behind the light mortar battery (LMB) in the courtyard on the north end of town. From this new location, they were able to continue firing to help pin down the enemy. Locations for other 60-mm mortars and the 81-mm mortar fires were relayed by walkie-talkie from units around Hosingen.

The lookouts posted in the water tower continued to scan the area around the town diligently, and as the fog lifted, they observed an entire company of white-clad German soldiers from the 77th Grenadier Regiment charging across an open field from the east, trying to force their way into the town. Despite the lookouts' surprise, they alerted their fellow GIs on the ground in time to stop the direct assault on Hosingen.

Contrary to Manteuffel's orders, two enemy companies attempted a direct assault from the east. Pvt. Edward Gasper, positioned in the large foxhole with Tom on the north end of town, was covering the area outside the barn where they had slept for several weeks. Gasper was pointing his M1 Garand rifle to the north, covering that side, while his two friends, privates Fox and Melvin Epstein, covered the east, with Tom positioned behind them: "This German…jumped up right in front of the foxhole. Private Epstein hit him with a BAR. He was dead before he hit the ground. "Private Gasper spotted two other enemy soldiers crawling up towards the farmhouse. They weren't more than thirty or forty feet from me. I saw 'em and I shot 'em." To the left, two more Germans were walking down the main road that led into Hosingen. Before Gasper could shoot them, another rifleman, nicknamed Tennessee, shot them down. The five dead enemy soldiers lay in defeated heaps."[6] Tom relayed the assault to Captain Feiker and he immediately relayed the report to Major Milton that the enemy had entered the outer edge of the town at about 0730.

Arbella quickly called out new target positions to his mortar team on the ground. The combination of mortar shells, BAR, machine gun, and rifle fire, shattered the advancing enemy companies, stopping the attack. It had only taken a few minutes for K Company's 1st Platoon and M Company on the north end of town to force the Germans to retreat to the shelter of the woods as scores of German soldiers now lay dead or wounded all across the open field.

While Tom and his riflemen were busy on the north end, the 77th Grenadier Regiment was also converging on Hosingen from the east and south. Capt. William Jarrett, the commanding officer of B Company, 103rd Engineer Combat Battalion, had gone up to the church tower and could clearly see the German movements from that direction. He observed the enemy moving along the Ober Eisenbach-Hosingen-Drauffelt road and crossing Skyline Drive on the south end of town. They had already overrun the K Company outpost on Steinmauer Hill, cutting off the 3rd Platoon, in addition to the thirty men of the 630th Tank Destroyer Battalion that were helping guard the crossroads south of Hosingen. Some of the men were able to retreat to the west, while others continued to fight to the death or were captured. No contact was ever regained with the men in these units while K Company still controlled Hosingen. The result was that K Company also lost the support of the 630th's three 57-mms and three .50-caliber machine guns and all their ammunition.

Captain Jarrett could see the steady stream of German infantry on foot, on bicycles, and on horse-drawn artillery caissons cutting across Skyline Drive to the south of Hosingen, so he contacted Lieutenant Morse, an M Company officer who controlled a section of 81-mm mortars on that end of town, and told him what he had

---

6   McManus, 67.

seen. Jarrett's information was exactly what Morse needed and his mortars pounded the Germans, also temporarily halting their movement.

From the command post in the Hotel Schmitz, Captain Feiker called for artillery fire, providing both coordinates and concentration numbers to his supporting artillery unit, Battery C, 109th Field Artillery Battalion, which was located directly to the west of the ridge. Battery C could not respond to his request, however, as it was also under attack by the German infantry that had bypassed Hosingen earlier that morning. Artillery fire was critically needed to stop the constant flow of Germans on main supply route (MSR), but as Tom noted, "Not one round of artillery was ever fired." Since the initial barrage had severed all phone communications and kept Captain Feiker from contacting any other units, the only support K Company had was from its own mortars.

During the initial artillery barrage, German troops had managed to enter the southern outskirts of Hosingen and Lt. Porter's men were involved in fierce house-to-house fighting. But K Company was able to hold them off and contain their progress. During this brief skirmish, one of the men captured a German officer who carried a map outlining Lüttwitz's XLVII Panzer Corps attack plan all the way to Bastogne. Recognizing the significance of the map and that the attack was actually part of a large counter offensive, Captain Feiker attempted to have a runner carry the map back to the regimental command post at Clervaux. But by then there were too many Germans between the two towns, and the runner only made it a mile out of Hosingen before returning with the map.

Tom contacted Major Milton at battalion headquarters to keep him informed of the situation and to let him know that it had become impossible to get the map to Colonel Fuller in Clervaux. At that point, Major Milton told Tom to hold the position and promised that L Company, waiting in reserve at the 3rd Battalion command post, would come forward to help and bring more ammunition. However, L Company became involved in its own battle and never made it to Hosingen.

> *Jarrett's and Feiker's transmissions were being overheard at the 110th Infantry Regiment headquarters in Clervaux but there was nothing that could be done. The 110th was still too scattered and confused by the sudden attack to mount a counterthrust. Before long, it seemed to be too late to help K Company, for at 0750 a radio operator in Holzthum intercepted a report by the executive officer of Battery C, 109th Field Artillery Battalion that reported Hosingen as quiet; this gave the false impression that the Germans had completely overrun the village and that resistance there had ceased. In fact, the silence was due to the fact that the attacking grenadiers had pulled back from Hosingen and ceased to cross the Skyline Drive within sight of the town. Having gained a new respect for the firepower commanded by the little garrison, they continued crossing the highway farther north and south, out of range of the American machine guns and mortars.[7]*

Enough information had gotten through to Colonel Fuller and General Cota by this time for them to realize that the 110th's frontline companies at Hosingen, Weiler, Holzthum, and Marnach were in the middle of a massive German assault and that most of his company positions were now surrounded or cut off. Fuller tried to convince General Cota to release his 2nd Battalion in reserve to bolster up his own defensive line around Clervaux but Cota didn't want to commit his key reserves so early in battle. However, at 0700, General Cota alerted the 707th Tank Battalion to be ready to counterattack and by 0900, Maj. R. S. Garner and sixteen Sherman tanks of the 707th's A and B companies moved out from their camps at Drauffelt and Wilwerwiltz, headed for Clervaux to support the 110th. This was all General Cota felt he could do.

---

7   Allyn R. Vannoy, Jay Karamales, Against the Panzers, United States Infantry versus German Tanks, 1944-1945, (North Carolina: McFarland & Company, Inc., 1996), 203

By 0800, Captain Jarrett and the officers of K Company believed that the enemy might now attack the town from the west, so the 103rd Engineer Company moved into position to help defend the west side of town. The engineers' assistance was now essential to establishing a perimeter defense. They dismounted their .50-caliber machine guns from their vehicles and set up a Final Protective Line (FPL) to impede enemy movement across the area by paired machine guns firing at an interlocked crossing barrier. K Company was already beginning to run low on ammunition, so Jarrett's engineers shared the 3,000 rounds each of .30-caliber and .50-caliber ammunition they still had. Even that would not last long once the enemy resumed its attack. The engineers also coordinated their defense with the mortar men of M Company so they could call for fire. They maintained contact with the engineer teams by radio. With the 3rd Platoon of K Company now gone, the rest of K Company needed all the help it could get.

> *Captain Jarrett sent his 1st Platoon under Lt. Cary Hutter to the western edge of the town, where two small roads from the west joined, and there they set up a roadblock. By doing so, they shielded the M Company mortar section under Lt. James Morse from any attack from the rear. Jarrett's 2nd Platoon, led by Lt. John Pickering, went to the southeastern sector of the K Company command post and a roadblock on the Skyline Drive facing south. The 3rd Engineer Platoon under Lt. Charles Devlin took up positions in the northeastern part of Hosingen, from where the soldiers could give fire support to the K Company outpost in the water tower. Captain Jarrett moved his company command post to a hotel in the northern part of town between the left flank of the 3rd Platoon and the right flank of the 1st Platoon. After they had taken their positions, the men of the garrison quickly ate a breakfast of hot cakes and coffee, still ducking the occasional German artillery round.[8]*

---

8   Vannoy, 201

Now moving outside of the range of the Hosingen weaponry, the German infantrymen continued to bypass the town to the north and the south as best they could through the forest and the cultivated fields. The GIs in Hosingen could do nothing to stop them. This situation continued throughout the day. The enemy made no attempt to enter the town.

Seeing a lull in the action, Captain Jarrett decided to prepare for the evacuation of his unit, which he believed to be imminent. He knew Hosingen was being cut off and he wanted to be ready when the order to move out came. The German artillery barrage had destroyed the tires on seven of his twenty trucks and any available men in his unit went to work replacing the tires and loading everything of value, such as barbed wire, food, and packs; leaving their mines, TNT, machine guns, demolition charges, and ammunition available for use, if needed. Jarrett's staff also began destroying the unit's maps and any critical papers that might be of value to the Germans. He planned to wait until the very last minute to remount on trucks the six .50-caliber and six .30-caliber machine guns that were dispersed around Hosingen.

Having just bolstered the perimeter with Jarrett's men, Captain Feiker tried to convince Jarrett to stay because K Company needed their help. Jarrett was not swayed, so Captain Feiker called Major Milton at battalion headquarters. Milton ordered Jarrett and B Company, 103rd Engineers to stay in Hosingen and support Captain Feiker's unit. He also told Jarrett not to evacuate anything or anyone without Captain Feiker's approval. Milton signed off by promising again that help was on the way.

Jarrett's men dismounted from their trucks and retook their positions on the western edge of town, where he and Feiker feared the Germans might soon attack. Together, the two captains inspected the defensive perimeter around Hosingen, talking with the men and making adjustment to squads and weapons positions where they deemed it necessary in order to give the best all-around coverage. Since the units were short on bazookas and anti-tank guns, they were thankful they hadn't seen any German tanks yet.

Cpl. George Stevenson, with the engineers, was positioned in a barn on the western edge of town with an 81-mm mortar crew and his .50-caliber machine gun. He helped the mortar crew haul the shells for the mortar and then they dragged sandbags from their trucks and placed them around his machine gun. When everything was set up the way they wanted it, they settled down to watch and wait, as did all the other men in Hosingen. It was clear that there was not much chance of breaking through the German lines, and they still had orders to "hold their position," but the men held out hope that the reinforcements promised by Major Milton would be able to break through to them.

Throughout the morning, they heard the sounds of fighting all around them, but except for the one attack earlier in the day, they were left alone. On the southern end of town, some of the GIs decided to test their skills, and sitting cross-legged in the middle of the Skyline Drive, spent the afternoon sniping with rifle and .50-cal machine guns at any Germans foolhardy enough to try to dash across the highway within range. A few GIs from 2nd Platoon also ventured out to reoccupy a farmhouse that had been captured earlier that day. It lay about 600 yards southeast of Hosingen. They, too, kept the Germans at bay, killing about thirty-five German soldiers and destroying some of their horse-drawn artillery.

The Tanks Are On Their Way

When the 707th Tank Battalion got to Clervaux, Colonel Fuller split the tanks into platoons and sent them out to help the different frontline companies. The Shermans of the 1st Platoon of Company B, 707th Tank Battalion, made their way along a winding trail up the west slope of the ridge from Wilwerwiltz to Bockholtz. When they reached the fork in the road at Bockholtz around noon, the first four tanks came to the rescue of Battery C of the 109th Field Artillery, which was under attack for the second time that day. Together, they drove off the attacking German infantry and recaptured one artillery piece that had been lost earlier in the morning, stalling Lüttwitz's 77th Regiment's drive to the Clerf for half a day. The rest of the tanks in Company B took the left fork and headed north to Munshausen and Marnach.

Once things settled down, the tanks took to the road again and fought their way through the German infantry line to the edge of Hosingen. For some reason, when the tanks reached the intersection of Skyline Drive on the south edge of town around 1300, they took up defensive positions and stayed there for two hours, not contacting anyone in Hosingen to make sure they were aware of their position, before the 77th Grenadier Regiment launched a counterattack against them.

Armed with *panzerfausts* (bazookas) and blasting small-arms fire, the grenadiers forced the tankers to button up and the platoon leader called for help over his tank's radio. In response, 1st Lt. Robert A. Payne led the 3rd Platoon of Company A of the 707th south along Skyline Drive from Marnach, three miles away. With machine guns blazing down the length of Skyline Drive, Payne's tanks entered the northern end of Hosingen an hour later to the cheers of the GIs in the town. Help had finally arrived! Based on radio reports heard earlier that day, Lieutenant Payne and his men were surprised to find the town still under the control of K Company.

At about the same time as Lieutenant Payne's tanks arrived, the four Shermans of the 1st Platoon, B Company, that had taken up position at the south end of town suddenly pulled up stakes and headed south down Skyline Drive toward Hoscheid accompanied by two more tanks of their outfit that had just come up from Bockholtz. With these tanks leaving, Lieutenant Payne scrambled to get his tanks into defensive positions before dark. Three tanks accompanied by a few infantry men sent as an escort by Captain Feiker, were sent to the high ground on Steinmauer Hill southeast of town and helped slow the enemy traffic coming up the east-west Ober Eisenbach road. Lieutenant Payne remained in town and moved his own tank to the southern end to cover the road to the south. Another tank strategically positioned itself between buildings that shielded it from the view of the enemy in the northern part of town and covered Skyline Drive to the north.

Captain Feiker, while relieved that he now had tanks to help defend the town, was disappointed that the tanks had arrived without the ammunition that Major Milton had promised. He contacted Major Milton on the radio. Milton told him he had intended for L Company to break through to Hosingen, supplying them with additional men and ammunition, but L Company had gotten caught in its own battles. Milton said that he would try to find someone else to bring more ammunition to Hosingen but his hands were full in Consthum.

At 1600, Lüttwitz's engineers finally finished construction on the bridges at Gemünd and Dasbürg, and the 600th Pioneer Battalion had completed the bridge at Ober Eisenbach, which finally allowed the heavy German Tiger and Panther tanks to cross the Our River. The engineers had experienced several unexpected obstacles that delayed the bridges' completion, stalling the tanks' forward movement for most of the day. The initial delay affecting construction at Gemünd and Ober Eisenbach for several hours was the result of a miscommunication between the engineers and the troops manning that section of the West Wall. The engineers also had to deal with a higher water level than normal due to recent heavy snowmelt, making the initial phase of construction much more difficult than anticipated. The bridges themselves presented challenges, as they had to be built in such a way as to allow access up the extremely steep banks on the west side of the river so that the armored vehicles could maneuver them successfully. Lastly, on the western side of the river, the roads were dotted with large craters from bombs and mines. The craters had to be filled in before the armored vehicles could get through the area. The teams also had to move obstacles that had been placed by retreating German troops a few months earlier to block the road. Once all this was achieved, the tanks still had to maneuver around tight curves alongside sharp drops that made the going slow and dangerous for large machinery. Despite all this, Lüttwitz's 216 tanks, assault guns, and tank destroyers finally moved forward, though at a snail's pace, and headed up the forest roads that led west to the stubborn American-held garrisons.

The delay in the bridges' construction was already causing major problems in Manteuffel's timetable. The tanks, assault guns, and tank destroyers of Lüttwitz's 26th VGD would now be needed to help the grenadiers capture the towns still held by the 110th, instead of making a fifteen-minute drive to the captured bridges over the Clerf, as originally planned.

Lüttwitz desperately needed to eliminate the stubborn American position in Hosingen, regain valuable lost time, and clear the 26th VGD's main supply route. So at 1700, three Mark IVs and elements of 26th VGD attacked Hosingen once again. Gen. Heinz Kokott of the 26th VGD had called upon his division reserve, the 78th Grenadier Regiment, to help eliminate the defenders at Hosingen. Armed with several flamethrowers and assault guns, I Battalion took positions two kilometers south of Hosingen, while II Battalion bypassed the town and headed for the Clerf, crossing at Wilwerwiltz. Two German Tiger tanks moved up to the high ground on Steinmauer Hill southeast of Hosingen and fired on the three Sherman 87 tanks that were covering the road. The Shermans withdrew from their untenable position on the hill and instead set up inside Hosingen near 2nd Platoon of K Company to cover the southern approaches into town. K Company infantry, which had covered the tanks, worked their way back into town as well, except for the few GIs who stayed in the farmhouse southeast of town. The German advance resumed on the Ober Eisenbach-Bockholtz road past Hosingen after the three Sherman tanks were no longer blocking the road and a steady flow of German traffic continued past Hosingen throughout the night. Lt. Payne's crew spent the evening sneaking out of their defilade positions, lobbing a few shells at the German positions, and then racing back to cover.

The Germans continued to fire semi-automatic and automatic weapons at Hosingen off and on all night, from the west, north, and south. Small German patrols were noticed moving in closer to town in preparation for another assault in the morning, but the main German attack was being directed in the north part of town, where Tom and the 1st Platoon were, near the water tower. The Germans continued to push forward, regardless of their losses, and eventually the Germans captured a few houses on the northern outskirts of the village. Vicious and often hand-to-hand fighting continued until around 2200. Tom became involved in one of these skirmishes, in which he killed a German officer. Tom quickly searched the officer's body and discovered a document that provided detailed information on all American dispositions along the entire frontline. Tom called the report in to Captain Feiker as soon as he was able.

One of Tom's squad leaders, Sgt. John Forsell, watched enemy artillery pound the water tower. But the GIs stayed put in the tower so they could continue to call down fire, providing the location of the enemy to the soldiers manning 81- and 60-mm mortars in the middle of town. To the west of the tower, Sergeant Forsell saw another squad from 1st Platoon lay down devastating fire with well-sighted .30- and .50-caliber machine guns from the eight buildings on either side of the road, but the enemy kept coming. Despite the grenadiers' repeated efforts to enter the town, the GIs kept firing with all their weapons as well as with the antitank guns located on the north end of town. They did a lot of damage and temporarily held most of the grenadiers at bay once again.

Cpl. George Stevenson, with the 103rd Engineer Company, was still on watch in the barn nearby with several other soldiers, when they spotted a small group of Germans about forty yards away. Lying on his stomach, Stevenson pointed his rifle out the window and fired a full clip. Several Germans fell and the rest scattered behind a nearby haystack. The men in the tower had called down the position of the haystack to the mortar team and shortly Stevenson heard the sound of an 81-mm mortar shell being placed down its tube. Within seconds, the shell exploded on the haystack, killing most of the Germans hiding there.

In the Hotel Schmitz, Captain Feiker evaluated their situation. During the day, the Germans had so far been able to capture only a few houses on the edge of Hosingen. The fighting had died down, although German patrols continued to work their way to the edge of town. Incredibly, there had only been a few American casualties so far. Hot meals had continued to be served all day to men who came to the kitchen by ones and twos, although food and ammo were both running very low. Most importantly, K Company and the Engineers still controlled Hosingen, causing as much interruption as they could to the movement of German supplies to Bastogne along the roads north and south of town.

Captain Feiker had heard reports throughout the day of Germans donning stolen American uniforms and driving American vehicles, and in addition to already severe communication issues, this added to the confusion within the 28th Division. In some cases, German commandos had switched road signs at crossroads, sending troops in the wrong direction. They had blocked off key roads with white tape, (erroneously indicating a warning of minefields ahead), and told many outlandish stories to the American troops intended to cause panic and fear. Only nine enemy teams had infiltrated through the American lines but they caused enough damage to have the Americans questioning everyone they met. Stories of "false" Americans spread like wildfire through the division. Feiker passed the word among his officers to beware.

What the men of Hosingen did not know at the time was how significant their accomplishments for the day were in the context of the broader German offensive. Their brave actions had considerably slowed the German advance and wreaked havoc on the strict timetable established for the action. Their spirited defense of Hosingen also forced many more German troops and resources to be used to take the town than Manteuffel had planned. In fact, the 300 men who were in Hosingen after the initial assault had cut off the 3rd Platoon had held up an entire division (twelve companies or approximately 5,000 men) from the 26th VGD.

General Manteuffel had a difficult time trying to put a positive twist on the situation when he reported to Hitler that evening. None of his units has reached the Clerf River at any point. Manteuffel reported that while the Americans definitely had been caught off guard by the attack, all units had put forth stubborn resistance, thereby delaying the German movements with skillful combat tactics—especially the men of Hosingen.

By the end of the day, enough information had reached General Middleton that he was finally realizing the Germans were attacking along his entire eighty-mile front and that his four and a half divisions were facing four times that number of German divisions. The commanding officers' calculated risk to have minimal coverage of the area had backfired on them. Middleton knew the only option was to delay the Germans as much as possible to allow Eisenhower and Bradley time to move reinforcements into the Ardennes, and particularly into Bastogne. Middleton reiterated the same orders to General Cota that the regiments of the 28th had already been told several times that day, to "hold at all costs." General Cota once again feared that his unit would be sacrificed to the greater cause, in particular the 110th, as it was the only major unit directly between the German army and Bastogne, a unit now in terrible trouble.

As the day ended, the fighting gradually tapered off and Hosingen prepared for another assault in the morning.

Sunday, December 17, 1944

On the night of December 16, 1944, neither the Germans nor the Americans got much sleep, if any. K Company and the Engineers kept a watchful eye in case more German patrols tried to work their way into town.

Just before dawn on Dec. 17, small groups of Germans from the 78th moved up to the high ground of Steinmauer Hill southeast of town and began to fire their semi-automatic and automatic weapons into K Company's southern-most positions in Hosingen. The GIs in the farmhouse outpost a few hundred yards farther south heard the shooting. Guessing that there were more Germans than they could handle on their own, they decided it was finally time to withdraw their position. Somehow, they managed to maneuver through the flow of Germans moving over the ridge and make it safely into town, thankful that it was still dark. Their practice patrols for the last month had paid off.

The German snipers firing on Hosingen had little effect on the Americans in town, as the GIs were too well dug in. When the sun finally started to rise, revealing the sniper positions to Lieutenant Porter and the 2nd Platoon, the machine gunners and riflemen opened fire and quickly cut the German snipers down. Any survivors capable of moving quickly escaped back to the east side of the big hill and out of sight. No other threatening enemy activity was observed on the south end of town, but gunfire had now been replaced by the faint sound of tanks and trucks. The Americans thought the sounds were likely the 2nd Panzer Division bypassing the town to the north but they could not determine the exact identity and location of the vehicles.

General von Lüttwitz was growing impatient. As long as the Americans occupied Hosingen, they blocked the 26th VGD's supply route, restricting the flow of supplies to the units in the front attempting to cross the Clerf River. If the seizure of this crossing continued to be delayed, the Americans might well win the race to Bastogne. Lüttwitz therefore made the decision to divert several Panthers and Mark IVs from the 2nd Panzer Division and moved them south to help the II Battalion, 78th Grenadier Regiment exert more firepower on the Americans who were still holding out in Hosingen.

About 0900, with Lüttwitz's additional tanks and grenadiers now in place, he was ready to attack once again. Artillery began to rain down on Hosingen for the second time in two days. Once again, the town was set ablaze. The weather had been bad enough to keep American fighter planes grounded since the start of the assault, but a spotter plane finally managed to make a reconnaissance mission over the area about this time. The crew relayed back to its command post the intensity of the artillery barrage it observed falling on the town.

During this bombardment, Captain Jarrett was hit in the foot by shell fragments and masonry when a 150-mm round landed in his hotel command post, exploding just after impact. Fortunately, Jarrett and his radio operators had just gone into the hotel's cellar and no one else was injured. Corporal Putz bandaged Captain

Jarrett's foot so that he could still hobble around. With the hotel in ruins, Captain Jarrett moved the Engineer's command post to the basement of a nearby dairy, which, to his satisfaction, was built of concrete and steel. That combination seemed to be protecting the men in the water tower.

As the artillery fell over the town, turning the beautiful old buildings into piles of rubble, German tanks and infantry once again began another assault, advancing toward Hosingen from their concealed locations in the forest surrounding most of the town. Captain Jarrett took up a position behind one of the machine guns that had been set up in the dairy's basement window. A German soldier moved in close enough to the building that he was able to fire his machine pistol into the window, striking Sergeant Groenveld in the upper thigh as he tried to shift the machine gun to shoot the German. Jarrett quickly put a tourniquet on Groenveld's leg to cover his shattered leg bone, which was protruding from the skin. Medical supplies were getting scarce, but Jarrett managed to locate two units of plasma for his sergeant.

The Americans' already depleted ammunition supply was beginning to run out. Captain Feiker got a radio call through to Major Milton, once again asking for artillery fire to break up the tank attack. But Major Milton informed him that the same elements that had been attacking Hosingen and Milton's own battalion command post two miles south in Consthum had forced supporting artillery batteries to retreat across the Clerf River. They held two of the few remaining American positions and both were now in the same perilous situation.

The assault lasted for another hour but the Germans remained unsuccessful at dislodging K Company, the Engineers, and Lieutenant Payne's Sherman crew from Hosingen. Once again, the Germans had suffered heavy casualties. Lüttwitz realized this new attack plan was not working, and began pulling his units back to their starting positions around 1000 hours, leaving the ground strewn with more wounded and dead. The artillery had much more significantly damaged communications and infrastructure this time, but like before, it had not inflicted many casualties on the Americans. The Americans all agreed that the Germans must have believed the town to be lightly held since they only made small-scale attacks time after time.

Thanks to the support of Lieutenant Payne's five tanks, Lüttwitz had failed once again to break through and capture Hosingen, so Lüttwitz resorted to trickery. Sometime around 1100 hours, two halftracks were observed moving rapidly down Skyline Drive from the north, as if coming from Monarch. Tom and his 1st Platoon in the northern part of town and the Sherman crewmembers in the area could tell that the lead vehicle was an American halftrack, but no one could make out the second vehicle clearly enough to make a positive identification. It didn't seem possible that an American vehicle had made it through the German defenses and that K Company had heard no shots fired. They were also suspicious after Captain Feiker's warning the day before of German impersonators using captured uniforms, equipment, and vehicles.

Tom had his men and Lieutenant Payne hold their fire to see what would happen next. Lieutenant Payne cautiously kept his tank in its defilade position, awaiting further developments. When the half-tracks were about 1,000 yards from town, the two vehicles quickly wheeled about and sped back up the road. The Sherman crew identified the second halftrack as German. Still suspicious of what the Germans were up to, K Company keep a vigilant watch and shortly thereafter, the lookouts still manning the water tower sighted two Tiger tanks hiding northwest of town in a position from which they could have blasted the American's Sherman tank had it revealed its location by firing on the halftracks. Thanks to their patience, Lieutenant Payne's tank had not been spotted and fired upon.

Lüttwitz and his officers were growing increasingly annoyed at the impact the water tower observation post was having on their attempts to overrun the town. At 1300, the Tiger tanks opened fire directly on the water tower, which was still being used as 1st Platoon's northern observation post and to call down mortar fire. The water tower took several direct hits but the Americans suffered no casualties due to the tower's unusual construction.

The outside walls were made of thick concrete supported by a steel shaft column enclosing a circular steel stairway in the center. This steelwork deflected any shrapnel from the shells that managed to penetrate the concrete walls. Even while grenadiers had swarmed the base of the tower, the GIs there had stayed at their post, protected from German fire by the sturdy construction of the tower. Tom found out later that the Germans had offered a substantial reward to anyone who could infiltrate into town and destroy the tower by demolition. The Tiger tanks' efforts were futile and the observation post remained in use.

Before long, six more tanks, Panthers and Mark IVs from the 2nd Panzer Division, had been pulled from their position three miles north in Marnach to join the two Tiger tanks. As they fired away at Hosingen, German small-arms fire once again increased from the woods to the north and west, and enemy semi-automatic and automatic weapons fire from the north prevented bazooka teams from getting in position to engage the Tiger tanks. Up to twenty tanks were reported throughout the day, surrounding Hosingen on all sides. It was very obvious to all that this was the beginning of a major assault on the town.

The fighting continued all afternoon. The eight German tanks in the north began to work their way closer to the north edge of town behind their infantry, wary of the Sherman tanks and bazooka teams, with four more tanks covering their advance with cannon and machine-gun fire. The houses, shops, and hotels in town were slowly and methodically being reduced to rubble as the tanks blasted hole after hole in their walls until the structures collapsed.

Lieutenant Payne proceeded to move the Shermans from the southern part of town to the north and west to engage the enemy tanks, but they were not having much luck against the Tigers. Tom's 1st Platoon machine gunners and riflemen once again opened fire on the attacking grenadiers and mortar shells, still directed by observers in the tower, pinning the enemy down north of town. Flying rocks and masonry added to the devastating impact of each explosion. The Americans continued inflicting significant casualties but more grenadiers just kept coming from the west.

Enemy infantry then began to work in from the north as well as from the west. There were just too many to stop them all. The Germans were finally successful in taking out both of 1st Platoon's machine guns covering Skyline Drive to the north and a .50-caliber machine gun. Eventually, all the 60-mm mortars either ran out of ammunition or were destroyed and even rifle ammunition began to run out.

The water tower went next. With the advancing grenadiers and the continual blasting by the German tanks, the tower was finally rendered untenable. Tom's 1st Platoon leader was wounded in the water tower and later evacuated by the Germans with the other wounded, but most of the GIs managed to get out and work their way south through town.

In the middle of all the chaos, Tom discovered that his radio in the 1st Platoon command post from which he had been reporting for almost two days had been shaken by the concussion of an exploding shell and would no longer transmit, although it could still receive transmissions. He needed to report 1st Platoon's situation and the enemy attack on the north edge of town to Captain Feiker, so he ran the gauntlet from his position, dashing from cover to cover through the rubble-strewn streets of Hosingen, even crawling on his hands and knees at times behind the little stonewalls the villagers had built along the roads. One of the German tanks spotted Tom and started shooting directly at him, but its position did not enable it to lower its aim enough to hit him. Tom thought it somewhat humorous as they continued to shoot over him. He dodged the German gunfire and shell bursts all the way to the Hotel Schmitz, Captain Feiker's company command post in the southern part of town, where he discovered the Germans had begun moving past the southern end of town again.

The Germans reached the north edge of town around dusk, armed with rifles, machine pistols, and panzerfausts. Enemy sniper and bazooka teams began taking houses one at a time and the Engineers and Tom's 1st Platoon, located in the outlying buildings, once again became engaged in hand-to-hand combat.

The men of the 1st Platoon continued to fire from the houses they occupied as long as possible, then after setting booby-traps with their hand grenades for the Germans soldiers entering from the front, escaped out the back door. Not only did this inflict more casualties on the enemy, but setting all the buildings on fire or blowing them up prevented the Germans from using them for cover. The fires also helped light the fields that surrounded the town, exposing any German advance to American fire. But despite the GIs' efforts, the Germans pressed forward and their numbers in the village grew.

In a farmhouse not far from the vacated water tower, 1st Platoon's 19-year-old rifleman Pvt. Edward Gasper, cornered an attacking German with the help of his buddies. The man wasn't wearing a helmet and appeared to be an officer but when he reached for his pistol at his side, the GIs instinctively shot him. They weren't sure if he was reaching for his pistol to shoot them or to surrender but after two days of intense combat, they weren't taking any chances.

Gradually, most of the men from 1st and 2nd platoons of K Company and Lieutenant Payne's Sherman crews worked their way back to the vicinity of the Hotel Schmitz. However, Captain Jarrett's engineers were now isolated in a small pocket on the west side, 1st Platoon had a few small groups of men cut off in the north, and 2nd Platoon had individuals and groups of two or three still scattered throughout the town.

Lieutenant Payne's five Shermans were restricted to movement on the main street, and finally worked into a perimeter defense of Feiker's command post. No dispersion was possible. Lieutenant Payne's radio was now either out of order or his 3rd Battalion command post had moved back out of radio range, as he got no response from them. One tank eventually got knocked out by a direct bazooka hit and one other was lost, probably hit by another panzerfaust, but Tom never found out for sure.

That night, Captain Feiker once again assessed the situation with his officers. Small pockets of his and Jarrett's men were cut off from their units, their ammunition was almost gone, and three of his machine-gun nests had been destroyed along with one of his

60-mm mortars. K Company's kitchen had continued to provide hot meals throughout the day as best it could but the power was now out, there was no running water, and the cooks were running out of food. The GIs were melting snow for drinking and cooking water. Lieutenant Payne was down to three useable tanks to use against the German arsenal surrounding the town. There would be no artillery support or relief force coming.

It was the end of the second day, and now only Hosingen and Consthum remained under the control of the Americans. They had followed the explicit orders from General Middleton and General Cota for two days to "Hold at all costs!" Hopefully, their efforts had bought enough time for the American forces to defend Bastogne and halt the German advance.

Monday, December 18, 1944

Monday, December 18 was going to be another cold, cloudy, hell of a day with the temperature just above freezing. Small pockets of fighting had continued all night long.

In one way, the men in Hosingen had been very lucky. Despite the extensive damage the Germans had inflicted on the town over the last two days, the Americans had experienced relatively few wounded or killed, although the medics' supplies had become just as scarce as everything else had and K Company was still under orders to "hold at all costs." Several of the wounded were in critical condition and in order to do as much as he could for his men, Captain Feiker dispatched Pvt. 1st Class Frank Smith and Corporal Putz, one of Captain Jarrett's medics, to slip through the German lines in the darkness to try to bring back some plasma or a surgeon. They made it less than a mile before they were spotted and captured by a German patrol.

Shortly after that, two groups of sixteen grenadiers stormed Captain Jarrett's command post in the dairy. Jarrett and his men fought them off with rifle and machine gun fire and by throwing their grenades. When the Germans retreated, Jarrett decided

to adjust his positions and Corporal Slobodzian moved into 3rd
Platoon's machine-gun position behind the hotel where their
command post had been. But Corporal Slobodzian was in the
wrong place at the wrong time. He was soon hit in the leg by
German small-arms fire. Several buddies carried him to the aid
station in the town church, and a runner ran through the German-
held streets to get some plasma from Feiker's company, but K
Company was all out as well. Several hours later, both Corporal
Slobodzian and Sergeant Groenveld, who had been wounded the
previous day, died from their injuries. Jarrett knew his two aid
men had done everything they could to save the men, given their
limited resources.

At 0400 on December 18, Captain Feiker spoke once again to
Major Milton, explaining K Company's situation and asking for
instructions. Much the same situation prevailed in Consthum,
and Major Milton finally gave the order for the men in Hosingen
to infiltrate westward through the German lines in small groups
while it was still dark. Captain Feiker said it was too late for that but
proclaimed, "We can't get out, but these Krauts are going to pay
a stiff price if they try to get in."[9] Feiker's several attempts to send
runners out of Hosingen for help over the past two days had been
unsuccessful. There were just too many German troops in every
direction around his position, and escape was highly improbable.
Feiker knew that by now Hosingen was as much as eighteen miles
behind enemy lines, if the Germans had made it to Bastogne.
Major Milton told Captain Feiker and his men to do whatever they
saw fit.

Captain Feiker promptly called a meeting with his officers
to discuss the situation. After a quick assessment, K Company
determined that it only had two rounds of smoke ammunition left
for the 81-mm mortars, the last 60-mm mortar had been knocked
out, and rifle ammunition was so low the men were sharing each
other's supplies. They each agreed with Captain Feiker that there
was little chance of escaping back through German lines. Major

---

9   "To Save Bastogne" by Robert F. Phillips, p. 160.

Milton was contacted again and he left the final decision to Captain Feiker.

As the officers' discussion ensued, 24-year old Tom recommended, as executive officer of K Company, that they surrender so the men would have a better chance of survival. There was nothing else they could do. Captain Feiker conceded and the other officers all agreed. Captain Feiker spoke with Captain Jarrett, briefed him on the situation, and asked for his help with the demolitions. Captain Feiker then issued the order that all weapons and materials that would be of any value to the enemy were to be destroyed. In response, Tom removed his personal weapon, a .45-caliber Smith and Wesson revolver, from its holster, and destroyed it while the other officers watched. He then laid the useless revolver on the table, turned, and left the room to get started on the rest of the demolition.

The Demolition

Feiker called Major Milton to tell him of their decision. In the meantime, Jarrett's engineers went to work and supplied the infantry and Lieutenant Payne's crew with TNT from their own supplies. All of the engineer trucks and road equipment were burned and tires were shot and cut. All K Company vehicles and their garage were set on fire and the tanks were rendered useless. The men demolished their own weapons and all functioning rifles and machine guns. Bulk rations, mail, and other papers were soaked with gasoline and burned. Field ranges and supplies were destroyed. All men who were able to get to the kitchen were issued one K ration and one D ration until the supply ran out. After handing out the rest of the food, the cooks destroyed all the kitchen equipment. The only items not destroyed by the Engineers were items lost to the Germans during battle the day before.

"Unfortunately the company records (morning reports, rosters, etc., covering a period of several months) fell into the hands of the enemy. These records had been prepared for burning with military police grenades. Shortly before these records were to be destroyed, the aid station next door to the command post caught on fire. The aid station was then moved into the basement of the command post, and as the wounded were still there at the time of the surrender, it was impossible to start a fire of the records which were there."[10]

The Last Hoorah

While the demolition was still taking place, men continued to guard the perimeter. Around 0700, Cpl. George Stevenson and several other engineers with 1st Platoon still stationed in the barn on the western edge of Hosingen, took their last shots with their .50-caliber machine gun. As the morning sun was coming up, they could make out several German horse-drawn ammunitions supply wagons traveling on the east-west road about 400 yards southwest of Hosingen. Gunner Lieutenant Hutter opened fire, pouring several hundred rounds right into the wagons, setting them afire. The engineers could hear the Germans cussing all the way from the barn and they had to cut the horses loose from the wagons. Captain Jarrett saw it happen and called it "a grand sight."

Surrender

Sometime between 0800 and 0900 hours, the German snipers and tanks once again began to fire on Hosingen. In order to prevent additional American casualties, Captains Feiker and Jarrett had a white flag hung from a building on the north end of town and had white panels hung on the tanks. The Germans ceased fire immediately. Captains Feiker and Jarrett then headed across the 1,000 yards of open ground between the two armies. Captain

---

10   1st Lt. Thomas J. Flynn interview, K Company, 110th Infantry Regiment, 28th Infantry Division, National Archives, Record Group 407.

Jarrett was still hobbling from his wounded foot, and this delay gave the soldiers a little bit more time to complete the demolition work.

When Feiker and Jarrett reached the German soldiers, they were thoroughly searched and one of the Germans removed Captain Jarrett's dentures from his pocket and kept them. They then met with the ranking German officer on the scene, a staff colonel from the 78th Grenadier Regiment, 26th VGD, and began to discuss surrender arrangements, which took about an hour.

Just before 1000 hours, a member of Feiker's staff radioed news of the surrender to Major Milton's command post. The man on radio told Major Milton's command post, "We're down to our last grenades. We've blown up everything there is to blow up except the radio and it goes next." What sounded like a sob came over the radio and the voice went on again, "I don't mind dying and I don't mind taking a beating, but I'll be damned if we'll give up to these bastards." Then the radio went dead.[11]

At 1000, captains Feiker and Jarrett returned at gunpoint, accompanied by German officers and troops. They gave their men one last order and told them to come out of their buildings in a column of threes with hands on helmets. German soldiers were now all over the place rounding up prisoners.

The Battle of the Bulge, as the Americans would come to call it, lasted until January 28, 1945, but for the Americans in Hosingen, their next mission was simply to survive.

Summary of the Battle

Tom summarized the casualties of the battle in Hosingen as follows:

> *"There were initially about 300 men, including the engineer company, which had been cut off west of town, and odd men*

---

11 Phillips, p. 160

who had been captured individually and eight officers. Three of the officers were from K Company (the 1st and 3rd platoon leaders were missing and the 2nd Platoon had been commanded by a T/ sergeant. Lieutenant Flynn later learned that the 1st Platoon leader had been wounded in the water tower OP and had been evacuated by the Germans with other wounded.) The other officers were a tank platoon leader, and four engineer officers. Known casualties with the town were seven killed, ten wounded, (two seriously), and none missing. ["12]

In defense of Hosingen, these brave men inflicted an estimated 2,000 casualties upon their German attackers and killed more than 300. They were often outnumbered more than ten to one and were provided no artillery support during the entire two and a half days of battle.

They had done exactly as General Middleton and General Cota had ordered and held their position at all costs, buying the precious time that the 101st Airborne and other divisions needed to arrive at and defend Bastogne. The title of John C. McManus's book on the battle, *Alamo in the Ardennes*, pretty well sums it up.

From the German's perspective, the regimental staff colonel and soldiers were extremely surprised when all of the Americans gathered in the street. They could hardly believe that such a small group of men had put up such a good fight, at times against 5,000 Germans, suffering so few casualties, while inflicting such enormous damage on their own forces.

---

12   Flynn interview

CHAPTER 6

December 18, 1944-April 29, 1945: 133 days as a German Prisoner of War

Appendix A contains maps that may be helpful to follow Tom's path.

Prisoners of War—Day 1

Unfortunately, word of surrender and the order to destroy their weapons was not relayed to all the men around Hosingen as quickly as it should have been. Sgt. James Arbella, the 60-mm mortar section leader, had received minimal communication from Captain Feiker over the past two days, so when he saw the other men from his unit coming out of the buildings with their hands on their heads, a buddy had to clue him in on what was happening. He nodded in agreement and headed to their garage to set his jeeps on fire. He then gathered the rest of his soldiers and prepared to surrender.

As he did so, he ran into eight of the mysterious Rangers who had been in the town this entire time. Those who had witnessed the Rangers in action for the past few days all agreed they really knew how to fight. Their commander asked Arbella if the surrender order was true. Arbella confirmed that it was, so it was no surprise that the Ranger responded that they were not giving up. He and his men took off west out of Hosingen, never to be seen again. Arbella watched them go and then he and his men joined the other American soldiers lined up on Hosingen's main street.

Pvt. Edward Gasper heard the grenadiers coming closer, as there was no longer any need for the Germans to be quiet. He took a deep breath and prepared to give up. He slammed his rifle down, venting his frustration and anger at the same time, breaking the stock and throwing the parts away. He then opened the door, put his hands up in the air, and joined the others falling in line. The Germans searched him thoroughly, taking anything of value, including his watch, cigarettes, and K rations.

Surrounded by the dead bodies of twenty-eight Germans soldiers, all but one shot in the head, one of the high-ranking German officers confronted Medic Wayne V. Erickson and demanded to know where all the rest of the Americans who had defended the town were. Erickson told him that he was looking at all of them. The German officer clearly was surprised at his response and told the medic he was not telling the truth, but Erickson reiterated, "This is it and there are no more." After a few moments, the German officer decided he was telling the truth and commented, "Nice shooting," to which Erickson agreed with a simple, "Yah." This was the second time since the 28th had started fighting in Europe that Medic Erickson was a prisoner. His first capture occurred while his unit fought its way through France. He had just been reunited with K Company in December.

The German officer was not the only one who was confused and angry. The grenadiers had watched many of their comrades be killed or wounded over the past two and a half days and many of them still lay unattended in the fields surrounding the town. Needless to say, the mood was very tense. All Tom and the other American officers could do was watch in silence as their men were yelled at, slapped around, searched, and stripped of their valuables. Unfortunately for the enlisted men, many of them were also forced to give up their combat shoes and/or galoshes in exchange for the inferior German boots of the soldier doing the trading. In most cases, the German boots did not fit very well and a number of the GIs found themselves with shoes that were to cause them nothing but problems.

The officers and enlisted men were allowed to keep their helmets and gas masks, and any toiletry items that they had brought with them.

While the men were being searched and boots were being exchanged, one of the German officers was intently questioning the enlisted men to find out who was responsible for killing one of his medics. First Lt. Bernie Porter had shot the weapon-carrying medic in self-defense and he knew he would be executed on the spot if anyone gave him up. The enlisted men also were aware that Lt. Porter would be punished if discovered, so everyone kept quiet and acted as if he didn't know what the German officer was talking about.

While all this was going on, the Germans mounted two MG42 machine guns, one on a trailer and the other on the ground just twenty-five yards away and pointed directly at the America POWs. All eyes were fixed on the weapons when one of the machine gunners opened fire. The accidental discharge caused a short burst of bullets to be expelled from the weapon killing two GIs and wounding two. The German captain in charge reprimanded the machine gunner responsible for the shooting. Captain Jarrett later reflected that the German captain had saved many GIs' lives that day by stopping the potential massacre.

The ranking German officer then ordered his men to take Tom and the other American officers to an isolated house at the south end of Hosingen. There they were crowded into a small room, searched, and interrogated. One by one, each officer was required to empty his pockets into his helmet so a German officer could inspect each item. For some reason, no physical search was made of their clothing. During this investigation, some of the officers were forced to destroy maps and papers which they had decided to keep or hadn't thought to get rid of before capture. Tom was allowed to keep a small brown, leather-bound book of German phrases that he had been carrying for several months. He was very glad he had studied German in high school so he could understand what the German officers were saying and to help his men understand what the Germans wanted.

The interrogation was relatively brief as the Germans were primarily concerned with details about the locations of minefields and booby-traps. The officers of K Company spoke only of a minefield the Germans had already discovered, as their vehicles had exploded several of the mines. The Germans threatened to march the prisoners cross-country to detonate possible mines, but fortunately, this threat was not carried out. At least there was some satisfaction in the possibility that the engineers' other minefields would still be wreaking havoc on the Germans long after the POWs were gone.

After the Germans were satisfied they had what they wanted from the enlisted men, and while the officers were being interrogated and searched, the enlisted men were moved out into the open fields around the town to tally and search through the dead and wounded. Medic Erickson was one of the men who was forced to help bury the three hundred dead Germans soldiers. He was told it was the German medics' job to bury the dead and now that he was a POW, it was his job. Once the dead were all buried, the medics were ordered to help take care of the wounded, both German and the POWs from Hosingen, until transportation could be arranged for them to a hospital.

The remaining officers and enlisted men were then corralled into a fenced-in, open area where they were held for the next four or five hours while the Germans tried to get confirmation as to what they should do with the prisoners. The POWs were exhausted, hungry, and cold and most of the enlisted men with ill-fitting boots already had problems with their feet. There was nowhere in the field to sit that wasn't wet, muddy, or snowy. Like Tom, many of the men thought about their wives and families, wondered what would happen to them, and whether they would make it through the rest of this war alive. Their survival would depend on the mercy of these German soldiers, who obviously hated them.

While the weather conditions had been bad enough to ground most planes over the past few days, the spotter plane's report of the intense shelling at Hosingen the day before had prompted at least one American fighter plane to be sent to the area for air support to defend the town. Unaware that the men of Hosingen had surrendered that morning, the American plane flew in from out of nowhere in an attempt to attack the German infantry, which the pilot had observed gathered on the ground below. He didn't realize that he was targeting the American POWs from Hosingen. Before the POWs had time to react, a German fighter plane came from behind and shot the American plane down. The plane crashed and exploded into flames close enough to the men for them to observe that no one made it out of the plane alive. The POWs assumed the pilot probably thought that they were Germans.

It was dark outside by the time Tom and the POWs were finally moved out in columns, with the enlisted men leading in one group and the officers following behind in the second group. As it had been for more than a month, the weather was rainy, the ground was wet and muddy, and the patches of snow that lay all around reminded the men of the winter weather to come. As the POWs moved out, leaving the Germans in possession of Hosingen once again, the Germans still could not believe that so few Americans had put up such an amazing fight.

Tom and the other POWs were marched to Eisenbach, the small border town just four miles away on the Ober Eisenbach-Hosingen-Drauffelt road, along the German's main supply route south. Even after three days, it was still jammed with westbound traffic in support of the massive German offensive. The POWs had to maneuver their way using the truck headlights that were shining right in their eyes. Because the road was very narrow they frequently had to move into the muddy ditches to permit the passing of motorized and horse drawn vehicles. The POWs were surprised to observe so many trucks towing two or three other trucks, as reserve vehicles.

It was late by the time the POWs arrived at Eisenbach and the exhausted, hungry men were jammed into a small church, where they lay tightly packed together on the floor with only straw to cover them. The cold and wet conditions had already caused frostbite to appear on some of the men's feet. The Germans had promised a hot meal when they got to Eisenbach but that did not happen. Those who still had their K and D rations shared them with their buddies. At least they were now sheltered inside a building and able to rest, as most had not slept for almost three days since before the fighting even began. They tried to get some sleep. The next day promised to be another long and miserable one.

On the Move—Days 2-7

The next morning, Tom and the other POWs were given only a small cup of hot coffee for breakfast. Observing only a few guards, some of the POWs contemplated an escape but at this point, they had no idea how far behind enemy lines they actually were. After all the men and equipment they had seen flowing past Hosingen for the past three days, they decided against it. Standing outside the Eisenbach church, they could also see large amounts of heavy artillery still moving up the road from the south on the west side of the Our River. It was not a good sign. Obviously, this heavy artillery was no longer needed along the German-Luxembourg border, since the Germans had recaptured all the frontline towns that had been held by the 28th Infantry Division.

The POWs once again were formed into columns to continue their march into Germany. As Tom crossed the small footbridge over Our River, he reflected on the significance of moving into Germany and farther away from any rescue attempt. He did not realize that despite their notification to Major Milton of their surrender yesterday, the Army had yet to reported K Company and the Engineer Battalion units missing in action.

The POWs were being marched to Prum, Germany, a 24½-mile, two-day walk away. The only food the POWs received before they got to Prum was from civilian supplies the *feldwebel* (sergeant) in charge of the column procured along the way. The German guards were anxious to impress upon the prisoners that they were in charge and it wasn't long before several of the German soldiers tried to take any money the enlisted men had on them for safekeeping. Captain Feiker protested to a German NCO that the Geneva Convention prohibited this and he insisted on speaking with the German officer in charge of the column. The disgruntled Germans protested but allowed the POWs to keep their money. As the day wore on and the weather continued to get colder, the German guards once again decided to flex their muscle and each enlisted man was forced to give up to the guards either his field jacket or his overcoat, whichever he chose. Most of the men chose to keep their overcoats but the missing layer of clothing intensified the cold and added to the misery of their frozen and blistered feet, thirst, hunger, and exhaustion. Tom and the other officers could do little to help their men.

As K Company and the Engineers got closer to Prum, they could see the small town was alive with activity; troops and equipment were moving in all directions. There appeared to be a marshalling yard in Prum that was being used to ship the American GIs to the German POW camps, along with the maze of tracks used to transport supplies to the frontlines. The German army had work crews everywhere (both slave labor and POWs). They were repairing and filling in bomb craters in the roads, removing rubble, repairing damaged railroad tracks, loading and unloading railroad cars, and working as field laborers. Despite the sophistication of much of the German equipment, the German army was still using horses for transportation at this stage of the war, which meant the roads were full of horse manure that the POWs had to continually step around.

When Tom's group made it into Prum late on December 20, other prisoners from miscellaneous units were added to the column, bringing the total to approximately 500. Some of the men who joined the group were from the 3rd Platoon of K Company, which had been overrun on the afternoon of December 16, south of Hosingen. Other POW columns could also be seen along the way and POWs from both the 28th and the 106th infantry divisions that had been stationed all along the frontline were now converging in Prum for transport to the camps. The men were all glad to see that their buddies were still alive despite their circumstances, and they caught up on what had happened to their units. The group did not get much rest, as the Germans rerouted them to Gerolstein, another 12½ miles away. The German soldiers guarding the columns also were beginning to feel the effects of exhaustion and hunger, but they did as they were told and lined the POWs up to continue their march. The weather continued to get colder and it felt as if a big storm was coming soon.

The POWs did not get rations before the column moved out for Gerolstein and many of them were in a lot of pain after the three day, 30-mile march from Hosingen on frozen feet with inadequate footgear. The column reached Gerolstein the following day (December 21) and only a small amount of hot soup was served them upon their arrival. The men were starving and what they were given did little to fill their empty stomachs.

The GIs were then issued some straw to sleep on and Tom and the other POWs were locked in an icehouse overnight. More prisoners were added to their group as the afternoon and evening wore on, and Tom observed many happy reunions taking place between the men from other units. There were no new POWs from the 28th Infantry Division, so Captain Feiker instructed the men of K Company not to speak to anyone they did not already know. Captain Feiker was still concerned the Germans would mix spies in with the prisoners in an attempt to gather more intelligence on the American forces. Thankful to be off their feet and out of the winter weather, the men tried to rest and tend to their aches and pains as best they could.

The next day, December 22, the Germans issued a two-day food ration for their next move. It consisted of two packages of German field biscuits per man and a fair sized can of cheese to be split between six men. The POWs were divided once again into groups of officers and enlisted men and then split into groups of about fifty to be loaded like livestock into boxcars, which were then locked. Their train was headed for Frankfurt, Germany, 147 miles away. The guards rode in separate cars and dismounted to patrol whenever the train stopped, as trains carrying supplies to the frontlines took priority on the railroad tracks. The men were let out only occasionally during these stops to relieve themselves, but because of the small amount of food they had been given, there was no major latrine problem in Tom's boxcar.

The train pulled into the Frankfurt marshalling yards later that day, December 22, but the POWs remained inside in the dark, cold, drafty boxcars and huddled together to try to stay warm. After a week of captivity, the men smelled pretty bad and each one longed for a hot shower; a hot meal; a soft, warm bed; and freedom. They could hear constant commotion outside but they were given no indication of what the Germans' plans for them were or when they would be fed again. Water and brief bathroom breaks, which afforded a breath of fresh air, were the only things they received frequently.

The POWs sat in the boxcars for two days—waiting, worrying, and wondering—and it was now Christmas Eve, December 24. The men were all thinking of their families at home celebrating the holidays without them. They were sure their loved ones had no idea of what they were going through or even that they had been captured.

Tom was glad that he had been able to tell his family in his brief letters in early December that he was okay after the Hürtgen Forest battle, but he, too, was sure they had no idea that he was now a prisoner. Tom's sister, Mel, never gave up hope that God would bring her three brothers home safely and she placed their photos underneath the Christmas tree. She took a photo to show them upon their return that they were with the family in spirit that Christmas.

Then it started. The air-raid sirens in Frankfurt went off and bombs began exploding all over the city, including in the Frankfurt marshalling yard. A number of boxcars exploded several rails away from where Tom's car was sitting, sending shock waves and shrapnel everywhere. The sounds of the explosions and pieces of metal shrapnel flying at high velocity through the air into the other boxcars nearby was deafening and terrifying. They had no idea if the next bomb would land directly on them. In a panic, one man tried to escape out the small window in the boxcar but was immediately shot and killed by a German guard. Fortunately, there were several other parked trains between Tom's boxcar and the strike area to absorb and hold back any shrapnel coming their way.

What Was Going On

It had now been nine long days since the German Ardennes offensive had begun. Due to the poor weather conditions, the Allies had not been able to use their superior air power to counterattack the German army. A break in the weather finally came on Christmas Eve Day as a high-pressure front moved across Western Europe, bringing with it clear skies and the opportunity for the Allies to strike back hard. The U.S. Eighth Air Force and England's Royal Air Force (R.A.F.) were ready, and launched the largest coordinated air strike in history, intending to cut off all communications and transportation routes for the German army. It was critical to eliminate access to supplies and replacement troops. Primary targets were German airfields, and secondary targets were marshalling yards (train yards). As part of this massive assault, one hundred and forty-three planes were headed to Frankfurt, Germany, to destroy the airfield. The marshalling yard where Tom and the other POWs were being held was not an official target on this mission; however, stray bombs obviously had landed near Tom's boxcar, causing massive damage, panic, and confusion.

Anna's older brother, Ole Bennedsen, with the 839th Squadron, 487th Bomb Group, was one of the pilots whose mission was to bomb the Gross Ostheim Airfield and the marshalling yard that Christmas Eve night. Ole was flying so deep into Germany that he didn't expect to make it back to England. He wished that somehow one day there would be a way for airplanes to refuel during flight. By the grace of God, Ole's plane made it back to England and he went on to fly many more successful missions. Ole had many friends who weren't so lucky and either were shot down over Germany or their planes ran out of gas on the return flight to England.

The Aftermath—Days 8-9 (Two days)

No one that Tom knew, besides the man who was shot trying to escape the boxcar, was physically injured that night, but the sheer terror of the Christmas Eve bombing would haunt Tom for the rest of his life. The next day was Christmas Day, and the men were given one Red Cross parcel per five men to share in lieu of German rations. The following day, the train finally headed northeast out of Frankfurt for Bad Orb, Germany.

Stalag IXB at Bad Orb, Germany—Days 10-24 (Fifteen days)

On December 26, after four days locked in the boxcar, Tom's train pulled into Bad Orb and he, along with hundreds of other GIs from the 28th and 106th infantry divisions captured on the Western Front, were organized into columns and marched up the mountain road to the POW camp, Stalag IXB. Before the war, the site had been a beautiful summer camp that children from all over Germany enjoyed. Located just thirty miles northwest of Frankfurt, Bad Orb was situated in a lovely valley surrounded by woods. But now instead of happy children playing and barracks filled with fun and laughter, the camp imprisoned thousands of POWs within its barbed wire fences.

Russian and Serbian prisoners had recently occupied the compound that was assigned to the American POWs. Tom's group was the first wave of American soldiers to be sent there and the German authorities of the camp were totally unprepared and unequipped for their reception.

Once inside the compound gates, the new prisoners were processed and issued numbered, metal prisoner ID tags. Tom's number was 25139. The prisoners were de-loused and allowed to have hot baths and then the officers and enlisted men once again were separated. Due to the large number of Americans, there was no choice but to pack them into sixteen of the dilapidated barracks. Tom was one of 250 officers jammed into a barracks they would temporarily occupy before being moved to another camp.

Most of the men were issued only one German blanket, many of which were worn and threadbare. Some men had no blankets and many had to sleep crowded on the bare wood floors in rooms that lacked bunk beds. In addition, one fifth of the men did not even have an overcoat since many had been forced to give them up to the German soldiers.

Each barrack had two large rooms fitted with only one small stove meant for heating the space. Many of the rooms had broken windows and the wood or cardboard covering the holes did little to keep the below-freezing temperature outdoors where it belonged. For the most part, the size and poor condition of the stoves really didn't matter, as the coal or wood provided to the prisoners each day produced only a few hours of heat. Lighting was also minimal as each room had only one very dim light bulb to illuminate the entire space during the long winter nights. Lights-out was at 7:30 p.m.

Hygiene was another major problem. The prisoners shared only three very primitive latrine houses and three latrine trenches. At night, the POWs were required to use the one equally primitive latrine in each room of the barracks. Toilet paper was scarce. There was no hot water, no soap, and no special washroom. The men had to make do with just the one or two taps of cold water that were in each room.

The German food rations for the POWs were also minimal and there was no stock of Red Cross food parcels, so the food available was barely sufficient. The POWs typically got a coffee-type beverage for breakfast. Some type of vegetable soup was served at noon. It usually consisted of field beets but sometimes five or six potatoes were added, although overcooking usually made them unrecognizable. On a good day, some form of black bread or sugar was included to supplement their diet. Occasionally, a dead horse would be dragged through the camp, meaning the prisoners might find a piece of meat in the soup. Even a dead bug in the soup was deemed acceptable, as it was just another form of protein to the starving POWs. Late in the afternoon, each man received one-sixth of a loaf of bread, a small portion of margarine, and occasionally, a little cheese or meat (horsemeat). Many of the soldiers had to use their steel helmets as eating bowls. Tom never saw a Red Cross parcel distributed while he was at this camp.

The POWs were losing weight rapidly and their strength seemed to ebb every day. It didn't take long for some of the heavier-built POWs to become too weak to leave their bunks, so Tom and the lighter-built men managed to get around and help take care of them.

The overall condition of Stalag IXB was terrible and it was considered one of the worst German POW camps that held American prisoners. POW doctors and medics ran a hospital in the camp and did the best they could for men needing medical attention, but their supplies and equipment were limited. The International Red Cross was allowed access to the camp but it had little impact on improving the living conditions for the prisoners. Unfortunately for too many POWs, Stalag IXB became a death camp. By the time the prisoners reached the camp, many were already rundown and suffering from unpleasant intestinal conditions. Lack of proper food, medical care, and sanitary conditions wreaked havoc on the POW population and some of the barracks displayed handmade crosses along the outside wall, bearing the names of the POWs who did not survive.

Due to the terms of the Geneva Convention, the officers were separated from enlisted men, but because of a lack of space, they were not kept in solitary confinement. Officers were not allowed on work details outside of camp, which meant there were no additional opportunities to supplement the minimal rations they were given, nor chances to gather firewood for the stoves in their barracks. This would be the case throughout their captivity.

Contact was made with other officers from the 28th Infantry Division while at Stalag IXB and the men tried to put together their stories to understand the events that had led them there. Not everyone from Hosingen made it to this camp. For various reasons, they were sent to other camps in Germany and Poland. Capt. William Jarrett, CO, 103rd   Engineers, Col. Hurley Fuller, commander of the 110th Infantry, and other officers of the 110th were marched to a POW camp in Poland, Stalag IVB at Mulburg, where they were liberated by the advancing Russians after just a month of captivity, in late January 1945. The medics that were required to stay behind and care for the wounded were initially sent to Stalag IVB at Mulburg, Germany and then marched again the Stalag VIIIA at Gorlitz near Poland.

Move to Oflag XIIIB at Hammelburg, Germany—Days 25-26 (Two days)

Besides separating the enlisted men and officers during their forced marches, confinement in the railroad boxcars and POW camp barracks, the Germans divided the POW camps into two types. Stalags were for the enlisted men and oflags were meant for officers. On January 11, 1945, Tom and 452 officers, twelve non-commissioned officers and eighteen privates were marched back down the mountain road, where they were loaded once again into boxcars and transported to Oflag XIIIB, thirty-four miles south near Hammelburg. The officers with whom Tom had fought in Hosingen and with whom he was relocated included:

- Capt. Frederick Feiker, CO, K Company, 110th Infantry Regiment
- 1st Lt. Bernie Porter, K Company, 110th Infantry Regiment
- 1st Lt. James D. Morse, Mortar Section Leader, M Company, 110th Infantry Regiment
- 1st Lt. Robert A. Payne, Platoon Leader, A Company, 707th Tank Battalion
- 1st Lt. Cary Hutter, 103B Engineers, 1st Platoon
- 2nd Lt. John Pickering, 103B Engineers, 2nd Platoon
- 2nd Lt. Charles Devlin, 103B Engineers, 3rd Platoon

The POWs were issued a three-day ration for the train ride. This time, the ration consisted of a 1½-pound can of beef and three-quarters of a loaf of bread for every two men. The train ride to Hammelburg took only two days (January 11 and 12) and, in anticipation of being fed upon arrival at the new camp, the men finished all the rations they had been given. Unfortunately, however, the Germans were true to their word and the men went without rations the first day at Hammelburg.

The civilians in Hammelburg were used to seeing prisoners being moved in and out and they displayed no reaction beyond natural curiosity as Tom and the other POWs marched from the rail yards to the enclosure on the hill three miles south of town. Tom and his group were the first Americans to be sent to this camp as well, and once again they were lodged in premises formerly occupied by Serbian POWs. By late March, there would be an estimated 3,000 Serbians in Oflag XIIIA and 1,500 Americans in Oflag XIIIB. Stalag XIIIC was nearby and it held an additional 10,000 NCOs and enlisted men. Former commanding officer of the 110th, Lt. Col. Theodore Seely, also was transferred to this camp in mid-January.

Like the rest of the POWS, Tom kept track of the days he spent in captivity. It was now the middle of January and in just a few days, it would be Anna's twenty-fifth birthday. This was not how he had pictured them celebrating it. He knew she was probably very worried about him and wondering if he was still alive.

Oflag XIIIB at Hammelburg, Germany—Days 27-100 (Seventy-four days)

The POW camp at Hammelburg was quite old and it had been housing Serbian prisoners since 1941. After the capture of so many Allied officers during the Battle of the Bulge, the Germans split this camp into two sections and hastily made some upgrades to the Allied side to make the buildings livable, although the conditions were still considered miserable. The Serbians were kept in Oflag

XIIIA and Allied officers in Oflag XIIIB. In the Allied compound, each of the seven stone barracks had five rooms and was set up with enough stacks of bunk beds to house 200 men—forty per room.

Camp Conditions

The winter of 1944-1945 was one of the coldest on record in Germany. The POWs tried to keep from freezing to death by wearing all the available clothing they could find and huddling around the stoves in each room. The Germans rationed the coal for each stove at a rate of just forty-eight 5-x-3–x-3–inch briquettes per three days. It was up to the POWs to ration their heat supply. Although some officers were allowed to search for wood outside the camp to supplement their coal, it still was not enough to keep the soldiers warm. As a result, the barrack temperature averaged about 20 degrees throughout most of the winter, despite the fact there were 200 bodies in each one.

The toilet facilities at Oflag XIIIB were completely inadequate at first but after the Red Cross's first visit in mid-January, the Germans made some much needed improvements. There were no washrooms and no hot water due to the fuel shortage. The officers had to carry water from the kitchen faucets to the washbasins in each room. Ventilation and daylight were adequate in the barracks but each room contained only two 15-watt drop light bulbs.

Tom kept his thoughts to himself. He tried to keep busy doing whatever he could to keep his mind and body occupied. His preference was to be outside whenever possible, and he spent his time talking to the Serbian officers in Oflag XIIIA through the fence that separated the two compounds. Tom developed a friendship with one of the Serbian officers and as a token of their friendship; the man gave Tom a beautiful, hand-embroidered silk scarf, which he handed to him through the fence. The scarf meant a lot to Tom, as he believed the Eastern Europeans in the camp were treated even worse than the American officers were. Tom kept the scarf in his dresser drawer for the rest of his life as a reminder of the man.

When Tom was alone, the uncertainty of survival as a POW was overwhelming at times. Tom experienced prolonged periods of fear, anxiety, depression, and feelings of helplessness. Since he had been shipped to Europe as part of the replacement forces, he had been with several units, had seen many of his men die in combat, and had taken the lives of a number of German soldiers. Seven years of training in the military could not have prepared him for what he had lived through in the last six months. Tom found it difficult to establish friendships.

Most of the men had the same concerns as Tom did and lived with the same demons. Within a month after their arrival at Oflag XIIIB, the POWs finally were allowed to send their first cards home to their families to announce their capture. POWs were issued three letter forms and three post cards per month for letters home, but there was no guarantee their loved ones ever received them, since the camp never received any incoming mail. Because of this complete lack of communication, many of the POWs believed as Tom did that their families had not even been notified that they were still alive.

In general, the extremely poor conditions of the camp and lack of any sort of organization amongst the prisoners seemed to create an overall feeling of carelessness and low morale. Morale improved in the camp in early March after Colonel Goode and the other evacuees from Oflag 64 in Poland arrived. Tom and the other officers at Oflag XIIIB were encouraged to see that even after enduring a ten-week forced march of 345 miles through the often sub-zero winter weather, the officers from Oflag 64 still had pride in their American uniforms. This served as a source of inspiration for the other officers in the Hammelburg camp.

Photo: Telegram to Anna on Jan 15, 1945 that Tom was identified as missing in action on Dec. 20, 1944.

International Red Cross

By mid-January, Anna had moved to Minneapolis and started work at her new job at the hospital. She had still not heard from Tom but continued to write to him and prayed for his safety. On January 15, the day before Anna's twenty-fifth birthday, her parents in Kimballton received a telegram from the War Department that notified them of Tom's Prisoners-of-War status, citing Stalag 9B as the camp where he was located. They got word to Anna right away to let her know that Tom was still alive but that he had been taken prisoner by the Germans. The Red Cross had identified him on the camp's records in late December. From thousands of miles away, Anna echoed Tom's sentiments that this was not the way she had pictured them spending her birthday. Anna was devastated and gravely concerned for Tom's safety.

The first visit to Oflag XIIIB by the International Red Cross was made by accident on January 22, 1945, when representatives of the Swiss delegation arrived to inspect Stalag XIIIC and the adjoining Serbian compound in accordance with previous arrangements. The International Red Cross reported many shortages in Oflag XIIIB and requisitions were made to fill those needs but supplies did not arrive before the camp was liberated later in the spring.

Treatment of the Prisoners

At the time the Oflag XIIIB camp opened, it was already apparent that Hitler's thrust through the Ardennes had not gone as planned and the German army continued to be squeezed from all directions by the Allied forces. Tension between the American POWs and German personnel was ongoing and treatment of the prisoners by the guards was only fair, at best.

One camp rule that caused a great deal of dissension between the Germans and the POWs was the commandant's order that all American officers were required to salute all German officers first, regardless of their rank. There were many discussions on the inappropriateness of the rule by the senior American officer (SAO) and General von Goeckel. Colonel Goode finally persuaded the commandant to revoke the order in March after he arrived in the camp from Oflag 64.

The tension between the prison guards and POWs was never more evident than when a POW was shot and killed for what appeared to be frivolous reasons.

One situation occurred when the air alert sounded twice within an hour. All winter and spring, the Allies continued extensive aerial assaults throughout Germany. Protocol for the POWs during the air raids was rigidly enforced. The rules required that once the air alert was sounded, all POWs were to be inside their barracks within three minutes in order to clear the open areas between the buildings.

When the alarm sounded the second time, four American officers who were standing at the fence talking to some Serbian officers, were slow in ending their conversation and returning to the barracks. They were still within their three-minute window to move indoors when a guard about seventy-five yards away saw them and fired at them just as they were about to enter their barracks. One of the officers was hit in the back, the bullet piercing his lung and chest. The officer died the following day of the wounds.

Red Cross reports also documented the shooting of 2nd Lt. George Vaream by a guard while he was going from one barrack to another on January 22, 1945. According to the American spokesman, the guard fired without good reason.

As the air raids over Oflag XIIIB increased in frequency, it sometimes became necessary for the men to be confined to their barracks for six or seven hours at a time. The SAO complained to the camp commandant, General von Goeckel, saying it was detrimental to the health of the men to be confined over these long periods with no indoor toilet facilities. The commandant later rescinded his strict orders and gave permission for the POWs to be able to use the outdoor latrines during these extended air raids. Communication between General von Goeckel and his guards, however, was lacking. On March 24, Lt. Charles Weeks was shot and killed returning from the latrine during an air-raid alert. The guard yelled a command at Lieutenant Weeks in German and when he did not respond promptly, the guard shot him in the back of the head. The camp commandant, General von Goeckel; Colonel Goode, and Major Berndt, who were approaching the area, witnessed the shooting. However, when they reached Lieutenant Weeks, the guard merely said he did not know about the new rule. He was not reprimanded for his actions.

Food

The only item that was provided in enough quantity during Tom's captivity was water. Initially, the men in the camp were given a diet of 1,700 calories a day, but as supplies ran low and the camp population increased, food rations were cut to less than 1,100 calories a day. There were no dairy products, nuts, fish, fruits, grain products, or rice. POWs received just enough broth, with the occasional piece of meat or vegetable, and bread to keep them alive. Many men in the camp lost more than fifty pounds during captivity and their muscle strength deteriorated significantly due to lack of food, leading to immobility or death, in some cases. Dysentery was a major concern due to the unsterile conditions and lack of hot water to sterilize the kitchen utensils, further weakening many men in the camp.

The normal daily menu consisted of one-tenth of a loaf of bread, one cup of ersatz coffee, one bowl of barley soup, and one serving of a vegetable per day. About three times a week a small piece of margarine was issued, and occasionally a tablespoon of sugar. Toward the end of March, many officers were in a dangerous condition due to malnutrition and the senior medical officer credited the generosity of the Serbian officers from Oflag XIIIA and the sharing of approximately 1,800 Red Cross packages over the three-month period with the saving of many American lives. Unfortunately, Tom never received a Red Cross parcel during this time.

The POWs developed their own way of making sure the bread was equally divided for each meal. Each day a different man in each group was responsible for slicing the bread into portions as equal as possible. Crude measuring tools were created and the man who sliced the bread was the last man to get his piece. The process usually took an hour and no bread crumbs were ever brushed onto the floor. Every last morsel was consumed. A rare piece of meat or vegetable in the soup was always cherished and worth bragging about.

Life at Oflag XIIIB had been reduced to getting enough food just to stay alive and finding ways and means to keep warm. The main topic of conversation was often food, favorite recipes their moms and wives made, and the best restaurants and favorite items on the menu.

Health Conditions

Like most of the POWs, Tom experienced occasional periods of dysentery, and he suffered from extreme vitamin deficiency and body lice. He also reported experiencing occasional chest pains, impaired vision, cavities, toothaches, occasional numbness or weakness in the arms and legs, occasional nausea, vomiting, and diarrhea, occasional aches or pains in the muscles and/or joints, and fever. Tom received no medical or dental attention while in the POW camps. The poor diet of the POWs and his deteriorating health only intensified the emotions he felt. Standing 5 foot 10, Tom weighed 165 pounds when he was captured and 125 pounds when he was finally liberated.

Tom was not alone in his misery. Most POWs experienced the same psychological and physiological issues—some better and some worse. The threat of being shot if one made the wrong move was always present and when combined with their poor heath and sub-standard living conditions, the POWs' mental health also declined. The result was that cynicism took over and Tom and many of the other officers began to believe they had been used as bait in the Ardennes to draw out the German reserves. Tom also felt that General Patton was not concerned about the welfare of his men, and his opinion would never change.

March 1945

Anna's parents received a second telegram from the War Department in early March that told her the International Red Cross had once again identified Tom as a Prisoner of War on February 14, and while that was not good, at least she knew that he was probably still alive. The telegram did not say at which camp he was being held.

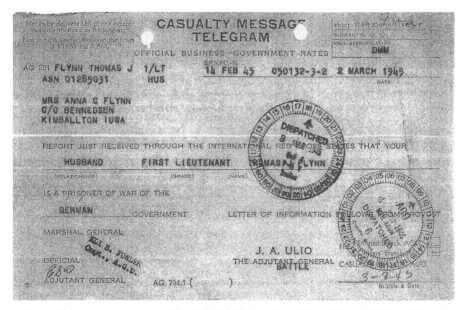

Photo: Telegram to Anna on March 2, 1945 that Tom identified as POW on Feb. 14, 1945.

The International Red Cross made another visit to Oflag XIIIB on March 25, 1945. Acute shortages were once again reported and supply requisitions made. All seven barracks were now filled to maximum capacity, with approximately 210 officers in each. Each officer had a wooden bunk bed, a pillow, and two German blankets. Coal issue for heat had ceased. Out of thirteen taps for running water, only eight were in working order. There was only one hot shower provided per month. Delousing was obviously not very effective as lice were prevalent in all the barracks.

Near the end of March, the POWs began hearing stories that the Americans were on their way to liberate the camp. In fact, Oflag XIIIB was now only sixty miles from the advancing American frontline. Military intelligence had informed General Patton that his son-in-law, Lt. Col. John Waters, who had been captured in the fighting in Tunisia, North Africa, in 1943, was now at Hammelburg. Waters had been imprisoned at Oflag 64 in Szubin, Poland, but arrived at the Hammelburg camp on March 6 with the rest of Col. Paul R. Goode's group.

The Escape from Oflag XIIIB at Hammelburg—Days 101-104 (Four days)

On March 27, the POWs heard gunfire and saw black smoke in the distance. By late afternoon, Capt. Abraham Baum, approximately two companies of Sherman tanks from the 4th Armored Division, and a 293-man task force appeared over the hill in view of the camp. The tanks quickly demolished the camp's guard towers and broke down the camp's gate. It did not take long for the German camp commandant, General Von Goeckel, to surrender to Colonel Goode, the ranking U.S. officer prisoner.

There had been German resistance along the way and Tom observed that the task force was already pretty shot up by the time it arrived at the camp. Some of the tanks had been destroyed. Baum's intention was to take as many POWs back to the American lines as possible. But Tom and some of the other infantry officers who knew how much artillery fire the tanks usually attracted, did not see how the task force, in its condition, could possibly make it back to the American lines with so many POWs.

Colonel Goode marched the men out of the camp and onto the road with the tanks, in hopes that transportation would be available for all, but the tanks were the only vehicles there. The tanks had no radio contact with the rest of the unit as the rear elements of the tank unit had been lost, but the tankers said some of their elements were not far away in Aschaffenburg. As many of the men as possible climbed onto the tanks. Colonel Goode briefed the others and gave the Allied prisoners permission to strike out cross-country on their own, if they chose, to try to reach the Allied lines.

Some of the men were too weak to travel and opted to stay at the camp. They were hopeful that other American units would be coming soon and they just had to hold on a little bit longer.

About a dozen officers decided to try to make it back to the American lines on foot. Tom and four other officers made plans to head southwest. A second group decided to head north toward the British lines. A third group of three men led by 2nd Lt. Donald Prell of the 106th Infantry Division headed west.[13] Before leaving, each group gathered any supplies they could find that might aid their survival. Several officers picked up pistols to carry with them. Tom's group also canvassed the tank column for weapons and food. They secured a compass and a case of C rations and filled their pockets with everything they would hold. Two of the men had gotten hold of German pistols from the guards. Tom wanted them to leave them behind to avoid complications should the group be recaptured, but he had no luck at persuading them to do so. Tom was against being armed. He believed that if they were recaptured without weapons, they would just be rounded up and taken back to the camp. But if they were armed, their fate would be far less certain and they probably would be shot on the spot.

Tom and the four other officers headed southwest through the woods toward Gemunden. They soon came upon a small house near the edge of a stone quarry. After some discussion, they decided to approach it. An older German couple lived there.

---

13   Phone interview with 2nd Lt. Donald Prell on June 9, 2010

Using his high school German, Tom convinced the couple that they meant no harm and that they were only trying to get back to the American line. They had heard of the U.S. Armored Force attack but the man was friendly to Tom. Judging the situation to be safe, the officers went in and sat down in the kitchen. The wife gave them milk and the first good cup of coffee they'd had in months and heated some of their rations for them.

Tom learned that the only other Germans in the near vicinity were two men guarding some Polish prisoners. With Tom as interpreter, the German couple and the officers talked about a variety of topics and found many interests in common, including religion and the fact that Tom's grandfather had emigrated from Germany in the late 1800s. Friendly conversation went on far into the night. The German couple gave them a military map of the region and pointed out the best route for the officers to take. Ultimately, they decided it was best not to follow that route in case the German couple was questioned and revealed their escape plan. The men almost had decided to rest at the house until the following night when someone knocked on the door. (It was approximately 0500 hours on March 28.) The woman quickly turned off the lights and the man went to answer the door. When he returned, he told Tom that it was another guard from town who was looking for the two guards in that area to tell them that there were SS troops in town.

Tom and the other officers quickly changed their plans and the German volunteered to lead them over a back trail before daylight. The German pointed out a secluded section of woods before leaving them on their own. However, to play it safe, Tom's group selected another position and then bedded down for the day. They studied the map and initially made plans to attempt crossing the Main River at Gemunden. After more discussion, this plan was changed in favor of attempting to cross the Frank Saale River north of Gemunden to avoid having to recross the Main River further west. They stayed hidden all day on March 28, as they had decided to move under cover of darkness. They all agreed it would be best to lay low during the day when they could be more easily spotted. The men remained in this hiding place the following day, March 29, as well, because one of the men was sick.

On the night of March 29, two of the men worked their way north along the Frank Saale River to the nearest bridge. As they observed a road running through the small town, a guard posted near the bridge spotted the patrol and sounded an alarm. Luckily, the men got back to the group safely. They reported back to the others that the river was only thirty to forty yards wide in that area but had a depth of approximately eight to ten feet. Given their poor physical condition and the cold weather, they knew they would have to risk crossing the bridge on foot rather than attempt to swim across the river.

Tom's group decided to try another approach. Early the next day, March 30, the men worked their way onto higher ground overlooking Gemunden. It was Good Friday. They had made it more than thirteen miles so far. The town was full of activity but they discovered a footbridge just below their position, so they considered the possibility of crossing there instead. Two of the men once again went out on reconnaissance while the others observed, taking notes about the German traffic along the road. They intended the notes to be for their own use as well as for that of the U.S. units they hoped to contact soon. They noted that there was a checkpoint at the footbridge, so they tentatively decided to attempt a crossing that night. However, when the two-man patrol returned late in the afternoon, they reported that the Germans were setting up a defensive position between the bridge and their hiding place. Based on this information, Tom and his group thought it possible that American troops were near. They needed to find a safer hiding place or risk getting caught in the potential cross fire.

Tom and his group started back to the stone quarry by a different route than the one they had used a few days before, but while passing through an open field where search parties were looking for escaped East European prisoners, they were spotted by German soldiers. When Tom realized there was no chance of escape, he quickly hid the map under some leaves and loose dirt to avoid getting the old couple in trouble and he advised the two officers with pistols to hide them the same way. Most of the soldiers who captured them were only fifteen to eighteen years of age, or too old to be on the front lines. The young soldiers were enthusiastic, and still believed they were winning the war. Once again, Tom's high school German came in handy as he explained that they were unarmed POWs turned loose by the Panzers and that they were now lost in the woods. The young guards did not even bother to search them.

Tom's group was marched a short distance to a small village, where they were fed tea and a sandwich. Then they were taken to a command post where they were issued German frontline rations. They received good treatment during this second capture. That night, they were held in a barn with plenty of soft straw to sleep on. The next morning, other retaken prisoners joined Tom's group and were driven back to Hammelburg by horse and wagon. The men noted on their way back that the entire area was being prepared for anti-tank defense. They were happy to know that the American army was not far away and hoped they would be freed again soon.

When Tom and his group arrived at Hammelburg on March 31, they heard that the task force had been shot up trying to get back to the American line and that all the prisoners had either been recaptured or killed in the fight. Even though they, too, had been recaptured, Tom was glad they had gone out on their own. They had at least been free for four days.

The evacuation of the Hammelburg camp had been underway for several days since the escape, as the Germans moved the Hammelburg prisoners farther into the interior of Germany to keep them away from the advancing American armies. Captain Feiker and the other men who had stayed in the camp had already been moved out by train to Stalag Luft III at Nuremburg on March 29 and Colonel Goode's contingent of men, which had been recaptured, was being marched there on foot.

The Serbians who were tending to the POWs still in the camp hospital served Tom's group a hot meal, and there were suddenly plenty of Red Cross parcels available. Among the POWs left behind was General Patton's son-in-law, Lt. Col. John Waters. Waters had been shot by a German corporal during the initial escape attempt and was one of only seventy-five wounded and sick Americans who would be liberated from this camp by the American 14th Armored Division within the week.

Ninety-six Miles to Stalag Luft III at Nuremberg, Germany— Days 105-109 (Five days)

The following morning, Tom and all remaining POWs capable of being moved were loaded into unmarked boxcars once again, en route to Nuremberg. This time, the old prison guards were stationed in each car. Approximately 10 kilometers (6.2 miles) outside of Hammelburg, an American P-51 fighter plane strafed their unmarked train. The .50-caliber ammo slamming into the metal roof of the cars was deafening and sounded to Tom like someone hammering on the roof. The fighters flew up the length of the train to shoot up the engine at the front. As the train slowed to a stop, Tom and the other POWs convinced the old guards to open the doors before the fighters came back. The guards jumped out first, and the POWs followed, taking cover far away from the train. The fighters returned to rake the train again but the men were far enough away by then to be safe.

The senior U.S. and British officers protested that their men would not ride farther unless the next train was plainly marked as a prisoner train. The German commander then gave the men the choice of walking or riding the remaining ninety miles. The majority of the men chose to walk the rest of the way to Nuremberg. The guards organized a column and they headed out on foot. It was now getting close to spring, so the march was easier than before. Tom was more than happy to be out from behind the barbed wire fences and locked gates, and he chose to be a straggler at the end of the column, and he walked as slowly as the guard would let him in order to delay their arrival at the next camp.

When Tom's group reached Nuremberg and Stalag Luft III, he found out that thirty American POWs who had been in the first group to be evacuated from Hammelburg, including Captain Feiker, had been killed during an Allied air raid of Nuremberg on April 5 as their POW column was being marched through the city. Tom was saddened by the news, as Captain Feiker had been a good officer who had really cared about his men.

Stalag Luft III at Nuremberg, Germany—Days 110-111 (Two days)

By the time that Tom's group reached Stalag Luft III at Nuremberg, the 14th Armored Division had arrived in full force at Oflag XIIIB in Hammelburg, liberating the camps there for good. The German army continued to fall back towards Berlin and kept moving the prisoners with it in an attempt to keep the advancing U.S. force from recovering its POWs. As a result, Tom was only kept at this camp for two days. The Americans were less than sixty miles away.

Once again on foot, Tom was marched through the city of Nuremberg en route to Stalag VIIA in Moosburg, another ninety miles away. By this time, the American fighters and bombers had destroyed much of Nuremberg and as the POWs were marched through the bombed-out sections of the city, the German civilians were hostile and angry with the American POWs. The Germans were especially angry with the pilots and called them "terror flyers." (Tom later said the phrase sounded like *tier pfluger*). Tom understood what they were saying and told all the pilots around him to hide the pilot wings on their uniforms. When a group would press too close to them, Tom would point to the crossed rifles insignia on his uniform coat and tell them, "*fuss soldaten*" (foot soldiers or infantry). Tom saved all the pilots in his group from harm in this way, and they made it safely through the city with no injuries. Unfortunately, some of the POWs in other groups were not so lucky and were pelted with stones by the mobs.

Ninety-four-mile March to Stalag VIIA at Moosburg, Germany—Days 112-119 (Eight days)

Near exhaustion, Tom lost track of time on the march to Moosburg. The prisoners walked as slowly as the German guards would let them in an attempt to prolong the journey. Anything was better than confinement. By this time, both the prisoners and guards had to scrounge for food along the way from the Bavarian farmers, and thankfully, in the warmer weather, they could sleep in the large stacks of hay in the fields at night.

Yet they still were not safe, and once again, Tom's POW column came under attack by an American fighter plane. This time it was near a railroad overpass. Tom wasn't sure if they had been the primary or secondary target this time, but some POWs at the front of the column were injured. Tom remained content to be one of the stragglers at the back of the line.

Stalag VIIA at Moosburg, Germany—Days 120-133 (Fourteen days)

Tom's POW column arrived at Moosburg Stalag VIIA around April 15, 1945. Once again, the men had to register upon arrival. This camp held by far the largest number of POWs of any camp that Tom had seen. There were men from every nation Germany had fought for the past five years. Fortunately, the International Red Cross was ever-present in this camp and it received more frequent delivery of Red Cross parcels than the other camps where Tom and the men of K Company had been held. Nevertheless, with so many new prisoners continuing to flood into the camp, it was hard for the Red Cross to put a dent in what was truly needed.

To put the conditions of the camp into perspective, the Moosburg camp was meant to hold 3,000 prisoners but as of mid-April 1945, the census had swelled to over 100,000. With such overcrowding, there was little food and no hot water for cooking or washing. The straw beds were infested with lice and fleas. There was one outdoor latrine for every 2,000 men. The fact that this camp had been built over swampland meant there was mud everywhere. At this point in the war, the buildings were old and many were just wooden shells because the POWs had been taking them apart gradually to burn the wood for cooking on their makeshift stoves. To accommodate the massive influx of new prisoners, tents had been set up and some prisoners chose to sleep out under the stars when the weather allowed.

When Tom and the other POWs were shown where they were to stay, the American and British airmen shared with each of the new arrivals an entire Red Cross package. This was quite the luxury to Tom, as it was the first time in four months of captivity that he had gotten a package just for himself. The airmen quickly shared all of the information they had. With all the new prisoners pouring into the camp over the past month, they had gotten a steady stream new information about what was happening and where the U.S. Army was.

The airmen also shared the rumor that Hitler had ordered all American officers in this camp killed, rather than surrendering them to the American Army. Tom had no way of knowing whether this rumor was true. We can only imagine the thoughts that ran through his mind.

On April 28, there were clear signs that the American Army was not far away. Tom and the other prisoners could hear the artillery fire of American weapons in the distant southwest. The next morning at sunrise, April 29, sounds of American tanks and gunfire could be heard nearby as the 14th Armored Division moved closer to the camp. Like the rest of the prisoners, Tom was thrilled that the U.S. Army had finally caught up with him and the other POWs who had been evacuated from the Hammelburg camp.

Photos: Moosburg Stalag VIIA camp overcrowding during mid-April 1945; (top) courtesy of U.S. Air Force Academy, USAFA Special Library; (bottom) courtesy of Moosburg Online (www.stalag.moosburg.org).

Unfortunately, the excitement of the pending rescue was dampened by what was going on immediately outside the camp, as the prisoners soon discovered that the rumor of Hitler's orders to kill the American officers was true. At that point, the POWs had no way of knowing that their camp was the last POW camp to be liberated, so with the advancing American Army near, the SS troops began to fire their weapons into the camp in a last-ditch attempt to carry out Hitler's orders. Shots even came from the SS troops positioned on the roof of a cheese factory nearby. The POWs were told by the guards to stay inside with their heads down and "the prison guards and the German Army fought off the Gestapo and SS and saved all the prisoners' lives."[14] The fighting was over in less than an hour and Tom could soon feel the vibration of the army tanks headed in their direction. It didn't take long for the sound of the moving Sherman tanks to be drowned out by the sounds of euphoria erupting from every able-bodied man in Stalag VIIA.

The Sherman tanks of the 14th Armored Division soon crashed through the fences of the compound. Each tank was immediately engulfed by the sea of ragged, emaciated, and filthy POWs. Tom wanted to join the celebration on top of the tanks but there were already so many bodies covering every inch of the tanks that the tanks themselves were no longer visible. Brigadier Gen. Charles H. Karlstad received an unconditional surrender from the camp commandant and the Americans assumed control of the camp.

Unbeknownst to Tom, Anna's younger brother, Magnus Bennedsen, had been assigned to the 14th Armored Division's maintenance unit in October 1944 and his crew was not far behind the tanks that had just crashed through the compound fences. Unfortunately, with all the chaos, neither of them would discover the other was there, and the two men would never make the connection.

---

14   http://www.Moosburg.org/info/stalag/bilder/

Photo: Moosburg Stalag VIIA POWs cover the U.S. tanks in excitement. Photo provided courtesy of U.S. Air Force Academy, USAFA Special Library.

As Tom joined the celebration, he witnessed the most amazing expression of freedom. At approximately 1300 hours on April 29, 1945, 1st Lt. Martin Allain, a twenty-three-year-old bomber pilot who had been a POW for over two years, revealed the treasured American flag he had been hiding for almost two years. He had sewn it between two German blankets to conceal it from the guards. Lieutenant Allain now realized what his prized flag was destined to be used for and began shimmying up the German flagpole with Old Glory in hand. The entire camp went silent as Allain replaced the ugly swastika with his beautiful Stars and Stripes. Regardless of his nationality, each man immediately came to attention and saluted the American flag. The prisoners were overcome with the emotion that most had locked away for months, if not years, and almost every eye filled up with tears. They were safe at last and going home.

Photo: Lt. Allain's American flag flies over Moosburg. Photo provided courtesy of U.S. Air Force Academy, USAFA Special Library.

With Moosburg Stalag VIIA the last German POW camp to be liberated, the army now had the massive job of not only feeding all the starving men but providing proper medical attention, clothing, and transportation back home, and helping troops of other nations do the same.

The next day, April 30, Hitler committed suicide during the Battle of Berlin, and his replacement, the president of Germany, Karl Dönitz authorized the surrender of Germany.

General Patton arrived in the camp for a visit on May 1, spoke briefly to the men, shook a few hands, and then left again. Tom made no mention of Patton's visit to the camp after the war, but that is not surprising since he was not a fan of the general and he probably wasn't impressed by the gratuitous gesture and short stay. "His blood and our guts," was what Tom would say about him when his name came up in conversation in the years that followed.

Photo: General Patton visits two days later. Photo provided courtesy of U.S. Air Force Academy, USAFA Special Library

Tom was one of the first officers to be interviewed at Moosburg by Army Field Historian Capt. William K. Dunkerly on May 1 and 2, 1945, about the Battle of the Bulge and how he and the other POWs were treated during their captivity. These interview documents and numerous other historical accounts by authors, scholars, and other POWs, provided the details to recreate Tom's experiences in chapters 5 and 6 of this book. Tom received a general medical exam to attend to immediate issues. No psychological evaluation or emotional assistance was provided. Army personnel did not brief Tom on any events that had occurred while he was in captivity.

As the Army sorted through all the men in the camp, it made sure they were well fed to build up their strength and prepare them for travel. A field hospital was set up near the Landshut airstrip to provide them with hot showers, soap, delousing, and fresh clothing. The sick and infirm were quickly processed and forwarded on for treatment, as needed. As the men were processed and approved for travel, the ones who were healthy enough would wait near the Landshut airstrip until C-47s landed to resupply the 14th Armored Division with gas and ammunition. Each plane would then be loaded with soldiers for the return trip to the airbase in France. It was the first time many of them had had something to laugh about in months. One officer even purchased a couple kegs of beer in town to share with the soldiers while they waited their turn to go home.

Tom had his first plane ride in the bucket seat of a C-47 on May 7, 1945, en route to the 195th General Hospital outside of Paris for further processing. Tom was then transported by truck along the back roads into Paris that night, just before the big Victory in Europe Day (V-E Day) celebration on May 8. Tom would never see or hear from any of the men of the 28th Infantry Division again.

Tom was released from the 195th General Hospital to the Normandy Base on May 8, where he stayed until he received orders to be shipped home. On May 13, 1945, Tom boarded the U.S. merchant ship, t*he John Erisco* and headed for New York. The Army made sure the POWs had all the food they could eat on their two-week trip back to the states. Tom's emaciated body packed on 45 pounds in just three weeks and he weighed 170 pounds when he arrived in New York. This was the most he would ever weigh in his life. Thank God, he was free and on his way home.

Anna received a third and final telegram from the War Department on May 21 telling her that Tom had been liberated from the POW camps. She was ecstatic! Tom was coming home! She found out that he was on a ship headed for New York but that he would be going to his oldest brother Bill's apartment in Chicago from there. Anna immediately packed her bags and left Minnesota to meet Tom without telling anyone or turning in her resignation at the hospital.

WAR DEPARTMENT
THE ADJUTANT GENERAL'S OFFICE
WASHINGTON 25. D. C.

BATTLE CASUALTY REPORT

	NAME		GRADE			DATE CAS. REPORT RECEIVED
AG 201	FLYNN THOMAS J		1 Lt.			
	ASN 01285031		HUS			

NAME AND ADDRESS OF E A.	MRS ANNA C FLYNN C/O BENNEDSEN KIMBALLTON IOWA	DATE TELEGRAM SENT 21 MAY 1945

THE INDIVIDUAL NAMED BELOW DESIGNATED THE ABOVE PERSON AS THE ONE TO BE NOTIFIED IN CASE OF EMERGENCY, AND THE OFFICIAL TELE- GRAPHIC AND LETTER NOTIFICATIONS WILL BE SENT TO THIS PERSON. THE RELATIONSHIP, IF ANY, IS SHOWN BELOW, IT SHOULD BE NOTED THAT THIS PERSON IS NOT NECESSARILY THE NEXT-OF-KIN OR RELATIVE DESIGNATED TO RECEIVE SIX MONTH'S PAY GRATUITY IN CASE OF DEATH

RELATIONSHIP HUSBAND

GRADE	NAME	SERIAL NUMBER	ARM OR SERVICE	REPORTING THEATRE	F OR J STATUS	SHIPMENT NUMBER
1 LT	FLYNN THOMAS J	01285031	INF	ETO	V	137

TYPE OF CASUALTY	PLACE OF CASUALTY	DATE OF CASUALTY DAY / MONTH / YEAR	CASUALTY CODE
RETURN TO MILITARY CONTROL	IN	29 APR 45	PH

REMARKS:
CORRECTED COPY   MN

ACTION BY PROCESSING AND VERIFICATION SECTION: REPORT VERIFIED ___ FORM 43 ___ AG 201 REQ. ___

CASUALTY BRANCH FILE ATTACHED ___ OR CHARGED TO ___ DATE ___

PREVIOUSLY REPORTED ___ NO ___ YES ___ (AS INDICATED BELOW):

FILE NO.	MESSAGE NO.	TYPE	DATE AND AREA	E. A. NOTIFIED
AG383.6(14 Feb 43)	050132 POW	NS NS		2 mar 45

FORWARDED TO →

SPEC. IDEN. ___ TELEGRAM ___ WOUNDED ___ LETTER ___ CORRES. ___ S. A. W.D. ___ CERTIF. ___ M. & M. ___ NON-DEL.

REPORT NOT VERIFIED ___ NO FORM 43 ___ NO CAS. BR. FILE ___ CHECKED BY *Fields 21 may* REMARKS ___

DISTRIBUTION "A" □ 25 COPIES
(ALL TYPES OF CASUALTIES PERTAINING TO MILITARY PERSONNEL, EXCEPT WOUNDED.)
COPIES FURNISHED: SEE CASUALTY BRANCH MEMORANDUM NO. 48, 1944.

DISTRIBUTION "B" □ ___ COPIES
(ALL WOUNDED MILITARY PERSONNEL AND ALL TYPES OF CASUALTIES PERTAINING TO CIVILIANS WHO ARE W. D. EMPLOYEES, EMPLOYEES OF W. D. CONTRACTORS AND OTHERS SUBJECT TO MILITARY LAW.)
COPIES FURNISHED: SEE CASUALTY BRANCH MEMORANDUM NO. 48, 19___

W.D., A.G.O. Form 0305 { This form supersedes W.D. A.G.O. Form 0305, 16 June 1943 and W.D. A.G.O. Form 1 JANUARY 1945 302-3, 802-4, of 1 February 1944, and 802-5, 802-6, 1 August 1944, which may { until existing stocks are exhausted.

Photo: Telegram to Anna on May 21, 1945 that Tom was returned to military control on April 29, 1945.

As the *John Erisco* neared New York City, Tom could see the Statue of Liberty off in the distance. Tom watched eagerly as the ship passed all of the familiar landmarks of home and he couldn't wait to be off the ship and with his family. More than anything, Tom longed for news of Anna. The few photos in his wallet he had been allowed to keep were all he'd had to hold onto all these months. It had been nine long months since he had heard any word from her or he had been able to get word to her.

Every day while Tom was a POW, his little sister, Mel, had gone to St. Francis Church just across the street from her workplace to pray. The church had set up a special niche to pray for the soldiers and she had made nine-day novenas for Tom on every visit. Mel had not yet heard the news of Tom's freedom but as Tom's ship drew nearer to shore, Mel happened to look out her office window. For some reason, she had an overwhelming feeling that Tom was on the troop ship she was watching enter the harbor. God had answered her prayers and Tom walked in the door of their apartment that evening. Tom's family was ecstatic to see their Tommy again. They were surprised at how good he looked and they were thrilled to have him home, even if just for a day, before he left to reunite with Anna.

Tom had orders to report to the Palmer House at Ft. Sheridan, Chicago. He arrived at the Chicago apartment of his brother, Bill, on June 4, 1945. Anna was there waiting for him.

CHAPTER 7

June 1945-May 1950: Civilian Life and the G.I. Bill

After reporting to the Palmer House at Ft. Sheridan, Chicago, Tom was given a two-month leave from the Army, from June 5 to August 3, to rest and recuperate. Needless to say, Tom and Anna were very happy to be together again and they both knew there were many others who were not so lucky. Tom's brother, Bill, made arrangements with his boss to take an impromptu vacation and planned to take his wife and daughters to their cabin in Indiana for a week so Anna and Tom could have the apartment to themselves. Before they left, they took Tom and Anna to Lake Michigan for the afternoon. While Tom talked to his brother and sister-in-law, he watched his beautiful wife play along the shoreline with his two little nieces, Betty and Maureen. It was obvious how much Tom loved his wife and how happy he was to be back with her again. A number of photos of the two of them taken over the years show him staring lovingly at her instead of looking at the camera.

Photo: Anna with nieces, Maureen and Betty at Lake Michigan, June 1945

Even after what Tom had just lived through, the Army offered no counseling or assistance. Returning GIs were just expected to go back to their pre-war lives as best they could. However, fellow citizens treated the men in uniform like celebrities for a while when they first came back, and the GIs all seemed to enjoy the special attention. While staying at Bill's apartment, Bill's boss invited them—and all of the returning GIs and their wives that he knew—out to dinner to show his gratitude for their service to our country. Anna and Tom are shown in the bottom, left-hand corner of the photo below.

*Photo: Dinner for returning GIs in Chicago; Tom and Anna are in
bottom, left corner.*

Photo: Tom and Anna with other returning GIs in Chicago

Tom and Anna greatly appreciated their stay at Bill's apartment for the week as it gave them some quiet time to talk for the first time in nine months. Tom initially was very upset that he hadn't heard from Anna the entire time he had been gone. Then she explained to him that she'd written to him faithfully as she'd promised. He believed her, as he knew Anna would never lie, and it was obvious that her feelings for him hadn't changed. They never would find out what happened to all the letters she'd written. The Army never returned them.

Like many WWII veterans, Tom would never be able to tell Anna about much of what he had been through during the fighting and his four and a half months as a POW. He just tried to bury it deep inside. What he had experienced was too horrible and inhumane for him to even put into words.

Tom and the other GIs who had returned to Chicago also were given a week's vacation in Miami, Florida, at the Army's expense. But Tom and Anna decided to go to Kimballton to visit Anna's parents before heading to Florida.

Photo: Tom and Anna at her parent's home in Kimballton, Iowa, June 1945.

From Florida, Tom and Anna went back to New York in July to spend time with Tom's family, as his initial stop after returning from Europe had been very brief. Tom's youngest brother, Eddie, just seventeen, had been waiting anxiously to join the military like his older brothers and had finally convinced their mom to allow him to enlist. Eddie and Bill, the oldest, were the only two of the six brothers who had not enlisted during WWII. Bill did not qualify for active duty due to a bad heart from a bout with scarlet fever as a child, and Eddie had been too young. Eddie left for basic training before the end of the month and was stationed in Cuba shortly after completing boot camp.

On Saturday, July 28, 1945, Tom and Anna awoke to find extremely thick cloud cover over New York and New Jersey, which was not, in itself, unusual. However, the dense clouds that day caused a B-25 bomber pilot who was intending to land in New Jersey, to misjudge his flight path, taking him directly into the north side of the 78th floor of the Empire State Building instead. The pilot had tried to fly below the clouds to get a better sense of his position, only to find himself in the middle of Manhattan. He did his best to climb and managed to avoid several smaller buildings, but the Empire State Building was just too large to go around or over. The plane crash killed fourteen people—eleven office workers and the three crew members—and injured twenty-six. It also started three fires, two in the Empire State Building and one in the building next door, where flaming engine parts were catapulted onto the roof. Needless to say, there was a lot of excitement over the accident.

After a month in New York, Tom and Anna returned to Miami Beach, Florida, so Tom could report for duty on August 3 at the Army Ground Forces Redistribution Station. On August 7, Tom was awarded the Bronze Star for the Rhineland, Ardennes, and Central Europe campaigns; and the Purple Heart with Oak Leaf Cluster for "Ground Operation 123," which was the Hürtgen Forest campaign.

The Bronze Star Medal is a United States Armed Forces individual military decoration that is awarded for bravery, acts of merit, or meritorious service. When awarded for bravery, it is the fourth-highest combat award of the U.S. Armed Forces and the ninth-highest military award (including both combat and non-combat awards) in order of precedence of U.S. military decorations.

The Purple Heart is authorized for the first wound suffered, typically under combat conditions, and is an award that a soldier is entitled to upon meeting specific criteria rather through a recommendation. The knee injuries Tom sustained in the Battle of the Hürtgen Forest were the result of being directly fired upon by the Germans, which was considered a qualifying act of a hostile foreign force.

The additional Oak Leaf Cluster is a separate, small pin to attach to the ribbon of the Purple Heart and was the Army's way of denoting subsequent events that would merit receiving each additional award. Tom never mentioned what that second event was, nor is it specifically identified in his military files, other than by "Ground Operation 123." Because so many men suffered from frostbite and trench foot during the Battle of the Hürtgen Forest, the Army actually changed the medical conditions that qualified a soldier for a Purple Heart during this battle, which lasted from September 1944 until the end of January 1945. Frostbite and trench foot became non-battle related injuries and no longer qualified a soldier for receiving a Purple Heart. However, it remains unclear whether this was the case for Tom.

On Monday, August 6, the United States under the order of President Harry S. Truman, dropped the first nuclear bomb on the city of Hiroshima, Japan, and on August 9 dropped a second, larger nuclear bomb on the city of Nagasaki, Japan, killing approximately 100,000 civilians on the first day. More than double that number died within four months from burns, radiation sickness, and other related injuries in the two cities. On August 15, Japan announced its surrender.

Tom was assigned to Company C, 5th Infantry Training Battalion; Infantry Replacement & Training Center, Camp Wheeler, Georgia, (near Macon, Georgia) on August 15 and he and Anna once again relocated.

August 21 was Tom's twenty-fifth birthday. He and Anna were very happy to be together to celebrate the special occasion, since Tom had been a POW on her twenty-fifth birthday in January.

Once Tom returned to duty, he discovered that almost all of his personal items of any value, which were being held for him back in the States, had been taken by other soldiers assuming Tom was dead. The only items remaining were a couple of beaten-up Army trunks, a few Army blankets and sleeping bags, and other small, miscellaneous items. Tom submitted a combat loss claim for reimbursement on the items that he had lost in Hosingen, including his .45-caliber Smith and Wesson revolver. First Sgt. Donald K. Williams, who had witnessed Tom's destruction of his weapon in the K Company command post in Hosingen, had survived being a POW in Stalag 9B and signed an affidavit to that effect for Tom.

Though Tom had lost practically everything he owned in Hosingen, he had brought home from Europe several mementos of the war. He still had the hand-embroidered scarf given to him by the Serbian prisoner at Hammelburg's Oflag XIIIB, a ceremonial Nazi dagger, a German saber sword, and a bayonet that could be affixed to the end of an M-1 rifle, a pair of silver pilot wings, and his little brown handbook of German translations.

On September 2, 1945, Japan signed the Instrument of Surrender officially ending the war in the Pacific and, therefore, World War II.

During October, with the war over and the Army about to go through an enormous drawdown, Tom was required to take a physical exam. On October 11, he was assigned to the Separation Center at Fort McPherson, Georgia. On October 16, he was admitted to Lawson General Hospital in Atlanta, Georgia. It was determined his eyesight had deteriorated so drastically since his last eye exam in February 1942, that he was no longer fit for active duty. Medical records showed that his eyesight had gone from 20/70 in both eyes to 20/400 and 20/200, and the Army concluded the decline had not been caused by military service or mistreatment and malnourishment as a POW.

After Tom's physical, he was given leave and he and Anna returned to Kimballton. Tom decided to take advantage of the GI Bill and complete his college degree, but he wasn't sure if he wanted to be a doctor or veterinarian. With Anna's encouragement, he chose veterinary medicine. She knew how much he loved animals. Tom was admitted for the winter term (January 1946) at Iowa State College in Ames, Iowa, as was Anna's brother, Ole. Ole planned to get a mechanical engineering degree.

After a thorough review of Tom's military record, on November 2 Tom was promoted from 1st lieutenant to captain in the United States Army. At that time, it was also determined that Capt. Thomas J. Flynn was entitled to wear the following decorations and service medals:

- **Captain bars**
- **Combat Infantry Badge**
- **Bronze Star**: Reads "Heroic or Meritorious Achievement," *"Thomas J. Flynn" is engraved in the center of the back.*
- **Purple Heart with Oakleaf Cluster**: Reads "For Military Merit"
- **American Defense Service Medal**: Reads "For Service during the limited emergency proclaimed by the President on May 27, 1941."
- **American Campaign Service Medal**
- **European-African-Middle Eastern Campaign Service Medal**: Reads "United States of America 1941-1945"
- **WWII Victory Medal**: Reads "World War II United States of America 1941-1945," "Freedom from Fear and Want," "Freedom of Speech and Religion"

His dress uniform now looked as decorated as the officer's uniform in the mirror of the cartoon that Stan MacGovern of the *New York Post* had drawn of him in October 1940. To Tom's credit, it was clear to those with whom and for whom he'd served that he was a man of not only courage and integrity but also compassion and honor.

On November 25, Tom was given special orders and put on terminal leave. Tom's effective date of release from active duty was to be January 25, 1946.

By now, Tom's brother, Joe, who had been a medic in Europe during the war, had also returned home without any injuries.

Moving on with Life

Anna got a job working as a nurse at the McFarland Clinic at Mary Greeley Hospital in Ames, Iowa, to support the two of them while Tom was in college. The McFarland Clinic is now the largest privately owned doctor practice in the state of Iowa, but at that time, there were only ten doctors in the clinic and the original McFarland doctors still worked there. All of the doctors were also veterans, and in a gracious gesture, they delivered all of the babies of the nurses who worked in the hospital free of charge.

During the first school year in Ames, Tom and Anna shared a second-floor apartment with Ole, Betty, and their little girl, Bonnie, in a large, older home within walking distance of the hospital where Anna worked. Biff remained in Kimballton as he had been adopted by the Esbeck family. It was great to be with Anna's big brother and his family and to have their little niece to play with. Tom and Ole became very good friends over the next few years, but Tom and Betty didn't always see eye to eye.

The following year, each couple bought a trailer to live in while Tom and Ole finished college. Tom and Anna found a nice trailer park nearby that was full of other returning veterans and their wives. Their trailer lot had a nice shade tree to block the summer sun.

Tom and Anna's trailer had running water but they shared the community showers, bathrooms, and laundry facilities. They could wash their clothes with a conventional washer for free or pay 10 cents a load to use the automatic washing machines. There were no clothes dryers, so everyone had to hang their laundry out to dry on the clotheslines. And even though the trailer was small, Tom used one of the closets as a dark room, as he enjoyed developing his own photographs. Those years in Ames were very happy ones for Tom and Anna. Everyone they knew was in the same boat and they all appreciated the opportunities the G.I. Bill provided them.

Tom and Anna didn't have much to move and quickly were settled in their new trailer. It was apparent that their trailer was a little cramped and Tom wanted to get another dog, so he got permission to build a kennel in a shaded area next to the trailer. Tom enjoyed working with dogs so much that he decided he wanted to breed and raise collies to compete in local dog shows. His collies would go on to win a number of trophies over the next five years.

Just like his father, Tom also had a passion for fishing and it didn't take him long to find the best fishing spots in the area. One of Tom's favorite fishing spots was at a beautiful old mill near Frazier, a small town near Ames, Iowa. Anna often felt that Tom spent more time fishing than he did going to school and studying. But he was a speed-reader with excellent memory retention, so it didn't take Tom as long to prepare for class each day as it did the other students.

Tom also kept track of his New York Yankees and in 1947, they beat the Brooklyn Dodgers 4-3 in the World Series.

By now, Anna was getting anxious to have a baby but was having difficulty getting pregnant. She talked to Tom about the possibility of adopting a child, but Tom said, "No." Anna didn't argue, and fortunately, it wasn't long before she was pregnant with their first child. On August 20, 1948, Tom and Anna had a beautiful little girl whom they named Joyce Anne, just one day before Tom's twenty-eighth birthday, and nearly six years after they were married. Tom and Anna felt very blessed.

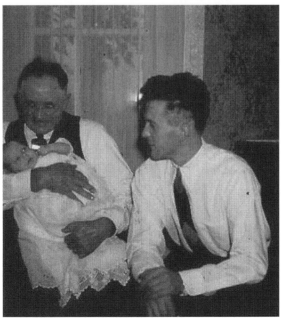

Photos: (top) Anna with newborn daughter, Joyce, and puppy, Coffee, August 1948; (bottom) Tom with Anna's father, holding Joyce; Joyce's baptism in Kimballton, Iowa, October 1948.

Anna's brother, Ole, graduated from Engineering School in May 1949 and moved his family to Seattle, Washington, for an engineering job at Boeing. Ole was very excited about his first assignment doing something that was very near and dear to him. Strategic Air Command (SAC) needed Boeing to design a better way for airplanes to refuel during flight and Ole had been assigned to the team already working on the project, known as the "Flying Boom" system. Earlier methods using flexible hoses did not allow for the transfer of fuel at a high enough rate of speed. Ole recalled his December 24, 1944, mission flying deep into Germany and how wonderful it would have been to be able to refuel in flight. This mission inspired Ole to develop his own ideas of how it could be done. The design would come to be known as the Boeing Boom and Ole was proud to be associated with its success story. This was the first of many government projects that Ole would be involved in during his long career at Boeing.

Photo: Tom's Iowa State graduation photo, May 1950

Nineteen forty-nine was another good year for Tom and Anna. Anna had become pregnant again in February and their first son, John Thomas, was born on November 4, 1949. Tom also was happy because his Yankees had once again beaten the Brooklyn Dodgers in the World Series, this time in a 4-1 contest. Tom graduated as a doctor of veterinary medicine the following May and Anna was already pregnant with their third child, due in October. There no longer appeared to be an infertility issue between the two.

Tom's brother, Bill, and his family came from Chicago to Ames to attend Tom's college graduation. Much to the pleasure of Tom's nieces, Betty and Maureen, the collies once again had two young puppies and they had a great time playing with the energetic balls of fur. Tom was now the first college graduate in his family.

After Tom's graduation, Anna's parents planned to take an extended trip to Canada and California to visit her aunts and their families and they asked Tom and Anna to stay at their house in Kimballton while they were gone and take care of the place.

Tom and Anna sold their trailer in Ames and Tom made the decision to start his veterinary practice and raise their family in Kimballton. He really enjoyed the friendly town, got along well with Anna's family, and he knew he needed the peace and tranquility that small-town life offered. After Tom's experiences in the war, he admitted to Anna that he would have difficulty working for and taking orders from anyone else.

PART II CHAPTER 8

June 1950-1959

In June 1950, Tom, Anna, Joyce, John, and the collies moved in with Anna's parents in Kimballton. With baby number three due in a few months, Anna wanted to stay at home and focus on raising their young family, although she planned to do whatever she could to help Tom with his practice. Anna knew almost everyone in the community and her husband quickly became a familiar figure in town. People seemed to like Tom and were willing to give him an opportunity to become their veterinarian.

Kimballton, Iowa, in 1950 was a small, picturesque, Danish community of 350 people surrounded by rolling hills. It was dotted with hundreds of farms planted in corn and soybeans and raising cattle, pigs, and sheep. With a town only six blocks wide and six blocks long, it didn't take long to get from one end of town to the other. Yet all the stores and businesses that a family would typically need for the day-to-day necessities were there. For other items, several larger towns were less than thirty minutes away.

Anna's parents had lived in the area since emigrating from Denmark in 1901. Her father, a brick and stonemason, had literally helped to build the community by constructing many of the brick buildings that lined Main Street. He was also one of the contractors who had helped to build the Lutheran church in town.

Doc Flynn

To most people, Tom soon became affectionately known as "Doc Flynn," or simply "Doc." It was particularly helpful to the local farmers to have a veterinarian who lived right in Kimballton.

Tom was well respected from the beginning, as his clients noticed how knowledgeable he was and how gentle he was with their animals. Tom was always reliable. Farmers who knew him commented that Tom would be there almost before you hung up the phone, no matter what time of day or night and no matter what the weather. Anna can also recall a number of times in late winter when Tom would get a call at 2 a.m. to go out to a farm to pull a calf from a cow laying in a snowy pasture or freezing cold barn. Even in these situations, Tom would often strip to the waist so he could get his whole arm inside the cow in order to reposition the calf for delivery. As was customary, Tom often was invited into the house when the work was done. It was never too late in the day or too early in the morning to accept a fresh, hot cup of coffee and a sandwich, cake, or cookies from the farmer's wife.

Tom was kind, friendly, and courteous to all of the farmers he worked for, however he inevitably ruffled a feather or two when he insisted the farmers clean out the spider webs in their farrowing houses or barns. Some farmers did not take kindly to a veterinarian telling them how to manage their businesses. On Tom's part however, after having lived in the bug-infested, substandard conditions of the POW camps, he had become highly allergic to insect bites. Tom always would experience excessive swelling after even the smallest insect bites and would cough black dust out of his lungs for days after spending hours in a dusty hog house.

Overall, Tom enjoyed the lifestyle Kimballton offered. His veterinarian practice took him all over the scenic southwestern Iowa community making house calls to help sick animals. Tom was happy with the profession he'd chosen and felt he was very good at his job. He also like the fact that he was his own boss and didn't answer to anyone, whether helping a sick or wounded animal or delivering a stubborn newborn when the normal birthing process wasn't going well. Making house calls also provided Tom with an excuse to drive by and check the ponds in the area for wild ducks and geese or to scan the sides of the roads for pheasants. A number of farmers let Tom and his friends hunt and trap on their land or allowed Tom to take his kids fishing in their ponds.

Since Tom and Anna wanted to build their life together in Kimballton, supporting the community was very important to Tom. From the beginning, he didn't hesitate to get involved in projects or to take a leadership role when he thought it would be benefit the community. Within a year after moving to Kimballton, Tom joined both the Kimballton Volunteer Fire Department and the Harry Albertsen AMVETS Post 51. He also committed to serving on the Audubon County Hospital Board for two years. Tom's willingness to volunteer his time and talents quickly earned him respect and appreciation and he became a role model and friend to many of the younger men in the community.

Tom also believed it was important to honor local veterans after witnessing firsthand the sacrifice that so many men had made defending our country. So after joining the AMVETS organization, Tom helped organize the first annual AMVETS' Memorial Day service at the Immanuel Lutheran Cemetery. For a number of years, Tom would dress in his uniform and join the other veterans from Post 51 and Kimballton residents in honoring not only those who had honorably served our country, but the loved ones of the community who were buried alongside them. As the years went by, Tom loved to tease other veterans that he was one of the few who would always stay thin enough to wear his original uniform. Odd as it may sound, no one in Tom's family or in the community would ever know much more about Tom's experience in WWII other than that he had attained the rank of captain, he had been with the 28th Infantry Division in the Battle of the Bulge, and he had subsequently been a POW in Nazi Germany.

Tom also enjoyed playing on the Kimballton men's softball team when he could, although his knee injuries from the war generally caused him problems after every game. Spectators at the games never would have guessed that Tom was hurting, however. He was always good for a solid line drive and with his speed, frequently earned singles and doubles. He never seemed to miss life in the city, although his family in New York couldn't imagine how their city boy could love living in southwest Iowa.

As was true growing up in New York, some of the young women in town during those years admit to being smitten with Tom. At thirty years old, Tom was still a very handsome man and stood out in a community full of blonde Danes. It didn't hurt that he was from New York, had beautiful sky-blue eyes, and dark, wavy hair. And the Irish name definitely stood out in a community where practically everyone else's last names ended in "sen" or "gaard."

One of Tom's first friends in Kimballton was Lars Larsen. Tom usually went to the Social Café on Main Street for his morning coffee and Lars Larsen, owner of the restaurant, was more than happy to show Tom all the local fishing spots. Good Friday was always the first day of fishing season and the two frequently entertained the other regulars at the café from spring to fall with their latest fishing stories. Sometimes the stories were so ridiculous that it was hard to tell if Tom and Lars were actually telling the truth. Tom also enjoyed fishing with his father-in-law, Niels, affectionately known as "Papa" to Tom and Anna's children.

Alvin Johnson became another of Tom's friends. Alvin owned the Johnson Bros. Implement, an Allis Chalmers dealership, on the west end of town with his brother, Chet. It wasn't long before he and Tom struck up a friendship. Tom frequently stopped at Alvin's shop late in the afternoon to see what was going on. If business was slow, a card game soon started, and Tom and Alvin sometimes would have a shot or two of Alvin's favorite schnapps before both went home for supper. Tom always maintained a two-drink limit, careful to avoid the excesses of his own father.

Alvin was as big a fan of baseball as Tom was and the 1950 World Series prompted the beginning of many friendly bets between the two men. Tom usually was able to bet on his Yankees and Alvin would always bet on the National League team in the series. Much to Tom's satisfaction, the Yankees were in the World Series seven out of ten times during the 1950s, winning in 1950-1954, 1956, and 1958. Tom had great fun bragging about his Yankees to Alvin and the other baseball fans in town, including Papa, who was a St. Louis Cardinals fan.

During the fall and winter, Tom and Alvin seemed to go duck, goose, or pheasant hunting every day. They were out of the house before dawn and back in time for work. Living in the middle of prime pheasant territory and within an hour of the Missouri River, they didn't have to drive far to get their hunt in for the day. During peak migration in the fall, Tom and Alvin also like to goose hunt near the DeSoto Bend National Wildlife Refuge along the Missouri River.

Tom and Alvin also were very active trapping fox in the area and would have a number of years of great success. Trapping foxes helped to protect the farmers' livestock and the furs provided Tom and Alvin extra income. Tom thought the fox furs were beautiful and so soft to the touch. Some farmers also asked the pair to help eliminate coyote and raccoons from their farms to help protect their property or livestock.

Through Alvin, Tom got to know Rex, the local Iowa Conservation Commission game warden. Through Rex, Tom and Anna would get involved in a program to raise quail for the Iowa Conservation Commission for several years during the mid-1950s.

The Early Years in Kimballton

In October, just five months after Tom's Iowa State graduation, his brother, Bill, died unexpectedly. The weak heart that had kept him out of the Army during WWII took his life at the young age of thirty-four. Tom and Bill had become very close over the years, and Tom was very glad that Bill and his family had been able to come to his Iowa State graduation in May. It had meant a great deal to Tom to have them there.

That same month, on October 24, Anna gave birth to another adorable baby girl. They named her Teresa Eileen. With the birth of Terry, Anna's parent's house had become too full. So in March 1951, Tom, Anna, and their family moved into the building next to the Social Café while they saved for a down payment on a house.

Photo: (l-r) Terry, Joyce, Anna holding John, January 1951

A year later, in March 1952, Tom and Anna bought their first home together. Situated at the north end of town, it was just a mile from Anna's parents. The house had been built in 1890, just seven years after the town of Kimballton was founded. The former owner lived in the upstairs temporarily until she bought a smaller home a few blocks away. Tom set up his new operating room and a medical supply room in the basement. He was happy he could give his children what he hadn't had growing up: a big house with a big yard to play in and—as time would prove—all the pets they could ever want.

That same month, Anna's sister, Helga, died of cancer, having been exposed to radioactive paint at her manufacturing job during WWII. Helga was buried at the Immanuel Lutheran Cemetery in Kimballton.

Photo: Tom and Anna's house, 1952

During this time, Tom also bought himself a small fishing boat and a couple of toys reminiscent of his Army days: a surplus Army jeep and a BC-348 N radio receiver that had been used in a B-17 bomber during WWII.

Anna did a lot to help Tom's practice, acting as not only his receptionist but with her nursing degree, assisting in operations on animals or dispensing medicine to farmers.

Having grown up during the Great Depression, both Tom and Anna were very frugal and accustomed to hard work. They put in a big garden to supplement the fruit trees already on the property, and Anna did a lot of canning. The storm cellar, or "the cave" as it was usually called, was perfect for storing large potato crops over the winter. Tom enjoyed hunting and fishing all year round, and this, too, provided food for his family. He would clean and Anna would cook everything he brought home—both game birds and fish. Anna also was an excellent seamstress and sewed quite a bit of clothing for her children and herself. But Anna's passion, like her mother's, was her flower gardens. Her yard was always full of all kinds of flowering plants—perennials, annuals, and flowering bushes. Like many avid gardeners, she spent any free time she had working in her flowerbeds.

After Tom and Anna were settled in their new house, Tom's younger brother, Joe, his wife Carole, and their mom, Josephine, came to visit from New York. Tom had not been home to New York since 1945. By this time, all of Tom's younger siblings—Chuck, Joe, Mel, and Eddie—were married and most of them had started their own families.

Tom's collie, Smokey, had puppies around this time and Joyce, John, and Terry all loved to play with them, especially Terry, who wasn't quite two yet. One day, Terry managed to crawl down the basement steps by herself and climbed into the large metal cage with Smokey and her puppies. When Tom and Anna realized Terry was nowhere to be found, Tom noticed the basement door ajar and went down the steps, only to find Terry cuddled up with Smokey and her family. They were very thankful that Terry had not fallen through the open stairway onto the concrete basement floor on her little adventure.

Photo: Terry and Joyce holding puppies, summer 1952

Tom learned a great deal about hunting and trapping from Alvin and eventually decided to switch from collies to Labradors. As hunting partners, Tom and Alvin agreed to be co-owners of their hunting dogs. Alvin would pay for the dogs and their food and Tom would keep them at his house, train them, and care for them. Their first Labrador was Boots, a large black male. As the newest member of the Flynn family, he lived in the house with everyone else. Boots grew to become a great hunting dog.

Photo: Joyce and Boots, 1952

With the three little ones, Christmas time at the Flynn house was full of fun and Tom was happy to go along with all of Anna's Danish Lutheran traditions. The night before Christmas Eve, December 23rd, Tom, Anna, and their family joined Anna's parents for a traditional holiday meal that included *Æbleskiver* (a small, round, Danish pancake) as the main course, served with Grandma's homemade jam and butter. Papa would bring out his homemade wine for the adults. There were always lots of Grandma's special Danish Christmas cookies to enjoy all evening long, as well.

Christmas Eve became Tom and Anna's time to have her parents over for dinner, and the first Christmas in their new home was the beginning of many special holidays. After the 5 p.m. candlelight church service, Anna served a wonderful Christmas Eve dinner for all. When everything was cleaned up and put away, the family gathered in the living room and sang their favorite Christmas songs. Before Santa came, the children had to get ready for bed, so Anna took Joyce, John, and Terry for their baths and to put their pajamas on. Somehow, Santa always happened to stop at their house just when they were in the middle of their baths, and the little ones were amazed that he seemed to know just when that was. You can just imagine the conversations between the three children and the fun that Tom and Anna had seeing the children's excitement when they discovered that Santa had stopped by and their presents were now under the Christmas tree.

Photo: Terry, Joyce, and John, Christmas 1952

1953-1954

As you can see from the photo below, Tom thought it was humorous to make headbands and other decorations for his children with the tail feathers from the pheasants he'd shot. John, Joyce, and Terry happened to be the victims in this photo, but rest assured, they would not be the only children or grandchildren to tolerate this pheasant-feather fetish over the next forty years.

Photo: Terry, Joyce, and John adorned with pheasant tail-feather headbands, 1953

On May 13, 1953, Tom and Anna were blessed with their fourth child, Joan Francis, another beautiful baby girl. Both Tom and Anna had wanted a large family. Anna was one of five children and Tom was one of eight. With the birth of baby number four, they were well on their way to reaching that goal.

Just a week after turning five, Joyce started kindergarten in 1953. At the time, Kimballton still had a small, rural schoolhouse across the street from the church parsonage. Most of the children in town attended it from kindergarten through eighth grade.

There were only seven students in Joyce's kindergarten class, including Joyce. Tom and Anna were happy that she could walk to school every day and come home for lunch. John started school the following year, and Terry, the year after that even though both had fall birthdays and neither was quite five when school started.

Anna faithfully attended church with her parents every Sunday and made sure the children attended Sunday school and Vacation Bible School in the summer. She also was involved in many church activities, although Tom only went with her for baptisms, confirmations, weddings, and funerals. Tom never said why he didn't go more often and Anna never asked him for a specific reason, although it seemed obvious that his many outdoor activities took priority and fully occupied his time.

1955-1956

In February 1955, Anna became pregnant with baby number five, who would be due in October. Tom and Anna had been hoping to have another child and were thrilled at the news that Anna was pregnant again.

Photo: Tom and Anna with Joan, John, Terry, and Joyce, Easter 1955

Their friends, Bonnie and Keith Poldberg, were expecting twins in July. Bonnie was the daughter of Tom's friend, Lars, and she and Keith lived just a few miles west of town. On April 22, 1955, Bonnie went into premature labor and gave birth to two baby boys; Larry weighed in at just two pounds and Terry weighed three pounds. Tom and Lars were the first to hear the news in Kimballton and they immediately dropped what they were doing to head out to Harlan to see Lars's new grandsons at the hospital. The two stopped at a flower shop along the way to buy Bonnie a plant and quickly decided on a large, blue flowering hydrangea to commemorate the event. Before leaving the shop, they asked the florist to remove one of the blossoms so there would be one bloom for each baby boy.

Tom and Lars came bearing big smiles and hugs for Bonnie when they walked into her hospital room. While they were glad to see that Bonnie was doing well, they both insisted on seeing the newborns right away. The nurse took them to the hospital nursery, but Tom and Lars soon returned to Bonnie's room with tears in their eyes. Neither had been mentally prepared to see what two- and three-pound babies actually looked like— their assessment was that the new babies looked like "skinned squirrels." Apparently, that was the best analogy that Tom could provide.

By mid-May, Bonnie and Keith were able to take Terry home. Larry joined the family a month later. Both infants were still very small and Dr. Larsen remained concerned that there could be medical complications. He told Bonnie and Keith that in an emergency, they should call the Kimballton Fire Department. The firefighters had first aid training, oxygen on hand, and would respond more quickly than he would be able to from Elk Horn. In those days, there were no EMTs or ambulances in the area and the hospital was seven miles from their farm.

When the babies were three months old, Bonnie woke up and discovered that Larry was not breathing. She immediately called the Kimballton Fire Department and Tom was the first person through their door to help. Even though the infant was probably past the point of revival, Tom took the baby out of Keith's arms and said, "Let's get going, Keith." As Keith pulled out of their driveway to head for Harlan Hospital, Tom performed infant cardio-pulmonary resuscitation (CPR) on Larry. Dr. Larsen was already at the hospital checking on other patients when he got the call about Larry and that Tom and Keith were on their way. Dr. Larsen got in his car and he met them halfway there. After performing a quick examination, Dr. Larsen told Keith and Tom that there was nothing more that could be done for Larry and there was no need to take the baby to the hospital. Dr. Larsen turned to Tom and asked him to take Larry to the funeral home in Kimballton instead. Dr. Larsen and Keith returned to the house to be with Bonnie and to wait for Tom to return with Bonnie's dad, Lars.

Deeply saddened by Larry's sudden death, Tom lovingly picked up the tiny, lifeless body again and did as he was asked. When Tom got to the funeral home, he left the tiny infant with the funeral home director, signed the death certificate, and then stopped to get Lars from work at his café. Tom gave Lars the bad news about his grandson and together they drove to Bonnie and Keith's farm. As in the hospital when the babies were born, both Tom and Lars had tears streaming down their faces when they walked in the house. Tom waited for either Lars or Keith to say something but both were too upset to speak, so Tom reached out and gently put his hand on Bonnie's shoulder. Bonnie could tell just by his body language that her baby was gone, and she broke down in tears.

Tom and Anna sat with the family at the funeral and did what they could to help them through the grieving process. Bonnie and Keith would always remember what a caring and compassionate man Tom was and how lovingly he had treated their tiny baby, as if the baby was his own. They never forgot his kindness during this difficult period in their lives. And as would become apparent to them over the years, Tom's compassion and genuine concern for everyone he knew would endear him to many others.

Photo: Tom holding a quail that he raised.

The next few months were very busy for Tom and Anna. In addition to all their other activities, Tom and the Flynn family had begun raising quail for the Iowa Conservation Commission (ICC), which was trying to build up the quail population in the southwestern part of the state. At last, the day came when Tom and his game warden friend, Rex, were ready to catch, band, and transport their annual quail flock for release into the wild. Tom and Rex worked all afternoon banding the birds, and then carefully placing each quail in a large box in Rex's truck for transport. Tom's Labrador, Boots, had been patiently watching all afternoon, but was suddenly overcome with curiosity about the cheeping noises coming from the box. As five-year-old Terry sat and watched, Boots slowly lifted the corner of the lid with his nose to see what was making all that noise. He must have lifted it just far enough for the quail to panic. In an instant, the lid of the box opened wide. Hundreds of quail shot into the air and flew off down the hill into the cornfields. Terry swore it was a better show than a Fourth of July fireworks display. Tom was relieved that Rex just laughed, commenting that Boots had just saved them a lot of work. Needless to say, the quail population around Kimballton grew substantially that fall and remained stable for many years after that.

On October 16, 1955, Anna brought another healthy, beautiful, baby girl into the world. They named this daughter Margaret Gail. One can only imagine how even more precious this little girl was to Tom and Anna after the recent loss of Bonnie and Keith's baby.

The following spring, the Kimballton Fire Department was called to a nearby farm to recover a body following a farming accident. A local farmer had tied himself to a rope and several men had lowered him into his grain silo in an attempt to clear out a clogged opening for his livestock's feed. Since the silos were known to be filled with toxic gases, the plan was that the man would tug on the rope to be pulled out if he ran into trouble. It wasn't long before the man pulled on the rope, but when his friends tried to pull him out, the rope was severed by the sharp edge of the metal opening. The man fell to the bottom of the silo and died. Details of the recovery effort by the firefighters are vague, but Tom was no doubt in the middle of the effort, as two or three firefighters had to go down into the silo to bring the man's body out. Tom took this senseless accident hard, as did many in the community, and Anna's typically unemotional husband was visibly upset when he came home.

Growing Up in Kimballton

As Tom and Anna's children grew older, it was clear how much Tom enjoyed the lifestyle that living in Kimballton offered, not only for himself, but for his family. This childhood was so different than the one Tom had experienced living in an apartment in New York. Like Tom, the Flynn children loved to read and they spent many hours perusing the books in the little Kimballton Library. While the selection was just a fraction of what Tom had had available to him in the New York public libraries, it was enough to keep his children happy and entertained.

For most of the decade of the 1950s, Tom and Anna did not have a television, so Joyce, John, and Terry did a lot of reading. Joyce liked to read to her younger sisters, Joan and Marg, and by age nine, she had already taught four-year-old Joan to read. Anna and Tom were very proud of both of them. John and Terry were also very bright children but they would find any excuse to be outside to avoid helping their mom with housework. Any excuse would do, even if it meant they had to shovel show, mow the grass, or work in the garden. Terry adored her big brother and usually could be found tagging along behind him no matter what he was doing.

Tom and Anna bought their first television in 1958. After having missed the televised events of the Korean War in the early 1950s and the Russian launch of Sputnik 1, the first Earth-orbiting artificial satellite, Tom was glad to be able to follow world news as it happened. Tom also was thrilled to watch Major League baseball games on TV, especially his beloved Yankees, rather than listening to the games on the radio. Anna, however, was not so pleased with the sudden impact that TV had on her young family as the children now wanted to watch TV more often than read. Unfortunately, she was too busy taking care of all of them to do much about it.

The Korsgaard family lived at the farm across the road from Tom and Anna's house, having built and moved into their new home just six months before Tom and Anna moved into theirs. Karen and Andrew were both Danish immigrants so it was great that Anna was fluent in Danish. The couple had five children close to the same ages as the Flynns, so there was always a friend close by for their children to play with. John and Terry loved watching the pigeons in the barn with Chris and Carl, and they would all shimmy out on the ledge at the top of the barn to see the baby pigeons when they hatched.

Once Tom and Anna thought that Joyce, John, and Terry were responsible enough to take care of animals by themselves, the children were allowed to have pets of their own. Terry had been asking for a horse, so Tom got a Shetland pony. This pony wasn't exactly what Terry had had in mind, though. It was mean and would buck them off when they wanted to ride it or bite them when it got angry. Tom didn't keep the pony very long.

When John was ten, he observed that several partially white pigeons were living in the Korsgaards' barn. Hoping to catch himself some new pets, he waited until the birds had returned to their roost for the night and then cautiously climbed in the darkness with a bag and flashlight in one hand, to the pigeons' roost. Tom had built a couple of bird coops for John in their own barn, and since Terry was his faithful sidekick, she helped him take care of them. John didn't know how to tell a male from a female pigeon, and apparently never bothered to ask his dad. So he was very happy when one of the birds laid several eggs and hatched three pure white offspring. John decided to keep just the three new white pigeons for pets, and Tom gave the other ones to Alvin. It seemed to John that Terry was the only one in the family who was interested in his pigeon project besides their dad. He eventually was bored with his pigeon project and decided to release the birds to join the wild flock in the neighborhood.

Then there was Cindy. Raising livestock didn't seem like it was very difficult to do, so Tom and Anna decided to raise a pig in their barn. Tom must not have made it clear to Joyce, John, Terry, and Joan that Cindy was being raised for slaughter, as they all believed Cindy was just the latest pet. It didn't take long for Cindy to grow into a very large sow, and then suddenly one day Cindy just disappeared. It was years before John and Terry ate bacon again out of fear that they would be eating Cindy. Needless to say, Tom and Anna didn't raise any more livestock.

Sometimes when Tom was out hunting and trapping, he would find abandoned baby animals and bring them home to take care of. In the late 1950s, he rescued both a fox and a raccoon. Tom showed the kids how to feed and take care of the tiny raccoon, keeping it in a box on the front porch. But after the baby raccoon had grown large enough to live outdoors, they moved its bed to the barn and the raccoon was allowed to run around in the yard on its own. The raccoon was very friendly and played with the children until one day the call of the wild became too appealing to ignore and the raccoon disappeared down the hill to the creek. No one in the family can remember what happened to the fox, only that they had one for a while.

Another time, Tom rescued a greyhound that had been retired from its racing career. Tom's original intent was to use the dog for raccoon hunting to help rid farms of stubborn raccoons. It turned out, however, that the greyhound was afraid of the sound of a gunshot, thereby making it useless for hunting. The animal also proved to be dangerous to have around the children. One night when Joan was outside playing with some of the new kittens under the west porch, the greyhound showed up and viciously attacked and killed two of the kittens as she watched in horror. She tried to rescue the kittens but was afraid the dog would attack her, too, so she ran inside the house to get her dad to help. Tom promptly got rid of the dog.

Then there were the cats. There always seemed to be at least two cats around the house, as everyone in the family, including Tom, loved cats and kittens. The family had so many cats over the years that they never even bothered to name them, other than the "mama kitty", which was known as just that. Tom's favorite cats, and the only ones he liked to keep, were longhaired female calicos, which he called tri-colors, and longhaired white cats. It was never hard to give away the other kittens, because all the farmers liked to have plenty of cats around to keep the rodent population under control. The only downside to having cats was the effect it had on the children's sandbox. The kids loved to play in the sandbox Tom had built, but Tom eliminated the sandbox when the cats started eliminating in it.

Outdoor life in Iowa is harsh, and one or two cats died or disappeared every winter. If the cats stayed close to the house, Tom would let them come in on the porch for warmth, but more often, they sought out neighbors' barns to be among the livestock in the hay instead, sometimes disappearing for months at a time. Often during the winter, the cats would climb under the hood of the car to warm themselves between Tom's frequent trips to and from the house. If Tom forgot to check under the hood before starting the car to leave again, they sometimes would be killed when he started the engine.

Despite the fact that Tom was a very strict father, his children all loved to spend time with him. Each of them had a favorite thing they liked to do with their dad. For Joyce, it was fishing. There was no lake close by, so the two would sometimes try their luck at a farm pond. Joyce was happy to use the simple cane pole her dad brought along for her. John liked fishing, too, but since he was a boy, he sometimes accompanied his dad and Alvin when they hunted. When he got old enough, Tom taught him gun safety and all he needed to know to be a successful bird hunter.

Photo: (l-r) Terry, Anna, Marg, Joyce, Tom, Joan, and John

Terry liked to go with her Dad on calls to the farms, especially when animals were about to give birth. If she wanted to go with him, though, she soon learned that she couldn't hesitate to jump in the car. Tom couldn't afford to wait for her when farmers often had waited as long as possible before calling him for help. Terry just loved watching him bring baby animals into the world. She also liked to help vaccinate baby pigs, catching them by their back legs and handing them to the farmer. The farmer would hold them upside down between his knees and Tom would swab and vaccinate them before releasing the piglets back to the sows.

They'd pay Terry a couple dollars for catching 200 to 300 pigs and she felt rich. When the farmer waited until the pigs weighted 40-50 pounds though, it wasn't so easy to catch them. Tom would always curse when this happened because it became much more difficult and dangerous work.

Joan didn't like going out to the farms much, preferring to stay around the house and play with the many cats and kittens. When the weather was nice, she and Tom often could be found sitting on the east steps in the shade of the house doing just that. Joan also like fishing with both her dad and Papa, and went as often as she could with both of them.

In the winter, the children spent many hours playing in the snow. After a big storm, they could be found riding their sleds or turning new snow drifts into snow forts and snow caves in preparation for the next big snowball fight. It was a good thing Tom and Anna had several long clotheslines in the basement to dry all those wet clothes and snow boots between frequent trips outdoors.

The Flynn children also spent many hours playing down by the creek near the house. The water wasn't usually very deep, but the tree-lined creek offered a year-round source of fun, adventure, and entertainment, especially when hot, humid Iowa summer days made it the only cool place to be. In the middle of winter, they could skate all the way from the culvert at the north end of town to the bridge on the south edge of town. Anna and Tom always thought they knew what their children were doing but like most children, plans often changed when they were playing with friends. Anna and Tom probably would have had heart attacks if they had witnessed the dangerous things their children did every day, thinking nothing of it.

Unfortunately, the only organized sport in town was summer baseball for the boys so John was the only one of the older Flynn children able to play on a youth ball team. John was happy that Terry was always a willing partner for playing catch and there were frequent ballgames going on in the yard with John's friends and sisters. Tom would sometimes join in their game, which was always a surprise and a treat for the kids.

The End of the Decade

By now, Tom knew pretty much everyone in the area. Besides Alvin, he fished with Paul Christensen, Jim Larsen, and Buzz and Christie Fredricksen. Tom and Paul's favorite spot was Black Hawk Lake at Lakeview, Iowa, about an hour north of Kimballton, where they liked night fishing for catfish. One especially successful night, Tom, Paul, and Christie all caught their limits before dawn, returning to Kimballton by 6:30 a.m. The men laid out their catch and made sure Alvin, who had been unable to make the overnight trip, stopped by before going to work so they could tease him about what he had missed out on.

Photo: Christie, Paul, and Tom after overnight fishing trip to Black Hawk Lake.

It had always been in the back of Anna's mind that when she had her own family, she didn't want to have an odd number of children. Anna had been the third of five children in her own family, and she remembered vividly the challenges of being the middle child. In mid-1958 when Anna became pregnant again with baby number six, she was happy at the prospect of again having an even the number of children. Joan was starting school soon, so Anna would only have Margaret at home all day, along with an infant. God had other plans for Tom and Anna though, and on February 28, 1959, Anna gave birth to twins. The older twin was Patricia Jean; William Michael joined the family twenty minutes later. With seven children in the household now, Anna still wasn't happy with an odd number but she decided seven children was enough. She and Tom would both be forty years old soon and she was ready to be done with having babies.

After the twins were born, Anna relied on Joyce's help when she was home from school to care for Bill because Pat wasn't happy being taken care of by anyone else but Anna. Anna also hired a young woman from town to help with household chores temporarily.

Tom helped Anna as much as he could but with seven children in the house, being at home was stressful for him. Being an early riser may have been a self-defense mechanism, enabling him to get out of the house while it was still quiet. If Tom wasn't headed out hunting or fishing at the crack of dawn or making an early morning call to a farm, he was usually out of the house running errands and catching up on the local gossip. After stopping to get a cup of coffee at the café, Tom frequently would pick up groceries and then stop by the post office to get the mail.

One day shortly after the twins were born, Tom ran into a former Kimballton resident at the post office who was in town visiting her father. She had two toddlers at her side, which prompted Tom to joke that she'd had her kids "boom, boom, boom." He was caught off guard when she turned to him and said with a smile, "At least I stopped." Speechless or just biting his tongue, we will never know, as he just turned and walked out without saying another word. After fathering seven babies in ten years, there was not much he could say.

Around this time, Tom's beloved dog had an accident. All his life, Boots had been an enthusiastic and reliable bird dog for Tom and Alvin, as well as a faithful companion for Joyce, John, and Terry. Once the children were old enough to walk around town on their own, Boots usually tagged along. One day when Boots was following Joyce and Terry, he was hit by a car on the south end of town. Tom was called about the accident and he quickly came to pick up his dog and the girls. Dropping Terry and Joyce off at home, Tom drove one hundred miles to the Iowa State Veterinary School in Ames to have a pin put into Boots's hip. The dog's broken bones soon healed but he was much slower after the accident. The entire family was very glad Boots was still alive, and probably no one was more relieved than Tom.

While Boots was recovering, Tom and Alvin decided to get another hunting dog for the fall. Alvin bought another black Labrador named Betty. By this time, Anna had had enough of sweeping up dog hair and keeping the little ones away from the dog food bowl on the kitchen floor, so Betty lived in the barn. Tom built her a nice doghouse and placed it inside the barn for extra protection in the winter. Betty was a quick learner and became adept at flushing pheasants out of the bushes. She spent a lot of time with Tom and Alvin hunting ducks, geese, and pheasants. Betty was very shy and gentle, and was good around the children. She would live until the mid-1960s.

The Christmas Season

In the late 1950s, Christmas time for the Flynn family was filled with many activities, including church festivities, school Christmas concerts, and all the practices each child needed to attend. Anna loved listening to her children sing in choirs and attended as many events as she could. As much as Tom loved music, though, he always found a reason not to go.

The house was filled to capacity on Christmas Eve with Tom, Anna, seven children, and Papa and Grandma. As usual, Anna always prepared a wonderful Christmas Eve dinner and the house smelled divine with a goose or ham baking in the oven. With so many people in the house at once, Anna and Tom had to set up two large tables in the living room to accommodate everyone. It was always a team effort to clean up after the meal and move the tables out of the living room so the rest of the evening's traditions could begin.

When Anna was ready, everyone would squeeze back into the living room, sitting together on the couches and the floor, as Christmas songbooks were passed out. Every year the number of Christmas songs that the children knew increased as they all learned new songs in school and church choirs. Their voices were also maturing and some of them had even learned to sing in harmony. Each person had a turn at choosing a song and the family sang every verse in the books. The scene must have reminded Tom of those Sunday dinners growing up when his family would sit around the table singing in harmony. Tom always insisted the last song of the night would be "Silent Night," as it was Anna's favorite. When Tom was finally satisfied he had squeezed every song possible out of his kids, he would hand out the presents one by one or appoint one of his children to do so. There were never many presents per child but with so many people, the tree was overflowing with gifts, and laughter, smiles, and love filled the room.

CHAPTER 9

1960-1970

1960

It was now January 1960. With seven children ranging in age from one to eleven, Tom and Anna knew their family life was going to continue to keep them very busy for the next decade. The twins had just started to walk and Anna looked forward to only one more year of washing diapers. By the time her fortieth birthday rolled around in mid-January, however, Anna discovered that she was pregnant with baby number eight. Feeling overwhelmed and exhausted, Anna was not very excited about this pregnancy. Who could blame her? Their large house was overflowing with children and the household chores were never-ending.

Tom did the best he could at being a good father. In his own way, he had developed a special relationship with each of his children. Tom continued to hunt, trap, and fish as often as he could with his friends, but more and more often one or more of his children tagged along. The children still loved to ride along with their dad for pretty much any reason: drives in the country, coffee at the café, fishing, running errands, or just making veterinarian calls to the farms. Tom rarely said "no" when one of them asked to ride along.

As the children grew older, Black Hawk Lake became a frequent weekend destination for the Flynn family, and Tom often took the older ones on daytrips to fish or to camp overnight. These camping trips didn't always go as planned, because Tom remained strict about his children's behavior and there was always the threat that they would go home if someone misbehaved. Much to their disappointment, Tom fulfilled his promise one time, packing everything up and heading home in the middle of the night.

Anna was happy to stay home to enjoy the comfort of her own bed, the convenience of cooking in her own kitchen, and a temporary reprieve from having all eight children under foot. However, Anna did have a good friend from childhood who had a house on Black Hawk Lake, so when Anna wanted to see her friend, the entire family would go.

Photo: Tom camping at Black Hawk Lake

Near the end of the summer, Anna gave birth to another baby girl on August 19, only two days before Tom's fortieth birthday. Anna decided once and for all that she had had enough children and was finally able to convince her Catholic husband that eight was enough. Joyce turned twelve the day after her new sister was born and was very excited that she was the only one allowed to go with her dad to visit her mom and sister in the hospital.

Tom and Anna did not name the newborn immediately. Tom wanted to name her Mary, after his grandmother, but John insisted he wanted to name her Alice. Tom and Anna decided that this time the baby's name should be a family decision, as there was at least one strong opinion against their choice! They took a vote and John's suggestion of Alice won. Tom's choice, Mary, came in second, therefore Alice Mary she became.

A week later, Margaret, not quite five, started kindergarten. Anna would have preferred that Margaret wait another year to start school but Tom insisted she was ready. As usual, Anna didn't argue and went along with Tom's decision.

In October, Tom's Yankees once again made it to the World Series after another great season. With a roster filled with great players such as Yogi Berra, Mickey Mantle, Roger Maris, Elston Howard, and Bobby Shantz, the Yankees faced the Pittsburgh Pirates for the championship. Once again, the bet was on between Tom and Alvin. Tom, Alvin, Jim Larsen, and John (who was now old enough to go goose hunting with his dad), sat in the goose blinds on several sunny October days, listening to the Yankees-Pirates World Series games on a transistor radio. Unfortunately, the Yankees lost the championship that year when Bill Mazeroski of the Pirates hit a home run to win the final game. Tom and John were devastated. The Yankees would return to the World Series in each of the next four years; winning in 1961 and 1962.

1961

It was hard to tell whether Tom or his children got more pleasure from having such a wide variety of pets. Tom continued to try his hand at raising different animals and birds and the kids loved having a variety of pets to care for and watch grow. Tom's next pet experiment was raising ducks and geese, and for this, he built a large pen near the barn under the pine trees. Anna, practical and resourceful as always, used the regular supply of brown duck eggs for her daily baking for the family. Thank goodness, she agreed with the rest of her family and only used chicken eggs for breakfast.

Tom would sometimes bring some of the warm, freshly laid eggs into the house and incubate them under a heat lamp. It was exciting for the kids to track the progress of the eggs, especially when the eggs started to hatch. Even Tom would get excited, gathering all the children to come watch. Little by little, the tiny beaks would break through the eggshells and little ducklings would eventually appear. Tom fed the ducklings oatmeal and kept them in a large box on the front porch so everyone could watch them grow, and to protect them from predators outside. When the ducklings got large enough that they could jump out of the box and run around, Anna put her foot down. It was time for them to be moved out into the big pen with the other ducks. She didn't want to worry about stepping on ducklings when she walked through the house with an armload of laundry from the clothesline or bags full of groceries.

Much to Tom's satisfaction, construction of an earthen dam that had begun in 1958 at the new Prairie Rose State Park, ten miles southwest of Kimballton, was finally nearing completion. The project would create a 218-acre lake, providing a new place to go fishing. It became apparent to Tom that the little boat he had been using for fishing and bird hunting since moving to Iowa just wasn't going to be good enough anymore. So in 1961, Tom purchased a larger one, measuring a whopping 11 feet 6 inches. Tom didn't have a trailer to pull the boat, but he could still transport it to the lake on the roof of his station wagon, just as he did with the smaller boat. Special brackets attached to the bumpers allowed him to easily load and unload the boat by himself.

When Anna joined Tom and the family at the new lake, Tom would take turns fishing with the children in the boat while the others stayed with Anna, fishing for bluegill and crappie from the shore or searching the shoreline for crayfish. Catching a big fish was always worth bragging about, and one summer Joan caught a large enough bullhead that Tom mounted the head, with its mouth wide open, near the storm cellar, where everyone who drove into the driveway could see it. It certainly earned Joan bragging rights, although it was hard to tell who was more proud of the catch— Joan or her dad.

1962

Joyce finished eighth grade and confirmation classes in 1962 and decided to go to Audubon for high school, as Audubon offered more college-prep classes than Elk Horn did. Joyce had wanted to be a teacher for as long as she could remember, so this seemed to be a logical choice. Despite the fact that all her life, she had only had seven classmates in Kimballton, she did very well in high school and joined the Future Teachers of America.

Throughout high school, Joyce volunteered to teach the younger grades in Sunday school and Vacation Bible School at church. Joyce also was busy working once she was old enough, earning enough money to buy her own clothes. She detasseled in the cornfields in the summers, waitressed at Simon's Café in town, and worked at the local grocery store. Tom was very proud of his oldest daughter and liked to stop for coffee at the café when Joyce was working, frequently bringing a little brother or sister along.

After twenty years of marriage, Tom had gotten to know Anna's family very well. At least one of Anna's siblings seemed to come home every year to visit Papa and Grandma. Though Ole and Betty still lived in Seattle and Ole continued to work as a mechanical engineer at Boeing, they seemed to come home to Kimballton the most often. Their oldest daughter, Bonnie, was six years older than Joyce, but Scott was about the same age as John, and Debbie was close to Marg's age, so together the cousins were always busy having fun during these visits. Tom and Anna very much looked forward to their visits, too. Anna thought the world of her big brother Ole.

Anna was also very close to her younger brother, Magnus, who lived in the San Francisco area, but his civil engineering job frequently took him away to large construction projects all over the world. Her sister, Eva, and Eva's husband had moved to northern Wisconsin to farm after World War II and were busy raising their own large family.

During Ole and Betty's 1962 visit, they invited Joyce and John to return with them to Seattle so they could attend the World's Fair. It was the first World's Fair in the United States since World War II and the Seattle Center and the futuristic Space Needle were supposed to be quite the sights to see. Tom and Anna were excited to have the older children go. Terry, however, was very disappointed with this arrangement because she had to stay home and mow the one-acre lawn while John was gone. When John got home, he surprised everyone with another new pet. He had caught a garter snake in Ole's yard in Seattle and had smuggled it home on the plane in his pocket. Anna didn't share his enthusiasm about having another snake in the house. Snakes tended to get loose, only to reveal themselves at inopportune times, such as when Anna had her friends over.

Over the years, the community had come to rely on Tom for many things, particularly when there was an emergency of some kind or an animal control problem. Tom was known to respond promptly and calmly. One such emergency was when an angry bull broke out of the Kimballton Sale Barn and ran loose around the south edge of town. Kimballton residents feared the bull would hurt someone, so Leland Kaltolf called Tom to help control the situation. Tom jumped in his jeep and met Leland and his eight-year-old son, Bernard, where the bull had last been spotted. Leland used his shotgun to bring the bull down and Tom then moved in closer and shot the bull in the head to end his pain. The owner of the bull was probably very upset when he found out what had happened but when the safety of the community was at stake, Tom always did what needed to be done.

Photo: Another successful hunt for Tom (Canada geese), December 1962.

In 1962, Tom's dog Boots died and Betty was getting too old to hunt, so Tom and Alvin acquired a new black Labrador named Casper. However, Casper did not turn out to be a very good hunting dog and Tom quickly grew frustrated with his hunting skills. Patience was not necessarily one of Tom's virtues and he had a difficult time getting Casper to work the pheasants in the field as he and Alvin walked.

Instead, Casper liked to run out in front, scaring the birds up before Tom and Alvin were in shooting range. Tom finally reached his boiling point one day after Casper had once again taken off out of control and scared all the pheasants away. Waiting until Casper had run far enough out that he wouldn't be injured seriously, Tom shot Casper in his hind end to teach him a lesson. The buckshot didn't hurt Casper much; it just stung his backside. Tom and Alvin only kept Casper a couple of hunting seasons before they decided that this Labrador was meant to be a family dog and Alvin found him a new home.

1963-1964

As the community continued to grow, Tom and his friends began to consider better ways to manage the fire department to meet the needs of the community. In the hope of implementing these ideas, Tom, Alvin, and several other volunteer firefighters assumed responsibility for the management of the volunteer fire department on December 30, 1963. Within a few weeks, the Kimballton City Council negotiated with the surrounding Township Trustees to provide fire protection for their areas under a new state law. The trustees of each township could now levee a tax and contract with cities and fire departments for fire protection. The result was the Kimballton Volunteer Fire Department was now responsible for covering a one hundred-square-mile area. In addition, the Kimballton FD had an agreement with Elk Horn to assist with any fires in town as well as the surrounding rural area in return for its assistance in Kimballton when needed. This was quite a responsibility for the small group of volunteer firefighters to manage, but they knew the community did not end at the city limits; the farms and homes outside of town needed their protection as well.

Tom and Anna tried to imbue their children with this sense of responsibility for family and community. The Flynn children were expected to work to help to pay for extra things they wanted, even though there weren't a lot of job opportunities in the area—particularly for young ladies—with the exception of babysitting and detasseling corn in late summer. Starting at age fourteen, each Flynn girl except Terry took her turn detasseling for the large seed corn growers in the area or walking the bean fields cutting the weeds out of every row. Terry opted to babysit to earn her extra spending money and then worked at Dairy Queen when she turned sixteen. Summer farm work was grueling for teenagers. Up at the crack of dawn and out the door armed with their small cooler of food, a bandana on their head and a corn machete in hand, they crawled half-asleep onto a bus filled with the other girls from Elk Horn and Kimballton who were just as tired as they were. They all worked long days in the hot Iowa sun or sloshed through the rain and mud, removing the tassel from each female stalk of corn, row after row after row. The best part about late-summer detasseling and walking the bean fields was when the job was over and they were paid for their hard work.

The boys typically would bale hay and walk the bean fields all summer for their spending money during their junior high and high school years. Baling hay generally paid much better, but it was very physically demanding. They loaded the heavy bales of hay from the fields onto the wagons and then unloaded and stacked the bales in the dusty barns, where it always seemed to be twenty degrees hotter than the already hot and humid summer outside.

Although it wasn't intentional on Tom and Anna's parts, having their children work physically demanding jobs in the fields all summer would ultimately help motivate each of them to pursue a college education. None of them wanted to do manual labor for the rest of their lives.

In the spring of 1964, Tom and Anna took in a small housedog, a female terrier named Mickey. It didn't take long for Mickey to become known as Pat's dog, since she slept under the covers near Pat's feet every night and was by her side everywhere she went.

Unfortunately, Mickey became pregnant before Tom had had time to spay her. During the pregnancy, she gained so much weight that she was no longer able to jump up on Pat's bed. To Pat's delight, Tom put together a small bed for Mickey on the floor beneath Pat's bed. It was no surprise, then, that Pat woke up when Mickey went into labor in the middle of the night. As Pat watched, Mickey seemed to be having difficulty giving birth so Pat finally woke up her dad around 3 a.m. Tom helped Mickey deliver her pups because they were too big to come out on their own, but it was too late. Both pups were already dead. Once Mickey recovered, Tom spayed the dog so she wouldn't get pregnant again, as they could have very easily lost Mickey during the difficult delivery, too.

The Flynn household was never a quiet place. To find a few moments of peace and solitude, Tom frequently could be found sitting on the steps on the east side of the house, especially between late spring and early fall when the weather was mild. The view to the east overlooked the creek a half mile away with farmland stretching over a mile and a half to the crest of the next big hill. Each season brought its own special beauty, and sitting in this spot was almost magical for the tranquility it brought to the soul. Whether enjoying the sunrise, or savoring the cool reprieve on a hot, summer afternoon, the east steps offered a retreat from the noise and chaos that could be overwhelming inside the house. Tom loved this view and the landscape and took many photos of it over the years.

Photo: (front) Bill, Pat, Marg with Mickey, Joan holding Alice, (back) John, Tom, Terry, and Joyce in summer 1963

Joan was a shy, quiet little girl, and the east porch was one of her favorite places, too. Sometimes Tom would join her there and the two would sit together quietly, petting the many cats and listening to the sounds of an Iowa summer. From the hill on which the house sat, they could often hear the cheers rising from a ballgame at the Kimballton baseball diamond, the Wednesday night Sale Barn auction, or the sounds of crickets and frogs serenading the firefly show at dark. Tom was always a good listener when one of his children wanted to have a serious conversation. Joan recalls one time when she was mad at her mom and Tom came out to sit with her on the steps. Venting her frustration, she told Tom that she was prouder of being Irish than she was of being Danish. To her, being Irish was unique because EVERYBODY around Kimballton was Danish, just like her mom. Tom listened to his little girl express her opinion, but his only words of advice to her were, "Don't tell your mother that."

That summer, Tom and Anna took one of their family drives to Lake View to visit the Scotts. The car was packed and Alice was still small enough that she sat in Anna's lap for the one-hour drive. It seemed to Alice that all her brothers and sisters were yelling at her, so she decided she didn't want to be in the car with them anymore. She reached for the door handle to get out just as Tom drove around a curve at 40 mph. The door flew open and Anna reacted by grabbing Alice tightly, but she didn't have her seat belt on. Mother and daughter tumbled out of the car and rolled down a steep embankment together. Tom was paying attention to the road with his head turned to the left so Joan yelled at him to stop the car. Anna was not badly injured, as she was wearing a long sleeved coat but Alice was all scraped up. By now they were closer to a doctor in Lake View than to Dr. Larsen back home so they continued on their way and sought medical attention for both once they got to the lake. Needless to say, Alice's brothers and sisters never let her forget that she ruined their trip to the lake that day.

In October, the 1964 World Series saw the New York Yankees taking on the St. Louis Cardinals. Once again, the bets were on, as Tom and Papa each cheered on their favorite teams, who were playing each other in the championship series for the first time. Of course, bragging rights for the next year were at stake. The

Cardinals won the series 4-3, making Papa a very happy man, especially after having listened to Tom brag about his Yankees for the past twenty years. After the 1964 series, the Yankees would only make it to the World Series four more times while Tom was still alive.

Photo: Tom and Alvin's winter harvest of thirty-nine fox furs.

Tom and Alvin continued to trap fox in the area, and they usually had quite a string of furs to sell by the end of the season. Tom had mastered the skill of skinning the animals and tanning the furs, and the furnace room in the basement typically was filled with dozens of furs drying out each winter. Tom had special metal hangers that stretched the fox skins as they dried. As you can imagine, the furnace room in the basement was not a pleasant sight to see—or to smell—during the winter. Amazingly, Anna never complained.

When Marg was in fourth grade, she decided she wanted her dad to bring one of the furs to school for show and tell. All Marg's classmates got to touch the fox fur, and the teacher wrote down the students' observations as they shared what they knew about fox. Marg's only comment about the fox fur was that she was used to seeing them all the time. Tom must have been pleased that Marg wanted to show one of his furs to her classmates, and he took this photo for her to remember the day.

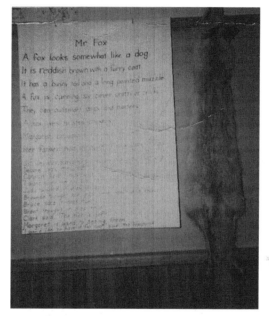

Photo: Marg's fox fur display for show-and-tell at school.

1965

In January 1965, Tom increased his commitment to the community and joined the Kimballton City Council. He was also elected fire chief after having spent fourteen years as a volunteer firefighter. Tom's friends, Paul Christensen and Don Madsen (also a City Council member), were appointed assistant fire chiefs. Like Tom, both men were reliable and dedicated to serving the community. At this time, they determined the fire department would need additional equipment in order to adequately serve the surrounding townships. The department ordered a new fire truck (a 1965 Dodge with a 400 gallon-per-minute (GPM) front-mounted pump and a 1,000-gallon tank) and a 5-horsepower warning siren for their fire alert system. Tax levies from the surrounding townships now included under their protection would help defray the cost of the new equipment. However at this point, the fire department did not have an official fire station so the fire trucks and equipment had to be stored inside other buildings in town.

In addition to Tom and his assistant fire chiefs, the 1965 Kimballton Volunteer Fire Department roster included only twelve additional residents and local businessmen. An emergency phone line for the Fire Department had been installed to each volunteer firefighter's home and/or business. When a call came in, the firefighters made sure everyone knew where to go as there were no radios or cell phones to rely on once they left home. If someone happened to miss the call but heard the siren go off, he would immediately call Anna, and she would tell him what the emergency was and where to go.

The fire department also utilized the new siren to alert the community in times of emergency, such as when the National Weather Service issued tornado warnings. Tom would diligently scan the TV and radio for news when threatening weather conditions existed for Audubon and Shelby counties or when a tornado was reported in a neighboring county. If there was a report of a tornado touching down in the area, Tom would go to where the fire trucks and equipment were stored to be ready in case of an emergency. Anna would stay home with the children and take shelter in the southwest corner of the basement until Tom returned or he called her to tell her it was safe.

Tom was very proud of the fire department and his role as fire chief. From time to time, there would be a dance at the Kimballton Town Hall. When Anna could convince Tom to go, he always wore his dress fireman's jacket. All the women were impressed by what a graceful dancer Tom was when he took Anna out on the dance floor. Sometimes he would even dance with his daughters. Alice recalls that her dad tried to teach her to dance when she was very small by letting her stand on his feet as they danced around the room together.

On August 25, 1965, Papa and Grandma celebrated their fiftieth wedding anniversary. Anna's parents planned a big party in August at their house when all their children and their families could be home to help celebrate. Tom and Anna didn't have any extra room for overnight guests, but Ole and Eva's families came to the house often while they were in town. John and Scott decided that with all sixteen cousins together, it was the perfect opportunity to have a touch football game in the yard. Tom even joined in their friendly game. The entire family had a lot of fun that day and John was impressed by how well his dad could catch passes and how fast he could run.

Just after Alice turned five in August, she started kindergarten and Anna finally had all her children in school. Joyce, John, and Terry were in high school fifteen miles away in Audubon, with Joyce starting her senior year. The younger five all walked to their school just a few blocks from the house.

In September, part of the new fall lineup on TV was a show called *Hogan's Heroes*. The show was a comedy about a fictional version of a Stalag 13 POW camp for captured airmen near Hammelburg, Germany, run by the Luftwaffe during WWII. *Hogan's Heroes* was a success, airing for six years. Tom failed to see the humor in the show. The Oflag 13B POW camp near Hammelburg, where he had been held for 2½ months, bore no resemblance to the prime-time family version. Understandably, Tom didn't allow his family to watch the show when he was home. It was an unwelcome reminder of a period in his life that he wanted to forget. Tom would occasionally talk about his WWII experiences with his children and Anna if they asked questions, but he very rarely went into detail, preferring to keep his comments and stories brief and often vague.

Soon after Tom took over as fire chief, there was a series of suspicious fires at abandoned farms around Kimballton. Tom and his men noticed that a particular individual kept showing up to watch the fire department put out the fires and Tom reported the man as a possible arson suspect to the Audubon County sheriff. When the man found out that Tom had named him as a suspect, he threatened Tom's life.

John remembers coming home from school one day that fall to find his dad and an Audubon County deputy sheriff standing in the driveway with loaded guns at their sides. Someone had called Tom to warn him that the suspect had been drinking heavily; the caller was worried the man might go after Tom. The deputy sheriff had driven from Audubon to provide extra protection for Tom and his family in case the man showed up at the house. John admits to being very scared at the time, but he had no doubt about what his dad and the deputy sheriff would have done if the man had been dumb enough to follow through on his threat. Tom told John to go in the house and not to say anything to his younger siblings. Fortunately, nothing happened, and the deputy sheriff returned to Audubon later that evening.

1966-1968

Tom and Alvin's next hunting dog was a yellow Labrador named Ginger. Once again, the new hunting dog did not have the hunting skills the two had hoped for, so in the spring of 1966, they decided to try to raise new hunting dogs from puppies. Tom's children were ecstatic when he brought home two female Labrador puppies. The kids named them Goldie and Blackie, and both turned out to be great hunting dogs. But at Anna's insistence, Tom kept them in the barn.

Joyce graduated from Audubon High School in May 1966 and made National Honor Society. She planned to attend Grand View Junior College in Des Moines in the fall. She was almost eighteen. Tom finally took Joyce and John to get their drivers licenses a week before Joyce left for college. The family still had only one car, so the licenses wouldn't have been of much use to them earlier, even if they'd gotten them at sixteen, like most of their friends had done.

When it was time to pick up Joyce for Thanksgiving vacation, rather than make the trip to Des Moines alone, Tom asked Marg if she wanted to skip school for the day and go along. Marg didn't get to do too much with her Dad by herself, so she was very excited and felt very special. He even treated her to her first trip to McDonald's once they made it to Des Moines!

The following spring, the Kimballton School closed its doors. The town had decided it was no longer feasible to support its own school. Both Audubon and Elk Horn already sent buses to Kimballton to pick up schoolchildren. So in the fall of 1967, the remaining seven of Tom and Anna's children all boarded the school bus together to attend Audubon. John was starting his senior year and Terry was a junior. Joan was in eighth grade; Marg, in seventh; Pat and Bill were in third; and Alice was in second grade.

Tom and Anna attended the first parent-teacher conferences in Audubon to make sure their children had transitioned into the new school without any problems. Tom was not a parent who often spoke words of praise or encouragement to his children, but he did try to inspire his children when he thought a pep talk would be beneficial. The older children had always done well academically, but Tom sensed that Marg doubted her own abilities. So after meeting with her new teachers, Tom shared with Marg that one of her teachers felt she could very well be one of the smartest students in her entire class. It was obvious Tom was proud of Marg and this was his way of trying to build up her self-confidence so she would try harder to live up to her potential.

During John's last two years of high school, he was very involved in school activities as well as sports. He participated in two musicals and in his senior year, both he and Terry ran for student government positions; John was voted Student Council president and Terry became treasurer.

John played football as a junior and senior, and played enough on specialty teams to letter. Those two years, Audubon was ranked 6th and 7th in the state, 1965 and 1966 respectively, which was before Iowa schools were divided into classes based on size. Even though John didn't get to play as much as he wanted to, he was still excited to be a part of the team. John also ran track his junior and senior years, lettering both years and setting the Audubon High School record in the 4 x 100 relay team event. He also played his last baseball season with his Audubon friends.

As much as Tom enjoyed sports and seeing his children succeed, he rarely went to see them compete in sporting events. Tom never explained why he didn't go, other than to say that he needed to be available if someone called for him for work—this was long before answering machines and cell phones. However, he did take Alice to watch the big rival high school football game— Audubon versus Harlan at Audubon—during John's senior year. Tom parked on the hill overlooking the football field, where he could watch the game from the car with binoculars. The football bleachers were packed for the big game. John didn't get to play much during that game and he didn't know that Tom and Alice had come to watch. For some reason, Tom never told John he had gone to see the game. John assumed his dad had never seen him play until Alice mentioned to him in 2009 that she remembered going to the game and watching from the car on the hill.

John graduated second in his class from Audubon High School in May 1967 and was accepted to Iowa State University for the fall quarter. He planned to major in physics. Tom and Anna were very proud of John and happy that he had chosen to go to Tom's alma mater.

Terry had a different focus in high school. She realized that getting good grades and a college education were the only way she was going to have a rewarding career. Terry was a firm believer in the women's rights movement and strongly believed that men and women should be treated and paid equally for doing the same jobs, and that they should have the same opportunities available to them. It was obvious to her even in high school that her brother had a lot more opportunities than she did as a female, and she didn't think that was fair. In support of her beliefs, she refused to take a typing class in high school, reasoning that she didn't want to get a secretarial job (although typing would have been a handy skill for all those high school and college papers.) Terry worked hard, excelled in the classroom, was on the debate team and involved in student government.

The following year, Terry graduated as valedictorian of the Audubon High School Class of 1968 and starting working at Landmands National Bank in Kimballton right after graduation. She had been accepted at Grinnell College starting in the fall and planned to major in economics. Terry, Tom, and Anna all thought she was very fortunate to be able to work at the bank in town, since there were not many jobs in Kimballton. She could also live at home and save her money for school. Terry would work at the bank for five summers and for a month during every Christmas break.

That summer, John moved home after his first year at Iowa State as Tom had helped him get a maintenance job with the City of Kimballton.

One of the benefits of attending a larger school was the sports program, and Marg decided to play junior high girls' six-on-six basketball in Audubon. Because gym time was limited and four teams had to share the space, Marg frequently had 7 a.m. basketball practices. As there were no other girls from Kimballton on the Audubon team, Tom drove her the fifteen miles to and from every practice and game when the activity bus wasn't available. No matter what the Iowa winter weather was like, by the time Marg was ready to leave each morning at 6:30 a.m., Tom had scraped the snow and ice from the windshield and warmed up the car. Tom never complained about taking her or sitting for extended periods in the cold and dark, waiting for her school bus to return from an away game. Whether Marg returned from games happy or sad, Tom was always there to hear how the game had gone and to find out how Marg felt she had played.

Marg also felt very lucky to have her big brother John around. They spent a lot of time playing basketball in the park in Elk Horn or in the makeshift basketball court in a neighbor's hayloft. Sometimes they took their little brother and sisters swimming in Elk Horn while they played basketball or tennis together. John also taught Marg how to play softball. He even went to her games, and she knew how hard it must have been for him to sit and listen to her high school softball coach yell at her. Marg often wondered if that's why their dad didn't watch her games. What parent wants to hear his child yelled at? And Coach Taylor liked to yell a lot!

Frustrations with His Practice

Although Tom loved caring for animals, there were definitely times when he became frustrated and angry with some of his farmer clients. Good or bad, Tom was never shy about voicing his opinion to his clients. As a result, there were a few instances in which Tom and a farmer just didn't get along. In those cases, Tom was happy to have the farmer seek the services of another veterinarian in the future.

Tom understood how financially difficult it was to manage a farm, but several clients repeatedly tried to save a few dollars on a veterinary bill by attempting to handle a difficult birth on their own. Time after time, they would wind up calling Tom as a last resort after it was already too late to save the baby. Tom would get upset and lecture the farmers. It was hard for him to understand how they could chose to let their animals suffer in hopes of saving a few dollars. Somehow, it never seemed to sink in to those clients that the ultimate cost was higher if they lost the calf, lamb, or piglet or sometimes even the mother.

One time, a farmer whom Tom considered a friend accused Tom of making an incorrect diagnosis on his sick cattle, which, he claimed, resulted in the death of at least one of the cows. John recalled that this was the most upset he'd ever seen his dad. Tom believed the cows were sick from eating nightshade. But the farmer got the opinion of another veterinarian, who disagreed with Tom's diagnosis. John felt very bad for his dad but he was too young to know what to do to help him.

As with any business, Tom had clients who simply didn't seem to think it was important to pay their veterinary bills. It was frustrating to Tom to see these same people spending their money on other things that seemed frivolous to Tom. Eventually, Tom would decide to cut his losses and refuse to do anymore work for clients with poor payment history.

Adjusting to the Shrinking Family

As Tom and Anna's children grew older and the oldest three left for college, Tom began to relax and spend more time at home, and his daily routines gradually changed. More frequently, Tom opted to make his morning coffee at home and could be found sitting at the kitchen table working on the daily crossword puzzle from the newspaper. The puzzles in the Des Moines and Omaha papers were generally very challenging, but Tom was usually able to complete one by the end of each day. The following morning, before starting the next day's puzzle, he'd study the answers for any words he'd struggled with the day before. It was always amazing to his children how much their dad knew. He always left the puzzles in progress sitting by his chair in the kitchen or living room throughout the day and anyone at the house was welcome to help complete it. Only rarely could anyone else in the family come up with more than an answer or two.

Tom also enjoyed listening to the radio when it was quiet in the house and while he worked on the daily crossword puzzle or read. Tom loved solo artists and groups with great vocals and harmony, as much as popular songs that were fun to sing and dance to. Some of those included *California Girls* by the Beach Boys, *Kansas City* by Trini Lopez ("They got some crazy little women there and I'm gonna get me one" was his favorite line), or any song performed by Simon & Garfunkel. *Bridge over Troubled Water,* released in January 1970 would be one of his all-time favorites by this duo. Tom also enjoyed the music of Kenny Rogers & The First Edition after Mary Arnold, an Audubon high school classmate of Terry's, joined the group in 1968 just prior to its worldwide hit, "Ruby, Don't Take Your Love to Town" in 1969. Quite frequently, when a song came on that he really liked, he'd crank up the music and sing along or whistle, or if he happened to be standing up working on something, he might dance a few steps to the music. If Anna was within reach, he sometimes pulled her into his arms for a spin around the room.

Since there were only so many opportunities to spend time with their dad each day, Alice liked to take advantage of TV time in the evenings. She frequently parked herself right next to her dad on the couch. They both enjoyed watching police and detective shows, and they had a long-standing contest of trying to be the first to figure out the plot. *Hawaii 5-0*, which started in 1968, was one of their favorites. Tom always liked the hula girls dancing at the introduction to the show, but being only eight years old, Alice didn't understand the attraction. Alice and Tom frequently played card games together to pass the time when her older brothers and sisters weren't around.

As much as Alice didn't like being treated like a baby by her family, she could tell that her dad was sometimes extra patient with her. She liked to fish, but she hated to put the squirmy, squishy worms on the hook. So after several failed attempts resulted in mangled night crawlers, Tom always baited the hook for her. He knew she wouldn't sit still very long anyway, preferring to play on the shore while Tom watched her line. When they were at home, Tom would go all the way upstairs to kill a spider for Alice when she called him to save her. He never got mad or frustrated with her or told her she was ridiculous. He'd just squash the spider with a tissue, throw it in the garbage, and go back downstairs with a smile.

Tom brought a second baby raccoon home in the late 1960s and the family named this one Ricky. Tom showed his younger children how to bottle-feed their new pet and they all had a lot of fun taking care of him. Tom switched Ricky over to dog food when he was big enough to eat on his own, and moved his bed into the barn. Ricky was a much more entertaining raccoon than the first one they'd had ten years before, and he stayed around a little longer. Ricky loved to climb in the fruit trees in the yard, helping himself to all the fresh fruit he wanted. He often could be found in one of the apple trees. Whether intentional or not, Ricky frequently knocked apples onto the children passing below on their way to a friend's house or to the school bus stop.

Ricky was very attached to Pat and loved to ride around the yard on her shoulder. Tom had Pat put Ricky in the barn at night when it was time for bed, but Ricky never stayed there long. Pat learned that she had to shut her bedroom light off before she put him in the barn or he would be hanging on her first-floor window screen by the time she got back to her room. When Ricky was eight or nine months old, Tom started leaving the barn door open at night and Ricky began to explore the area by the creek. Ricky went back and forth between Indian Creek and the house for about a month, enticed back each morning by the steady supply of dog food, but one day he just didn't come back. Tom and the kids all missed Ricky after he left.

Tom and Anna celebrated their twenty-fifth wedding anniversary on September 13, 1967. What an event-filled marriage it had been so far.

The Patient Teacher

One of Bill's earliest memories is of Tom coming home from a duck-hunting trip. Tom had returned home later than usual that day, after the sun had set and the miserable rainy day had turned into a dark and rainy night. By the time Tom opened the door and stepped onto the front porch, he was soaked to the bone. Beads of water ran down his face and the warmth of the house fogged his glasses. Nevertheless, there was a big smile on his face when he saw his little boy looking up at him, as he stood there holding two mallard drakes he had shot that day. It was then that Bill knew he wanted to hunt with his dad.

Bill started out riding along with Tom and sometimes Alvin, as they would drive around checking all their favorite ponds for mallards. After pheasant season started, Bill would scan the ditches for pheasants as they drove through the countryside, and he got very good at spotting them scurrying through the tall grass in the ditch. After Bill had proven his value to his dad and Alvin, he was invited along all the time. If he spotted a rooster, Tom or Alvin would stop the car and try to flush the pheasant up in the air. More often than not, they would succeed in shooting the rooster and Bill would end up playing bird dog, too. Sometimes the pheasants weren't dead and Bill would end up chasing them. As Bill explained, "It is hard to catch a pheasant on the run. It isn't so much that they could out run me, but that they could turn on a dime. I was usually pretty worn out by the time I made it back to the car with the rooster."

Bill became a fanatic about hunting, just like his dad. He would even watch the sides of the roads for pheasant and the ponds for ducks and geese as he rode the school bus home. On the sunny afternoon of October 2, 1968, when Bill was on the school bus coming home from Audubon, he spotted a flock of Canada geese on a pond. At that time, Canada geese weren't very abundant in the area, thus they were highly prized. Bill told his dad about the flock when he got home and Tom immediately called Alvin. The three rode out to the pond to see if the geese were still there. Alvin knew the farmer who owned the pond and they got permission to try their luck. Tom and Alvin got as close to the flock as they could, but the geese saw them and took off flying. The geese were just barely within range of their shotguns, so Tom and Alvin each took a few shots. Bill watched a couple of geese fall and then he heard his dad calling for him to come to the pond. Two of the geese had fallen into the water just a few yards from shore and they needed Bill to play bird dog again. The water wasn't deep, but the two men weren't about to step into that mud to retrieve the geese when Bill was around. Bill took off his shoes, rolled up his pant legs, and happily waded in to retrieve the birds.

Photo: Tom and Bill at 5 p.m. October 2, 1968.

Eventually, Tom decided it was time to teach Bill to shoot. Before Bill was allowed to touch a shotgun, he first had to do some homework. Tom made Bill memorize the ten rules of gun safety. Then he had to learn about shotguns, what the shotgun shell was like, what made the shell work, what came out of the barrel when the gun was fired, and the differences in choke patterns. Tom also made flash cards for Bill with the profiles of ducks that he had to learn to identify. Sometimes they would sit in Tom's duck blind and watch the ducks until Bill became proficient at identifying them. While they watched the ducks, Tom would make sure that Bill was also listening to the sound of their wings, listening for the distinct difference between the soft whistle of mallard wings and the roar of a flock of teal that had their wings set for landing. Bill was excited to be learning all these things from his dad, but most of all, he just liked being around his dad. Bill was always impressed by how tuned-in to his surroundings Tom was and how he seemed to know all kinds of interesting things.

When Tom felt that Bill was ready to learn how to handle a gun, he drew the profile of a flying duck in the center of a paper bulls-eye a yard in diameter. He hung it up in the field behind the house. Bill saw it immediately when he came home from school. Tom brought out the single-shot, 20-gauge, modified-choke shotgun that Bill was going to be allowed to use. He demonstrated how to stand to shoot, and had Bill hold the unloaded shotgun and practice bringing it up to his shoulder to aim. Tom then instructed Bill how to look down the barrel and line up the sight on the target. By this time, Bill knew that with a modified-choke shotgun, 90 percent of the pellets should hit within a one-yard diameter circle at a distance of thirty yards, so they paced off thirty yards from the target. Tom then instructed Bill how to load the shotgun. Bill lined up the sight at the target and took his first shot, surprised at the gun's kick. Tom then showed Bill how to unload the used shell and they walked to the target to look at the result. Bill was disappointed that his first shot was low rather than dead center, but Tom pointed out how many pellets had hit the profile of the duck on the target. Bill's shot would have brought the duck down. There was a lot more to learn about hitting a moving target, but Bill was excited that he was now on his way to hunting with his dad.

Tom made sure Bill learned how important it was to obey hunting laws and have good hunting etiquette. Tom also passed on his love of wild animals and the great outdoors. The two of them were perfectly happy just watching the wildlife together whenever they could. Bill thought his dad was the best shot he would ever meet, but Tom always thought that Alvin was a better marksman then he. Bill watched both men make beautiful, difficult shots. When Bill got older, there were moments when he, too, displayed exceptional shooting skills, and both Tom and Alvin would brag about him to their friends. But Bill never thought he was worthy of being boasted about when compared to his dad.

Going on Vet Calls with Tom

As Terry grew older and became more serious about her education and work, she gradually quit going on calls to the farms with Tom. Neither Joan nor Marg ever seemed to have much interest, and they only went once in a while. It wasn't very appealing to hang out in the smelly barns with the livestock. Pat and Bill, however, were both very happy to spend this time with their dad, and one of them frequently rode shotgun as Tom pulled out of the driveway.

Pat loved to go on vet calls. It didn't really matter what animal needed help, as long as she was with her dad. She also loved to go for drives through the countryside to spot animals and birds, or go fishing. Tom always seemed to know everything about the animals and birds they'd see, and where every road led. Rarely did he consult a map. Tom had become a master at driving on the gravel roads surrounding Kimballton, knowing just the right speed to be going when he crested each hill to make his children laugh hysterically as he drove down the other side. They called the rollercoaster feeling "tickle hills." Tom especially liked to do this when Pat was along. Cruising along the gravel roads, he would often turn to her with a grin and ask if she wanted to go fast. She would smile and laughingly say yes because she knew exactly what he meant to do.

Bill started riding with Tom on veterinary calls when he was very young. He remembers that much his dad's business consisted of delivering difficult births for cattle, pigs, and sheep. Tom taught Bill how to work the jack when delivering calves so that he could concentrate on birthing the animal. Bill saw his dad do some pretty miraculous things. It never ceased to amaze Bill how Tom would strip down to his T-shirt, even in sub-zero temperatures, to wash up before putting his hands and arms inside a cow to turn her calf into the correct position for birth.

Two deliveries stand out in Bill's memory. The first one was a cow that had been showing the front feet of her calf for far too long before the farmer called Tom for help. Both the farmer and Tom were sure the calf would be dead. After Bill helped Tom pull the calf, Tom didn't give up. He tied the calf's back legs to a bar that they hung up in the barn. While the calf was hanging upside down, Tom reached into its mouth to clean out all the fluids. He then gave the calf a good thump on the chest and rubbed its chest and legs vigorously, trying to get the heartbeat and circulation going. Soon, the calf started moving its head and coming around. Bill helped his dad gently take the calf down. They laid it next to its mother. The calf survived.

The other delivery was for a wild cow. The farmer had been unable to catch her until she started getting sick from the dead calf inside her. The cow had mated with a large-breed bull and the calf was too large for her to deliver naturally. Bill worked the jack while Tom worked on getting the dead calf out of the cow. After the delivery, Tom reached back into the cow to remove the decomposing placenta. He felt something funny and pulled out his hand. He had cupped his hand and it was full of blood. The calf had torn the cow's uterus, cutting a large vein. The farmer thought he was going to lose the cow, too, but Tom didn't want to give up on her just yet. Tom reached into his surgical kit and pulled out a curved needle and thread. Tom was right-handed, but for some reason he took the needle in his left hand, reached inside the cow and sewed up the tear with only his left hand. The cow survived. Bill was proud of these feats and impressed with his dad.

Other Stories about Tom's Practice

While Tom's practice included working with farmers and large animals, he also had many clients in Kimballton who came to him with family pet concerns—often much more emotional issues. Tom handled with patience, caring, and understanding the trauma of having a pet fall ill. Tom made sure he answered all questions and concerns and let family grieve, too, when he needed to put a favorite pet to sleep.

Unique situations came up from time to time. Once, a bat got inside a home and bit the occupant. After catching the bat, Tom sealed it in a mason jar and put it in his kitchen freezer so he could prepare it for shipping to the state lab where it would be tested for rabies. The results would determine if the resident should be given the series of rabies shots. Imagine young Alice's shock, horror, and disgust when she opened the freezer the next morning to get a can of orange juice concentrate only to see the grotesque, frozen face of a scrunched up bat staring back at her. Nothing totally shocked the Flynn kids, however, so following her initial reaction, Alice shut the freezer door and went on with making her orange juice.

1969

After a few changes in her college plans, Joyce met Gary French in January 1969 while working as a waitress at a truck stop in central Iowa. Gary had enlisted in the Army in 1965 and had just returned from Vietnam a few months earlier. It was love at first sight for Gary and it wasn't long before the two were engaged. The entire family loved Gary right away and it was great to see Joyce so happy.

Over the years, Tom had become interested in astronomy. Sometimes on clear summer nights, he'd set up his telescope to look at the moon, stars, and constellations with his children. When he couldn't sleep at night, he would often sit on the corner of his bed, smoking a cigarette, and gazing through the window at the northern sky. One evening in the summer of 1969, Tom woke up Alice in the middle of the night to show her the beautiful Northern Lights display. He explained what the Aurora Borealis was (a name she remembered from *Frosty the Snowman*) and commented on how rare it was to see such a display as far south as southern Iowa. They sat and watched together until Alice couldn't stay awake any longer. She gave her dad a kiss goodnight and went back to bed while he continued to watch.

Tom was fascinated with the success of the NASA space program and he made sure his family watched the historic Apollo missions on TV as they unfolded. After the Apollo 11 crew landed on the moon on July 20, 1969, followed by Neil Armstrong and Aldrin's first walk on the moon on July 21, NASA decided it needed a motorized vehicle to use on the moon during the Apollo 15 mission. NASA awarded Boeing the contract to design and build the Lunar Roving Vehicle (the "LRV," also nicknamed the Moon Buggy). The design and development of the LRV took place at Boeing's Kent, Washington, facility and Anna's brother, Ole, was assigned to the team of engineers that would develop the guidance system for the vehicle.

On December 1, 1969, the U.S. started a lottery draft to bolster the military in Vietnam. Volunteers were not filling vacancies in the armed forces. John was still in college at the time, so he qualified for the student deferment.

Christmas

As the 1960s came to an end, Tom and Anna were happy to see all their children growing up happy and healthy. There were sibling rivalries over the years, but in general, they all enjoyed spending time together. Both John and Terry had been able to spend summers at home in between their years at college, so all the younger siblings missed them when they left each fall. Their return in December, as well as Joyce's arrival with her fiancé, Gary, added to the excitement of the holidays and made Christmas even more special. Christmas was no longer just about celebrating the birth of Christ; it was about celebrating the family being together.

Photo: Tom and Anna, Christmas mid-1960s

Tom always enjoyed watching Bing Crosby's *White Christmas* during the holidays and he loved to sing along. Listening to Bing still reminded Tom and Anna of how they met at the USO show in 1942. As Tom sometimes liked to do, he would take Anna by the hand, pull her off the couch, and dance for a few moments in the middle of the room while the family watched; that is until Anna got embarrassed and made him stop.

The highlight of the evening was always singing their favorite Christmas songs. With all the mature voices in the family, it was fun to sing in harmony. After the gifts were opened and the younger children went to bed, Joyce, Gary, John, and Terry would often stay up and play cards with their dad at the kitchen table.

CHAPTER 10

1970-1980

1970

City Council business would keep Tom busy for the next two years now that the federal government was requiring the city of Kimballton to install a sewer system. The Environmental Protection Agency (EPA) had inspected the creamery south of town and discovered that the creamery was discharging its manufacturing waste directly into Indian Creek. Council members spent many hours coordinating every facet of the sewer installation project; working with engineers and planners on the design and scope of the work, developing cost estimates and budgets and determining the best method of financing. They held town hall meetings, and then selected a contractor to complete the project.

The town ultimately received a grant from the EPA for some of the cost and the city of Kimballton issued a municipal bond to cover the rest. Once the sewer system was complete, each homeowner would be required to pay to hook up to it. The plan was for installation to begin the following spring.

Joyce and Gary were married in January and the newlyweds soon decided to move from Ames to Iowa City so Joyce could complete her teaching degree at the University of Iowa. At least Tom and Anna had one child they didn't need to worry about anymore.

In April, Tom made his first trip back to New York in twenty-five years when his brother, Richard, passed away. Tom took the train from Atlantic, Iowa, to New York. Despite the sad occasion, the family enjoyed spending time with Tom and they were very glad he was able to be with them.

Photo: Chuck, Tom, Grandma Flynn, Eddie, and Joe Flynn, April 1970

Another significant event in 1970 was the settlement of a long-standing dispute regarding the school boundary between Audubon and Elk Horn school districts. There had been many heated discussions and legal proceedings on the subject following the closure of the Kimballton School in 1968, and each family had made its own decision about which school their children would attend. Unfortunately, Tom and Anna's family would be heavily affected by the boundary decision. They had sent their children to Audubon, but the ruling officially placed them in the Elk Horn-Kimballton School District.

Marg, Pat, Bill, and Alice started school in Elk Horn in the fall. As a sophomore, Margaret immediately got very involved in school, going out for fall softball and being elected as a student council representative for her class. Marg had worked hard playing softball in Jacksonville and with John's extra coaching, had become a pretty good catcher. Tom was proud of how good she was, but his lack of attendance at her games gave her the impression he really didn't care.

Joan had a lot of friends at Audubon and had been involved in a number of activities during high school, including several musicals. She was reluctant to change schools until she absolutely had to. She started her senior year at Audubon but then switched to Elk Horn after the first quarter. Fortunately for her, she knew most of the girls at Elk Horn already because she had detasseled with them every summer. But it was still awkward changing schools in the middle of her last year of high school. In the spring, Joan surprised everyone by getting engaged to her boyfriend from Audubon. They planned a June wedding after graduation.

Softball ended and Marg went straight into basketball season. As a sophomore, Marg played on the junior varsity team but was able to suit up for varsity games, as well. Tom listened to as many varsity games as he could on the local radio stations, hoping to hear that Marg got some playing time. It was tough being only five foot four inches tall, but Marg was quick and played hard. It was obvious that all that time she'd spent playing against her big brother John had been good practice.

1971

In March 1971, the Elk Horn-Kimballton Lady Danes made it to the Sweet 16 in the Iowa Girls High School State Basketball Tournament led by seniors Rita Paulsen and Pat Wolken. Marg was very excited that she was one of the few younger players who were able to go with the team for the week in Des Moines. Many residents of Elk Horn and Kimballton drove to Des Moines to support the team for their games, but Tom felt that he and a skeleton crew should stay behind in case there was a fire or other emergency.

Christie

It was late winter when Tom received a call from a farmer who lived four miles north of Kimballton asking for help with a coyote problem. The farmer had seen a very skinny and sick-looking female coyote on his farm and was concerned that the coyote might attack his livestock. This type of call was not unusual, and Tom and Alvin set out the following Sunday morning to see if they could track the coyote down. They hadn't been walking the fields very long when they heard some coyote pups crying not far away.

Tom and Alvin soon found the den with four coyote pups inside. It appeared that the mother hadn't been back to the den for quite a while and had abandoned the pups, which looked very weak. Tom knew they couldn't be much more than a week old because their eyes had not yet opened. They were so small that all four fit into the palms of Tom's two hands. The hunt was over for the rest of the day. Without hesitation, Tom got back into his car and took them home. It was still very early in the morning, so Tom woke up Pat first to show her the tiny pups, since she was the only one who still slept in the downstairs bedroom. He then scooped them up and took them upstairs to show everyone else. The house was now alive with excitement.

Tom and the kids tried to warm the pups and get them to drink some milk from an eyedropper. Tom put soft rags in a small box for the pups to sleep in, and used a heat lamp to warm them. He then placed the box on the floor next to his chair at the kitchen table so he could keep an eye on them all day. Much to their sadness, the pups had been left alone by their mom for too long. Two died within a day or two. A third one was very sick and Pat asked her dad to put it to sleep so it wouldn't continue to suffer. The fourth pup survived, and Pat named her Christie. Tom kept Christie in the house under the heat lamp to keep her warm and brought in a lactating mother cat to nurse her. Amazingly, the cat let Christie nurse for a few weeks until her teeth got too sharp. At that point, Tom and the kids took turns bottle-feeding Christie and holding her. Tom let Christie stay in the house for several months, taking her out frequently to relieve herself, until her wild side started to assert itself.

Tom made sure to get permission to keep Christie from the state game warden. He then built a large pen attached to the barn and a double-insulated doghouse. Christie's kennel was right next to Tom's hunting dogs in the barn but they seemed to co-exist without any problems.

Photo: Christie; Pat and Christie, December 1973

The family loved having Christie around. Even after she was full grown, she would let Tom and the children pet her while they were cleaning her pen or when they reached through the fence. One time, however, Tom made the mistake of squirting her with the hose and Christie wouldn't let him touch her after that.

The kids all helped keep Christie's fur combed and clean, especially in the spring when she was shedding. Her back legs seemed to be a tender area on her body and she would let them know when to stop combing her with a gentle bite on the hand. Staying calm, talking softly, and petting and scratching her for a few minutes always seemed to calm her down. Then they could resume combing her fur.

Anna Returns to Work

With such a large family, making ends meet had always been a challenge for Tom and Anna. During the late 1960s, Tom's veterinary practice was on the decline. Fewer and fewer farmers were raising livestock while many more were taking care of routine veterinary tasks themselves, such as vaccinations and helping livestock through the birthing process. In addition, Tom generally chose not to do surgery on small animals and would refer clients to one of the other veterinarians in Elk Horn when the need arose. Tom looked into other job opportunities in the area, like inspecting meat at the meatpacking plants, but he wasn't interested in joining a union or working for anyone else.

So, in May 1971, Anna took matters into her own hands and decided that it was time she went back to work. The Salem Nursing Home in Elk Horn was looking for a registered nurse and the timing seemed perfect. Anna didn't discuss it with Tom, but he didn't argue with her once she had made the decision. Anna felt that Pat, Bill, and Alice were old enough that Tom could manage taking care of them when she was at work. So she reactivated her RN license and started working part-time.

Photo: Tom and Anna, mid-1970s

Most days, Anna worked the swing shift, so Tom needed to be home when school got out. Tom didn't seem to mind this role reversal and did his best to care for the children. If Marg had a ball game in the evening, Tom would prepare an early supper and make sure he got her to school on time to play or catch the team bus to the game. Then he'd pick her afterwards. If she needed her uniform washed for another game the next night, Tom would have it ready for her to take to school in the morning.

For a number of years, Tom and Anna only had one car, so Tom did a lot driving, taking the women in his life where they needed to go. If Tom wasn't waiting to pick up Marg from her game, he was usually waiting to pick up Anna from work at 11 p.m. The *Tonight Show* started at 10:30 p.m. and Johnny Carson's monologue was his favorite part of the show. Luckily, it lasted just long enough that he could still make it to Elk Horn to pick Anna up on time. If Anna had to work the morning shift, Tom made sure the car was warmed up and ready to go by the time she was ready to leave, just as he had always done for his daughter's early morning basketball practices.

Spring and Summer

May of 1971 was a busy month for graduations. Joan graduated from Elk Horn-Kimballton High School, Joyce graduated with a B.A. and her teaching certificate from the University of Iowa, and John finished Iowa State University with a B.S. in political science and minors in history and sociology. John also got his teaching certification in case he decided to pursue that route later on, but he had been accepted to law school at the University of Iowa in the fall.

Tom and Anna were excited to go to John's graduation at Iowa State, and since Joyce had chosen not to go through the big graduation ceremony at the University of Iowa, she and Gary met her parents in Ames to celebrate together instead. After the ceremony, John returned to Kimballton for the summer to work for the contractor that was installing the new sewer system. After Joan was married in June, she moved to Audubon and got a job as a dental assistant.

As summer began, Grandma had concluded that she was no longer able take care of their home or Papa, who was now 91. Tom and Anna helped them sell the house and move into a room at the Salem Retirement Home, just across the street from Anna's workplace. It was wonderful that Anna was able to stop in and see them frequently, but Papa was confused by the change and quite unhappy.

In the fall, Pat and Bill started playing junior high basketball and Tom started all over with running his children to early morning basketball practices and games.

The Moon Buggy

On July 26, 1971, Apollo 15 left the Kennedy Space Center en route to the moon with the new Lunar Rover Vehicle inside. After four days, it landed and the astronauts prepared the Moon Buggy for its inaugural mission. Tom told Anna and the kids to come in to watch the news with him. Tom was very excited. Pointing to the moon buggy on the TV screen, he told the children, "Your Uncle Ole helped build that." Tom was glued to the news coverage of the LRV missions over the next several days before the astronauts headed back to Earth on August 2. It was clear that Tom was very proud of his brother-in-law, as it was amazing to think that something that Ole had helped create was sitting on the moon. They all took turns looking at the moon and stars through Tom's telescope over the next few nights and it crossed Tom's mind that while he was content to look up at the moon, Ole was helping build equipment for NASA to explore it. Now *that* was impressive.

Apollo 15 was the fourth mission to land men on the moon. Thanks to the LRV, it was the first flight during which astronauts could explore the geology of the moon beyond the landing site. The LRV added so much value to the space program that it also would be used during the Apollo 16 and Apollo 17 missions, covering just over a hundred kilometers on its final excursion on the moon.

1972

On March 11, 1972, Papa passed away in his sleep. Grandma had him buried next to their daughter, Helga, in the Kimballton Cemetery.

Terry graduated from Grinnell College in May 1972 with a B.A. in economics, and she was accepted to University of Chicago's M.B.A. program in the fall. She returned home and worked at the bank in Kimballton one last summer.

After Joyce completed her student teaching, Gary re-enlisted in the Army. Unfortunately, he had waited long enough after returning from Vietnam that he was required to go through Basic Training again. When Basic Training was complete, Gary was stationed at Ft. Bragg, so he and Joyce packed up and moved to North Carolina in January 1973. While everyone was very excited for them, the parting was bittersweet as Joyce was two months pregnant with Tom and Anna's first grandchild.

In the fall, John and Terry went back to college once again and the Flynn household was down to just four children. Marg started her senior year and as usual, got involved in a number of school activities in addition to her sports. Soon after school started, she was honored with a nomination for Homecoming Queen. Tom knew how disappointed Anna was that she had to work the night of the crowning ceremony, so Tom had Marg get ready early and then took her, dressed in her Homecoming formal, up to the nursing home for Anna to see. He then took Marg to the retirement home to show off his daughter to Grandma. Tom did his best to make Anna feel like she wasn't missing out and he knew how much stopping to visit Grandma would brighten both her day and Marg's. He then took Marg up to the high school and watched the ceremony from the doorway to the gym. Pat, Bill, and Alice sat in the bleachers not far away.

1973

Marg graduated from Elk Horn-Kimballton High School with honors in May 1973 and made plans to attend Grand View College in Des Moines. She had already accepted a summer job in West Des Moines as a live-in nanny, and it wasn't long before Tom was driving her to her new job.

That summer, for the first time neither Terry nor John lived at home because both had gotten summer internships through school. Terry would be working for Xerox in Rochester, New York; and John, at the Carroll County, Iowa Attorney's office.

On July 29, 1973, Joyce gave birth to Melissa Jean, Tom and Anna's first granddaughter. It was hard with Joyce and Gary living in far-away North Carolina, but they had made plans to come home on leave in January. Joyce made sure she sent home plenty of pictures of the adorable little girl for their families to see.

With only three children at home, the house was much quieter and it was apparent to the older four children that their dad was much more relaxed and less strict than he had been with them. Pat and Bill started high school in August and Alice was in eighth grade. Bill went out for football and track. He was too busy hunting with his dad in the winter to care about basketball or wrestling. Pat followed in Marg's footsteps and went out for softball, basketball, and track and sang in the school choir.

Tom planted a rose garden that Anna could see from her kitchen windows. He carefully nurtured it every year, replacing any plants that died off during the winter. Anna loved having fresh-cut flowers all summer long, and now she had beautiful roses to add to her bouquets. All of Tom's daughters thought it was sweet of their dad to do that for their mom.

Photo: Tom and Anna by the roses, July 4, 1976

Alice, now in junior high, was enjoying her growing relationship with her dad. One day she decided to ask him a question that she had been pondering. Patiently, she waited until he was seated at the kitchen table working on the daily crossword puzzle. She sat down in the chair next to him, still not sure if she really wanted to know the answer. Out of her mouth her question came, "Dad, since I was the youngest of eight kids, was I a mistake?" Without missing a beat, he looked at her and with a smirk on his face, and replied, "You all were," and then went back to his crossword puzzle. Alice didn't see the humor in this and taking him seriously, she continued to probe. "How can that be? You're a vet and Mom's a nurse? Don't you know what causes babies?" she asked, even though she wasn't quite sure she knew the answer to that question either. Tom didn't answer. He just looked at her, chuckled, and went back to work on his crossword puzzle. Alice walked away confused.

Tom and Bill continued to spend a great deal of time together, and in addition to weekend hunting trips, Tom frequently took Bill bird hunting before school, making it home just in time for Bill to change his clothes and run to the bus stop. Bill ultimately chose not to play football with his friends so he could hunt with his dad more often in the fall.

1974

The Kimballton Hotel

At 1 a.m. on Tuesday, January 15, 1974, the Flynn family awoke to the ringing of the fire phone. Its sound was distinctive: one continuous ring until the receiver was lifted. It didn't take but a few seconds for Tom to hop out of bed to answer the call. Since it was the middle of winter, all the leaves were gone from the trees and as he ran to the phone, Tom could see the blaze from his living room window. The three-story Kimballton Hotel, just five blocks away, was ablaze. Flames were already shooting out of the first-floor windows. He immediately got dressed, grabbed his firemen's hat, coat, and boots, and was out the door. Once on the scene, the firefighters checked to see if all the residents were accounted for, and quickly realized that an elderly, male resident was still inside his second-floor apartment.

Tom and Leland Kaltoft headed in the front door of the burning building to save the man. The fire was already burning out of control in the rear of the first floor. As the photo taken the next day of the smoldering structure shows, the stairway was near the front entrance to the building. Tom and Leland climbed the stairs and crawled down the hallway to avoid the thick smoke as much as possible until they reached Peter Sorensen's apartment on the second floor. The floor was very hot beneath them with the main fire directly below, but the apartment was small and they found him right away. Mr. Sorensen was in shock and unresponsive, but together they laid him on the floor. Crawling once again, they pulled him out of the room and down the hall. When they reached the stairs, Tom, now fifty-four years old, picked Mr. Sorensen up, lifting him into a straddling position over his shoulders. With Leland leading the way, Tom carried him down the stairs and out of the building. Mr. Sorensen was treated for shock and smoke inhalation at the hospital but made a full recovery.

By 1:45 a.m., the Audubon and Elk Horn fire departments had been called in to help control the stubborn blaze and keep it from spreading to nearby buildings. By that point, there was no saving the twenty-five room structure. By morning, only the walls remained standing. The hotel where Tom and Anna had spent their first Christmas together no longer existed.

Photo: The Kimballton Hotel when first built in 1900.

Photo: The Kimballton Hotel the morning after the fire.

Anna had no idea that Tom had put himself in such danger as she, Pat, Bill, and Alice watched the fire from the living room window. Since they were on the north hill overlooking the town, they had a pretty good view.

As usual, Tom didn't talk about what he had done, not even to his family. John, Joan, and Marg all read about their dad's heroic act the next day in the *Des Moines Register*.

The hotel fire convinced Tom that his fire department was under-equipped to handle such situations. Six days later, Tom purchased two thirty-minute Air Paks for the department, something he and Leland could have used when they went into the hotel to rescue Mr. Sorensen. Tom also got the Kimballton Town Council to approve funding to purchase a U.S. Forest Service surplus truck. They remodeled the truck in Kimballton to add a 1,000-gallon tank and a portable, high-pressure fire pump to serve as an off-the-road fire truck capable of getting to and extinguishing fires in hard-to-reach areas. The truck was finished and ready for service by Christmas that same year.

The Family

John graduated from law school at the University of Iowa in May 1974. He had met a young woman while in law school and the two planned to be married in August in Kalamazoo, Michigan. He also had accepted a position at a law firm in Davenport, Iowa.

Terry graduated from the University of Chicago in June with an M.B.A. and she, too, was engaged with plans to be married at the end of the month in New Jersey, the home of her fiancé, Chuck. Anna, Joyce, Joan, and Marg all went to the wedding, determined not to miss a chance to see the Flynn family in New York. But Tom decided it was best if he stayed at home with Pat, Bill, and Alice. Both Terry and Chuck had been hired by Procter & Gamble to work in their Green Bay, Wisconsin, plants and they moved there shortly after the honeymoon.

Marg got a summer job on a maintenance crew for the college, cleaning dorms, working in the kitchen, doing grounds maintenance and various building-maintenance projects.

In August, Tom and Anna drove the family to John's wedding in Kalamazoo. It was the first time that Tom had taken his family anywhere out of the state of Iowa, so to Pat, Bill, and Alice, it seemed more like a vacation.

Joan moved to Iowa City in the fall with her husband so he could go back to college. Joan got a job as a dental assistant at the University of Iowa's College of Dentistry to help support them.

Just out of eighth grade, Alice planned to play high school sports like her sisters, Marg and Pat, starting with summer softball. She and Pat played together on the junior varsity team in the summer and fall, as there weren't enough girls to have more than two teams. Once basketball season started, Tom and Anna realized that Pat wasn't getting as much playing time as they had hoped she would and they thought it would be more productive for Pat to get a part-time job at the nursing home where Anna worked. Though Pat was disappointed her parents didn't support her desire to keep playing sports with her friends, the decision gave her more time to spend with her dad, which she loved. Tom would tell her stories about growing up in New York and sometimes he would talk about being in the war. Many times, they just sat out on the front steps with the cats and dog. Pat also loved to go the cafe and to Arnold's Tavern just to hang out with her dad and his friends.

Photo: Anna and Tom, Christmas 1974.

Photo: Terry and granddaughter Missy with Tom, Christmas 1974.

Joyce and Gary came home again for Christmas in 1974 and everyone had fun playing with their little girl. It was easy to see that Missy would always hold a very special place in Tom and Anna's hearts as their first grandchild—and the only granddaughter they would have for the next fourteen years. Tom made sure Missy knew she was his very special little girl, and the two of them would always have a very special bond.

1975

In May 1975, Joyce had a second child and the first grandson, whom they named Timothy Brian.

That same month, Marg completed her two-year associate's degree at Grand View College. After she received her semester grades from Grand View College, she found out that she had received an academic scholarship to the University of Northern Iowa. She was thrilled. Tom made sure to remind her, "See what you can do if you put your mind to it!" In his eyes, there was never a reason for limits or boundaries on what his children could achieve. She decided to finish the four-year program with a B.A. in fashion merchandising at the University of Northern Iowa in Cedar Falls.

Joyce and Gary came home for the holidays once again and Tom enjoyed playing with his new grandson.

After losing both Goldie and Blackie in the mid-1970s, Tom and Alvin decided they weren't done hunting yet, so they bought yet another puppy, a yellow Labrador that Tom named Mike. Tom got busy training him right away and soon Tom and Alvin had another great hunting dog to accompany them on their trips.

Photo: Tom training the new puppy, Mike

1976

In the early morning hours of March 7, 1976, Tom once again awakened Alice to look at the night sky. Although it wasn't highly publicized, Comet West surprised stargazers by coming brilliantly into viewing range and remaining visible to the human eye for several days. The comet had a very bright head and a huge tail.

Because of the lack of news coverage, Tom assumed it was probably Haley's Comet. He and Alice sat together and watched the natural phenomenon in awe of its beauty. Scientists estimated that the last time Comet West had come that close to earth was over 500,000 years ago, well before the appearance of man on the planet.

Bill and Alice both competed in the Iowa High School State Track Meet in May; Bill in the high jump and Alice as part of a relay team. Neither of them placed, but it was exciting for Tom and Anna that the two had qualified to compete at the state level. Trying to set the bar high, Tom liked to remind Alice how fast her brother John was and that he had a set school record in Audubon. Tom gave his camera and several rolls of film to Alice to capture the special moments of her stay in Des Moines.

After summer softball was over for Alice in August, Tom and Anna took Pat, Bill, and Alice on their one and only official family vacation. They headed up to Green Bay to see Terry and Chuck. During the trip, they went fishing at Door County in northern Wisconsin and watched a preseason Green Bay Packers football game. Terry and Chuck had become big Packer fans.

In 1976, Tom's Yankees finally made it back to the World Series, but with four straight losses to Cincinnati, the series was soon over.

Joyce and Gary moved back to Iowa shortly after Timmy was born, after Gary's four years in the Army were complete.

While working at the University of Iowa's College of Dentistry, Joan decided to take advantage of being at the university and enrolled in night classes and summer school. She also came to the realization that her marriage to her high school sweetheart wasn't working and she filed for divorce.

1977

In January, Marg received a college internship at a women's retail clothing store, and in May, she graduated from the University of Northern Iowa with a B.A. in fashion merchandising and business. Marg had been offered a position into the retail store's management training program and would work in Waterloo, Cedar Rapids, and Omaha over the next few years. All of Marg's brothers and sisters still living in Iowa joined Tom and Anna for her graduation ceremony in Cedar Falls.

Bill and Alice competed in the state track meets again in May; Bill in the high jump and Alice on the 880 medley relay team. Again, neither one placed, but their performances had definitely improved over those of the previous year.

Alice's Turn

In May, Pat and Bill graduated from Elk Horn-Kimballton High School and in August, as had become a family tradition, they both left for college. Pat went to Grand View College in Des Moines and Bill to the University of Iowa in Iowa City. Alice finally had the house and her parents all to herself, although Pat came home from college frequently on weekends to keep her dad company when her mom was at work and Alice was busy with sports.

Alice kept busy with sports year round. Besides doing well in track, she had been the varsity softball catcher for several seasons and had been a starting guard on the varsity basketball team her junior year. All summer and fall, her coach took the softball team to compete in a number of tournaments in order to play teams outside their conference and continue to improve their skills and build their confidence. The better they got, the more the local crowds grew, both at home and away games. By the fall, the Lady Danes were considered serious competitors, continually winning against schools much larger than Elk Horn-Kimballton and several team members were getting a lot of recognition. The Lady Danes finally met their match when they were beat 4-0 in Regionals by defending state champion, Urbandale, which went on to win the fall state title again. It was a hard loss for Alice and her teammates at the end of a great season. Urbandale was a Des Moines-area school with approximately 2,000 students, compared to Elk Horn-Kimballton's student population of 110.

All year long, Alice had been asking her dad if he'd come to watch her games. Sometimes he did, watching from the outfield fence, away from the crowd. He never attended her basketball games, though. Alice made several all-tournament teams during the summer and fall and even received an MVP honor. She knew Tom was very proud of her, as he'd gotten into the habit of perusing the Omaha, Des Moines, and local papers every day so when Alice came downstairs on her way to school, Tom would already have cut out any articles about her team to show her. He seemed to take great pride in pointing out her name when it was mentioned in an article. With Anna working full time now, Tom made sure Alice had everything she needed before leaving the house each morning. In Alice's opinion, her dad had adjusted to being Mr. Mom very well and she liked it.

As basketball season started and the Lady Danes began to win game after game, Alice finally sat down with her dad and had a heart-to-heart discussion with him to find out why he never came to her basketball games. Even though he listened to the games on the radio, she was tired of coming out of the locker room alone; with no family there to share the victory. Only her sister Pat, and sometimes her brother Bill, had been there to cheer for her for the past three years. But they were now away at college. Tom finally came clean and simply said, "I can't." He explained that after his POW experience, it was very difficult for him to be packed into any room with a large number of people, including a gymnasium. But he promised that if her team made it to the Iowa Girls High School State Basketball Tournament in Des Moines in March, he would be there. Alice understood, appreciating her dad's honesty, and didn't argue the point. Her team went into Christmas break undefeated and with each victory, Alice silently chalked another game off the list toward the day when her dad would come see her play.

1978

Early one morning in January, while Pat and Bill were still home on winter break, Anna had a seizure and convulsions, and Tom had difficulty getting her to wake up. Tom didn't say anything about the incident to Alice and she went to school as usual. Tom took Anna to see Dr. Larsen in Elk Horn. Not finding anything that could help pinpoint the cause of the seizure, Dr. Larsen referred Anna to a specialist at Clarkson Hospital in Omaha, an hour away. Tom checked Anna into the hospital, and then he drove back to Kimballton and picked up Pat and Bill at the house, as well as Alice from school. They then drove back down to Omaha to see their mom and cheer her up. Anna's abdomen was sore from the convulsions but otherwise she was feeling okay. Doctors did a number of tests on Anna over the next few days, but couldn't find any definitive cause for the seizures, so they sent Anna home. Tom was very concerned about his wife.

As the month of January wore on, the Lady Danes basketball team continued its undefeated season. Dressed in their orange and black uniforms, Alice and fellow guards Jana Petersen and Annette Hansen had been nicknamed the "Orange Crush" defense by a local newspaper because the three frequently held opponents to under fifty points a game. The team's forwards were unstoppable on the offensive end of the court. Tom listened to every game on the radio and cut out every article he could find for Alice's scrapbook. In March 1978, as her team took the court to warm up in its first state tournament game against Creston at Memorial Coliseum in Des Moines, Alice saw her family sitting right up front and center, even her mom and dad. That alone made that day one of the most amazing days in Alice's life. Unfortunately, it was a tough, back and forth game and they lost by just a few points. Alice was devastated by the loss, but was elated that her family, especially her dad, had come to see her play.

Then came track season and Alice's team continued its competitive run, with Tom happily cutting out articles for Alice's scrapbook. Her 880-medley relay team once again qualified for the state track meet and for the first time, it qualified for finals. The team ran its best time of the season, placing seventh overall.

In May 1978, Alice graduated from Elk Horn-Kimballton High School. Like her older brothers and sisters, Alice had done well academically and planned to attend the University of Iowa starting in August. Tom once again endured a packed graduation ceremony in the high school gym to watch his youngest daughter graduate with honors.

Photo: Tom, Alice, and Anna at Alice's high school graduation, May 1978

Once again that summer, Pat moved home to work at the nursing home and play on a slow-pitch softball team with her friends. Tom would sometimes go watch her play, but the dusty, Kimballton ball diamond bothered his lungs.

At that time, it was typical for seniors to continue to compete in summer sports even after graduation, and Alice's softball team once again went undefeated, winning every tournament in which it competed. In the state softball championships, held at the University of Northern Iowa in Cedar Falls, the team placed seventh. Alice was very happy that her dad made it a point to attend more of her home games that summer, and that he had come to watch her last game at the state tournament. Alice left the last game with her dad to go straight to her sister Joan's wedding rehearsal in Iowa City. Alice and Pat were singing two songs in the wedding.

Joan had met a young dentist while working at the dental school and decided to remarry. The couple was moving to Warrensburg, Missouri, where he would be stationed in the Air Force, while Joan would finish college at Central Missouri State University. Joan had worked hard, completing two years of college part-time, and she was looking forward to just being a student again and getting her degree.

Photo: Tom giving Joan a kiss at her wedding, August 1978.

The morning of Joan's wedding, Anna had another seizure. This one was not as severe as the first but because they were in Iowa City, Tom didn't take Anna to see a doctor this time. Anna didn't feel well for most of the day but managed to make it through the wedding and reception.

Three weeks later, Tom took Alice to her new dorm, Burge Hall at the University of Iowa. Tom and Anna finally had the house to themselves after thirty years of raising children!

In October, Anna had a third seizure. Dr. Larsen once again had her check into Harlan Hospital for more tests. The doctors there still couldn't find anything wrong, but Dr. Larsen finally prescribed Anna some medicine that he thought would help prevent further seizures. It seemed to do the trick, and Anna would never have another seizure.

1979

On March 23, 1979, after six years in the nursing home, Grandma passed away at the age of 96. All of Anna's family came to Kimballton for the funeral, as did all of Tom and Anna's children. The family had Grandma buried next to Papa and Anna's sister, Helga.

Pat decided to transfer from Grand View College to the University of Iowa in the fall and both Pat and Alice moved home for the summer. Pat worked in the kitchen at the nursing home one last summer and Alice worked part time at the nursing home with the activity director. Bill spent the summer working with his friends in Iowa City and Chicago.

John's wife had their first baby, named Ryan John, on August 15, 1978. Tom and Anna decided to make an impromptu visit to Davenport to see their new grandson.

When Pat and Alice returned to Iowa City in the fall, Tom did something that was very uncharacteristic. He had happened to run across an advertisement in one of his trade magazines for a T-shirt that said, "I Love My Vet," There were two versions, one with a cartoon drawing of a veterinarian preparing to give a smiling cow a shot and the other was a vet with a small dog. Tom let Pat and Alice pick the one they wanted and ordered one for each of them. They were both very touched that their dad wanted them to have one of these shirts. Was Tom—the dad who would never say, "I love you" back—getting sentimental on them?

Neither Pat, Bill, or Alice typically came home more the once a month now as Iowa City was 200 miles away and none of them had a car. Tom kept himself occupied with the fire department and work on the Town Council when Anna was at work. Tom and the older firefighters were recruiting younger members who could one day fill their shoes, and Tom got a great deal of enjoyment joking around with the new recruits to the department.

Fire department meetings took place once a month, but there always seem to be plenty to do in between meetings and fire calls. Members who recall those meetings agree that they sometimes became a bit disorganized, with opinions and ideas flying at random. Tom's attempt to curb sidebar conversations usually concluded with him telling the guilty parties, "Shut up, ya bastards," which only resulted in eruptions of laughter. The evenings usually ended with a friendly game or two of three-point pitch, and lots of bullshit flying around the room. Tom usually was right in the middle of the verbal exchanges.

On November 6, 1979, Tom's youngest brother Eddie died suddenly from a brain aneurism. Tom was unable to make the trip for the funeral. That same month, Alice flew to New York to meet her Grandma Flynn for the first time at her ninetieth birthday party. Tom arranged for Alice to stay with his brother, Joe's family, and her cousins were more than happy to show her around Long Island.

Accommodating everyone at Christmas was definitely becoming a challenge with in-laws and grandchildren added to the mix. Family members would either stagger their visits over the holidays or stay with friends and neighbors when too many arrived at one time for the Flynn house to accommodate. But regardless of who slept where, Christmas was a lively and cherished holiday for all and worth the cramped quarters.

CHAPTER 11

1980-1993

1980-1981

In the early 1980s, Tom finally decided it was time to find their pet coyote, Christie, a new home. No one else was around to help take care of her and give her attention, and her pen badly needed repair. While everyone in the area knew about Doc Flynn's coyote, no one would expect to see her running loose if she were to escape from her pen. Christie was used to being around people but typically, only wild animals with rabies or other diseases were daring enough to venture close to humans. Tom worried that people would fear she was dangerous and someone would shoot her.

Tom frequently had gotten offers to buy Christie because of her beautiful fur coat, which was thick and healthy. But the men only wanted her fur, so Tom had always refused, claiming, "Pat would kill me." Instead, Tom decided to sell Christie to a breeder in Missouri that his friend, Alvin, knew. Tom knew his children, particularly Pat, wouldn't be happy about losing Christie, but at least she'd have a new home where she would be well taken care of. Tom deposited the money he got for Christie into Pat's bank account as his way of making a peace offering. At ten years old, Christie gave birth to a very healthy litter of ten pups.

In May, Joan completed her four-year college degree at Central Missouri State University with a B.S. in biology and a minor in chemistry. Tom and Anna drove to Warrensburg, Missouri, for

Joan's graduation and her husband was able to arrange a tour of the Air Force base for them during their visit. Shortly thereafter, Joan and her husband moved to Davenport, Iowa, where she planned to be the dental assistant for her husband while he got his new dental practice established.

The Distinguished Visitor

In April 1980, Bill decided college wasn't for him and enlisted in the United States Air Force. After a year of basic training and technical schools, Bill received orders to report for duty to Strategic Air Command (SAC) at the Offutt Air Force Base in Omaha, Nebraska, just seventy miles away from Kimballton. Bill thought it was ironic that he had specifically requested an assignment that would allow him to travel but the Air Force sent him back home. He was assigned to the 55th Airborne Maintenance Squadron (AMS) and he worked on the EC-135 Airborne Command Posts. These airplanes were of similar design to Air Force One used by the president. They were equipped to be command posts in the sky in the event that the ground command post was attacked. Bill took the opportunity to go home to Kimballton frequently to see his parents, and, of course, to go hunting and fishing with his dad. It was obvious to everyone how proud Tom was of his son.

According to Bill, during one of his first weekend visits home, Tom told him he had seen a news report that the public relations office at Offutt gave tours of the SAC Underground Command Post. Tom thought that was something he would like to see, especially since Bill worked there and his job was so closely tied to the SAC Underground. Bill explained that he really didn't have anything to do with the SAC Underground but when he returned to the base, he would check with the public relations office to see what the procedure was for scheduling a tour. Bill thought his dad's chances of getting a personal tour were remote, because tours were probably only given to VIPs. Tom told Bill he didn't need to bother checking because he had already written a letter to the four-star general who was the current commanding officer of the Strategic Air Command program asking for a tour of the Offutt facility; not the Offutt Air Force Base commander who happened to be a colonel.

Bill didn't know what to expect when he returned to the base. He was a lowly airman first class, barely out of basic training and technical schools, and his dad was already making waves for him. Bill reminded his dad that he had to follow a chain of command for things like this, but Tom's reply was, "I don't have to do that." Bill knew he was right. His dad was a civilian and could write to whomever he wanted to, but he still couldn't believe Tom had gone straight to the top with his request.

Bill admits to almost being scared to go back to work as he kept waiting for the backlash following his dad's letter. But after a week or so of business as usual, he figured that his dad's letter had been ignored. How wrong he was. Bill knew right away the day the word came down because all the senior NCOs were waiting for him when he walked into work that day. Bill had received orders to report to the squadron commander as soon as possible. Everyone asked what he had done. He told them that he had no idea, but he thought to himself, "This can't be good."

Bill took a deep breath and entered the 55th AMS commander's office. His squad commander got right to the point. Apparently, Tom's letter had specifically mentioned both his son and his commanding officer, and the four-star general wanted to know more about Bill and his dad. Bill wasn't in his office more than five minutes before he was dismissed, although to Bill it seemed like it took a lot longer.

Shortly thereafter, the general agreed to Tom's request and arranged for a personal VIP tour for Tom, Anna, and any family members who could join them. Bill received a personal "invitation" to join "Distinguished Visitor Dr. Thomas Flynn and family" on a guided tour of the SAC Underground Command Post and the EC-135 Airborne Command Post. Bill really didn't need a tour of the airplane since he worked on them every day, but the invitation was one that he wouldn't refuse.

In June 1981, Joyce and Marg joined Tom, Anna, and Bill at the entrance to the base. The first hour of the tour provided general background on the facility and then they moved to the Underground Command Post. The tour guide explained that if the nation were under attack, the command post would be in the air communicating with the rest of the country, while the president would be kept safe in the air on Air Force One.

Then the communications officer gave a demonstration of how quickly they could contact other command posts. On the big board in the front of the room, a map of North America showed indicators for all the sites with which they maintained direct contact. There were dozens of bases shown and the communications officer asked Tom to pick three bases to call. The communications officer called each base in turn and identified himself. He would then tell the distant station that he was performing a demonstration for a "distinguished visitor" without mentioning any names. Then the officer on the other end would say, "Welcome, Dr. Flynn." Apparently, everybody on the board had been briefed ahead of the tour in case they received a call from the SAC Underground Command Post. It was a very impressive demonstration, and Tom was extremely pleased with the courtesy extended to him that day to show respect for his military service during World War II and his ex-POW status. Everyone in the room could see that it meant a lot to Tom and his family.

Before Tom left the room, a pilot from a plane in the air also addressed the family and recognized Dr. Flynn as an honored visitor to the base.

After the underground tour, Tom, Anna, and family were taken out to the flight line and escorted onto an EC-135 aircraft, where the female pilot gave them an hour-long tour of the Airborne Command Post jet. Bill knew several of the airmen, officers, and enlisted men on the airplane so he talked to a few of them while the rest of the family was briefed.

Photo: EC-135 Airborne Command Post at Offutt Air Force Base in Omaha (photo taken by Tom).

Tom was very pleased with the special treatment he and his family received that day. He felt it was especially nice that after all these years, his service to our country was still appreciated, respected, and acknowledged by his son's generation, which in turn had committed to defend our country.

On September 20, 1981, John's second son, Scott Jerad, was born. John and his wife brought the next generation of Flynn boys home to see Tom and Anna later that fall. Like Bill, John tried to sneak in a little bird-hunting with his dad every chance he got.

Alice moved to Boise, Idaho, in October with her fiancé and the couple was married on Christmas Eve. When Alice became pregnant with her first child, Tom took one of the baby cribs from the storeroom upstairs and refinished it for her to use. He made a new mattress and hand sewed a mattress cover. Anna then sewed bumper pads and a mattress pad. When they were done, Tom boxed everything up and shipped it to her in Idaho. Alice was very touched by all the work and trouble her parents had gone to and it was the only crib that all three of her sons would ever use.

New Fire Station for the Kimballton Fire Department

Tom continued to work on projects for the fire department. In 1980, Tom coordinated the purchase of a new, fully equipped pumper truck with a 1,000-gallon tank. In 1981, they replaced the old warning siren which, after fifteen years, was worn out. The arrival of the new tanker caused the department to outgrow its current storage facility, and with the increase in valuable firefighting equipment, it was time for the community to provide an adequate facility to house it.

Photo: Kimballton Fire Station, Kimballton Centennial, June 1983

The Fire Department launched a campaign to build a new fire station. Tom's hunting partner and friend, Alvin Johnson, donated the land for the proposed 60-foot-x-60-foot building, which would contain two full 60-foot bays and one 40-foot bay with a 20-foot-x-20-foot meeting room behind it. A successful fund drive collected almost $20,000 from 405 contributors and the building was completed in October 1981. The balance of $45,000 was funded by the issuance of City General Obligation Bonds. Tom drew the original sketches for the building and calculated the projected cost estimates and funding requirements. His friend, Leland Kaltoft, finalized the project working with the construction firm from Atlantic, Iowa. On November 14, 1981, the new building was dedicated in honor of Alvin and Esther Johnson, who had donated the land, with an open house for the public. Since Tom had started keeping records after joining the fire department in 1965, the Kimballton Fire Department had responded to 202 calls, most of which involved fires. Tom was very pleased with the new building and the fire department moved into its new home the next day.

Tom loved the new station and every trip to Kimballton his children and grandchildren made for the next twelve years would include a tour of the fire station, including photos with the grandchildren on the fire trucks.

Photo: Chief Flynn in the new fire station, June 1983.

Once again, Tom had had a busy and productive year. He was happy to see his Yankees in the World Series too, even though they lost to Los Angeles, four games to two.

1982

On May 13, 1982, Alice brought her first son, Robert Royce, into the world. Tom's baby, as he still called her, now had her own baby. She planned to come home to visit over the July Fourth weekend.

In June, Marg got married in Omaha. Marg had met her fiancé, Joe, several years before while he was still in medical school and they were now moving to Galveston, Texas, for his residency. Everyone was able to make it home to the wedding except for Alice, and Tom and Anna greatly enjoyed the celebration.

Photos: (l) Tom and Marg at her wedding; (r) Anna and Tom dancing at the reception, June 1982.

None of Tom's daughters lived close to home anymore, and they all gave Tom a hard time about not talking to them on the phone, as they loved to talk to their dad. Even more frustrating to them was the fact that when they told him, "I love you Dad," his frequent response was, "Ditto." All they really wanted was for him to say, "I love you," back.

When Alice came home a few weeks later, she was pleased to have time to catch up with her dad in person. Tom shared with Alice that there had been a couple of instances since the Offutt tour when Air Force planes (he assumed they were pilots returning to the Offutt Air Base) had buzzed the American flag that he always hoisted up high on the flagpole outside. Needless to say, Tom got a big kick of out of it.

By the end of the summer, after focusing the last two years on helping start her husband's dental practice, Joan surprised everyone when she decided to continue with her college education. She got a job in Iowa City so she could start taking the classes she would need to get into a graduate school program and started commuting from Davenport to Iowa City every day.

1983

On February 14, 1983, Terry gave birth to her first son. She and Chuck named him Bradley Matthews.

In June, Marg's husband, Joe, completed his residency in Galveston and they moved to Louisville, Kentucky, for a second residency in anesthesiology.

Tom and Anna's children had grown up not really knowing any of their first cousins very well, and they all agreed it was important to them that their children get know each other, despite the fact that they now lived all over the country. So, in September, six of the eight Flynn kids and five of the six grandchildren drove or flew home to Kimballton for a reunion. Tom and Anna borrowed several camper trailers from friends and the Korsgaards offered their empty beds.

As was typical when she was home, Alice joined her dad at the kitchen table with a cup of coffee, chatting with him while he worked on the daily crossword puzzle, his coffee and a burning cigarette within reach.

Tom's children frequently told him they wished that he would quit smoking but so far, no one had been successful in convincing him to quit. Alice decided once again to take her best shot at persuading him to give up the cigarettes. Apparently irritated by the topic, Tom looked at her, took a long drag on his cigarette and then with one quick, strong blow, exhaled a big puff of cigarette smoke right in her face. He then turned his attention once again to his crossword puzzle. Waving her hands in front of her face to dissipate the smoke, Alice stood up irritated, exclaiming, "Da-a-a-a-d," and walked into the living room, realizing he had just answered yet another question without saying a word.

By now, the wallpaper in every room of the house had a yellowish tinge as a result of the one or two packs a day Tom smoked. He was also drinking fifteen to twenty cups of coffee a day, as the two habits seemed to go hand in hand. All of the children were concerned about the secondhand smoke they had been exposed to for so many years, which might ultimately cause problems for their mother as well as themselves.

In September, Tom was admitted for outpatient surgery at Omaha Medical Center VA Hospital. He had a lipoma removed from the base of his neck on the left side of the spine. Tom had been experiencing severe pain in his left shoulder and weakness in the left arm all the previous winter, and hoped the surgery would relieve this. Tom healed without any complications but any medical situations always caused Tom a great deal of nervous stress, something the doctors called "chronic anxiety reaction." As a result, Tom didn't eat much for extended periods in an effort to minimize the nausea he experienced.

In 1983, at age sixty-three, even Tom realized that forty years of smoking had taken its toll on his body. His right shoulder had never been 100 percent after his rock-climbing fall and his knees were bad. He had also lost all his original teeth, and had a full set of dentures by his early forties. Tom knew the loss of his teeth at such an early age was probably due to the malnourishment he had endured as a POW, but getting the Veteran's Administration (VA) to admit that would be a challenge. He contacted the VA to determine what veteran benefits he was eligible for, but it seemed the only response he ever got were letters of rejection.

Tom was persistent with the VA though, because he knew that having been a heavy smoker most of his adult life, his medical problems were probably just beginning. He didn't want Anna to bear the financial burden of his poor health. Tom submitted a VA Medical Benefits Application on October 21, 1983, and for the first time in almost forty years, he wrote in detail about the events that had occurred during the Battle of the Bulge, his time as a POW, and his temporary escape from the Nazis. It was hard for the VA to deny that Tom's service record was exemplary, given the extreme treatment he'd suffered as a POW. Eventually, after several thorough medical exams and evaluations, the VA doctors conceded that Tom's assessment was correct: his medical issues were a direct result of his military and POW experience. Knowing that he now would have the medical coverage he needed lifted a great burden from Tom's shoulders.

In November, Tom and Anna made their only trip back to New York together since 1945 to see Tom's family. Tom's niece Judy, Joe's daughter, was getting married and Joe had lung cancer. It was time to put his personal demons aside and go see his little brother. It was also the only plane ride he would ever take since he flew out of Germany after liberation from the Moosburg POW camp in 1945.

Before leaving for New York, Tom sent a letter to the Adjutant General's Office of the Commonwealth of Pennsylvania, requesting a copy of a book entitled, *History of the 110th Infantry Regiment World War II*, which was compiled by Col. Daniel Strickler shortly after World War II was over. As always, Tom went straight to the top of the chain of command, contacting the acting commanding officer, General Scott. By the end of December, the book had been mailed to Tom. Tom read the book cover to cover and meticulously underlined every phrase, sentence, and paragraph in red ink that referenced K Company actions, starting with the Hürtgen Forest battle in November 1944 when Tom joined the 110th, and including K Company actions in Hosingen. He wrote comments in the margins, noted corrections that should have been made, and paper-clipped pages that he felt were significant. The letter written by Col. Hurley Fuller, commanding officer of the 110th during the Battle of the Bulge, to Gen. Norman Cota requesting that the 110th be given the Distinguished Unit Citation from the War Department, was especially important to Tom. Tom did not know that with all the changes that occurred near the end of the war, General Cota had never followed up to ensure his unit received this distinction. But the simple fact that Colonel Fuller recognized what his unit had accomplished obviously meant a great deal to Tom.

It is just as noteworthy to consider the passages Tom did not highlight or comment on in the book. As usual, Tom did not focus on his own personal actions—he made no note of that fact that his name was not listed near the end of the book in the Awards and Decorations section where each individual in the 110th Infantry Regiment receiving at least a Bronze Star was listed. Tom did not make a mark anywhere in this section where his name had been omitted, nor did he share this book with his children or his wife so they might finally know clearly what he had been through during the war. When Alice asked him one time where he had been during the Battle of the Bulge, the only response he would give her was, "In the bulge." He made it clear that the war was a subject he did not want to discuss.

1984

Tom's brother, Joe, passed away on April 8, 1984.

After three years stationed at Offutt, Bill's four years in the Air Force ended and he began working for a civilian contractor for the Air Force. He would finally leave the Midwest and head oversees to work at the Air Force base in Greece. From there, he made several trips to the Middle East during Desert Storm and met a beautiful Greek-American girl who would soon become his wife. He was going to miss his time with his dad though, as he had gone home frequently when he was stationed in Omaha. Bill left his Jeep Cherokee with his parents for them to use while he was overseas.

Terry gave birth to her second son, Tyler Birk, on June 25, 1984.

In early August, Tom and Anna's children and grandchildren returned to Kimballton for what was becoming an annual gathering. Their numbers just kept growing. Again, Tom and Anna borrowed camper trailers and accepted the Korsgaards' help to accommodate the overflow of Flynn kids.

Photo: Robert wearing Tom's fireman's hat and boots at fire station; August 1984.

Tom checked himself into the VA hospital for another surgery on August 20 after his children left, to repair an aneurysm in the left femoral artery near his groin. The procedure went well and Tom was home again in five days to rest and recuperate.

Alice and her husband moved to Portland, Oregon, in January and on December 23, 1984, Alice had her second son, Joshua Daniel.

1985

Marg's husband, Joe, completed his residency in Louisville and the two moved to Gadsden, Alabama, in January where he started his new job.

That spring, Joan was accepted to graduate school at Baylor College of Medicine, and she and her husband moved to Houston.

During the summer, Joyce and Gary took a long-overdue vacation for just the two of them and flew to Hawaii for a week. Anna went to stay with Missy at Joyce's house because she had softball games she didn't want to miss. Tim went to stay with relatives in Missouri. The weather was hot that week and one day, Missy asked her grandma to take her to the nearby lake to go swimming with a friend. After dropping the girls off, Anna drove back to Joyce's house. As she walked in the door, the phone was ringing. It was Tom calling to tell her to go back and pick the girls up at the lake right now because a bad thunderstorm was moving into the area. Anna was confused. No one had called Tom to tell him what they were doing that day, but nevertheless; Anna did as he had told her. Shortly after returning to the house with the girls, the thunder and lightning started. No one ever figured out how Tom knew that Missy was in danger. However, Missy always claimed that she and her grandpa had a special connection that went beyond words.

In August, the family had another mini reunion, this time in Green Bay, and the family made another fishing trip to Door County. Bill was home on vacation from Greece and the men had a great time fishing together.

Photo: Tom and Brad in fire truck at fire station; 1987.

Photo: Tom with Ryan and Scott holding their pheasant tail feathers.

On November 8, 1985, the United States military created an MIA-POW Service Medal that was retroactive for all military personnel back to April 5, 1917. Tom was glad that the time he had spent as a POW in Nazi Germany was finally acknowledged as being above and beyond the call of duty. The medal reads: "For Honorable Service While a Prisoner of War," "United States of America." Tom proudly added it to his medal collection and showed it to all his children and grandchildren when they came home. They were all glad for their dad, and felt the recognition was long overdue.

1986

Alice and her husband transferred to Spokane, Washington, from Portland, Oregon, in March and Alice was pregnant with her third baby in four years.

In May 1986, John argued a real estate case, Hancock v. City Council of the City of Davenport, cited at 392 N.W. 2d 472 in the Iowa Supreme Court. Tom and Anna drove to Des Moines to hear John's oral arguments, and John was excited to have his parents there. Tom agreed with John's oral arguments and after the hearing was adjourned for the day, he told John he should win. John knew he had done well if he had impressed his father. Tom was correct; John won the case, establishing new law in Iowa.

In July, two more grandchildren were born. Alice gave birth to a third son, Justin David, on July 7, and Marg gave birth to her first child, a girl, on July 16, 1986. Finally another granddaughter in the family after a run of eight grandsons! Her name was Laura Elizabeth and she was absolutely adorable.

The family all swarmed the Flynn house once again in September and everyone loved holding the two new babies, especially Anna and Tom. Thank goodness for the big yard where all the grandchildren could run around and play.

Photos: (top) Tom and grandsons, except for two-month old Justin, September 1986;
(bottom) Tom and Justin, August 1988

1987-1988

Tom's mother, Josephine, died July 18, 1987. Unfortunately, Tom was unable to attend the funeral.

Alice's family moved back to Portland, Oregon, again, in time for Robert, her oldest son, to start school in the fall. Terry and Chuck both accepted promotions with Procter & Gamble and moved to Georgia in October to work at the pulp mills. They were excited to raise their sons in a warmer climate.

Bill and Natassa were married in Athens, Greece, on Oct 24, 1987. Both Anna and Bill's twin sister, Pat, flew to Greece for the wedding. Tom was thrilled with his new daughter-in-law and was very happy for his son. Bill brought Natassa home to Kimballton to meet everyone the following July and naturally another family reunion resulted. Natassa had no idea how crazy being part of a big family could be but with her outgoing, friendly personality, she fit right in and everyone loved her.

Photo: Bill, Tom, and Alvin, July 31, 1988

Photo: Ryan watching Tom work on a crossword puzzle, Nov. 1988

Photo: Tom, Anna, and all ten grandchildren, August 1988

1989

Marg had her second daughter, Katherine Ann, on September 26, 1989.

In January, Tom again went to the VA for a checkup, weighing in at only 135 pounds, which was close to what he had weighed as a POW. Tom had been slowly losing weight over the years and a recent nine-day bout with the flu had exacerbated the situation. During this visit, the doctor noted that Tom had another aneurysm, this time on the right femoral artery on the opposite side of his groin from the first one. Tom was admitted to the VA a month later for another graft to repair the artery. He stayed in the hospital for two weeks. After his March checkup, the doctors determined that Tom had a vascular disease, having found two more aneurysms. They also found an enlarged prostate.

In May, Tom spent another week in the VA to have his right popliteal artery aneurysm repaired. Tom's doctors were getting frustrated with Tom's unwillingness to stop smoking, believing it contributed to the problem. The vascular surgeon finally told Tom he wouldn't operate on his other aneurysms unless he quit. Knowing he had no choice, Tom at last gave up his cigarettes. He spent another ten days in the hospital in September, and then again in October for two more surgeries. After recovering from both, Tom started smoking again.

With Tom in and out of the hospital frequently during 1989, the Flynn kids came home more often to spend time with their dad, or to drive Anna back and forth to Omaha to see Tom as much as possible. Pat was able to make it home the most often, and her parents and siblings greatly appreciated her steadfast support.

1990

In 1990, Tom decided it was time to relinquish his seat on the City Council after twenty-four years. Tom was tired and ready to let the younger generations do the job. This last year had been physically hard on Tom, although even at age seventy, he still impressed people. Some commented that his walk was so smooth, he seemed to glide.

Joan completed her PhD classes at Baylor College of Medicine by May 1990 and moved to Washington, D.C., for post-doctoral work at the National Cancer Institute, which is part of the National Institutes of Health. She and Tom got a big kick out of having another doctor in the family. Tom was extremely proud of his daughter and impressed with her dedication to her education and career.

In April, granddaughter Missy was hospitalized with the eating disorder bulimia. Tom wanted Missy to know that he supported and loved her no matter what and wrote her the following letter. It speaks for itself.

Sat. 5-12-90

Dear Missy,

Your mom let us know awhile back that you were hospitalized for a period of treatment and counseling. Grandma sent you a letter recently, but I thought that I should write my own note to you. You know that grandma and I raised 6 girls and 2 boys. They were not easy times but we all loved each other and made the best of each day as it came. We loved each child and helped them with individual problems when we could. However, a personal problem could not be aided unless that child was willing and ready to talk about the things that were bothering her or him. They had to confide in mom or dad so we could know how to help. Sometimes, the confidence was given to young friends, but they were not able to help, and sometimes made matters worse.

Well, our kids grew up and married in the process (in due time). (You know that Pat is the only one now who has not done so).

Our family grew and then something special happened. Very special. Joyce came home with her first child, her daughter, Missy. You were special! Our first grandchild, and even today, as you know, I still love you as my very special girl, even though I now have other grandchildren and all my original family. Grandma also feels this way. It is only because we love you that I dare make a recommendation to you.

You are at a center which specializes in helping young ones with your problem, and probably other problems. They can see how you behave but they can't know why, unless you are able to talk to someone you trust and tell them the things that you think about which may lead you to behave in a manner which has ruined many young ones bodies and lives. I hope you can find at least one person you will feel comfortable with as a counselor to you, and talk-talk-talk until you feel better inside. I'm sure everything you say will be confidential, unless you give her or him permission to repeat some of it to help your mom and dad help you. You know they want to do so.

You keep remembering that I and grandma also love you very much. As I said, you are SPECIAL to us. Please find one person to talk to and help yourself get better.

When you can, we would love to see you again at our house. I and grandma have some hugs waiting for you.

All my love,
Grandpa Flynn

If you wish, show this to a counselor and ask their opinion. TALK!

Love - Grandpa

Four days later, May 16, Tom checked himself into the VA once again for an operation to remove a hernia the size of a golf ball, which was right next to the old incision for the left femoral aneurysm that had been repaired previously. Routine radiology tests completed on May 17 showed a mass with increased density in Tom's right upper lung. Radiology pictures of the area over time led doctors to conclude Tom had Chronic Obstructive Pulmonary Disease (COPD) and the beginning stages of emphysema. He also had pneumonia in his right lung. Following this diagnosis, the doctors went ahead with the hernia operation on May 18 as planned, as Tom had needed it to be repaired for several months.

The day after the surgery, Tom told the nurse, "I'm going to drive myself home tomorrow." When she told him that he was not allowed to drive, he wouldn't take no for an answer and stated, "The doctor knows. I told him and he didn't say that I can't." One can only imagine how much his irritability was increased as a result of the bad news. The hospital did not discharge Tom until May 23. Before Tom left, he was asked about having a bronchoscopy to get a better picture of what was going on in his lungs, but Tom refused. His doctors would repeatedly ask him to have this procedure done for the next three years so they could better treat him and he would refuse each time.

Photo: Tom and Anna, spring 1990

On June 11, Tom was back at the VA hospital complaining of respiratory problems and shortness of breath. Lab results from Tom hernia operation had just arrived that day as well, and Tom had tested positive for Mycobacterium, some strains of which caused tuberculosis. The hospital couldn't take a chance that Tom had the contagious strain, so doctors admitted him to respiratory isolation and started him on a tuberculosis drug in addition to antibiotics, steroids, and inhalers, even while they continued to work to identify the exact organism in Tom's lungs.

Tom was very sick and weak, and irritable and frustrated that they wouldn't bring meals into his room. The staff would set his tray of food outside the door and he would have to get up and get it himself if he wanted to eat. Pat came home from Iowa City and drove Anna to the hospital, where the two of them would stay with Tom for the entire day. It was painful to see Tom looking so frail but there was nothing they could do to help other than simply be there with him. Anna called Alice in Oregon and told her she should come home to see her father, as he wasn't doing very well. She made plans to come home as soon as possible. This was the first of three times that Anna would make such a call for Alice to come home.

On June 19, the strain was identified as one not dangerous to healthy people. Since Tom was feeling better, he was discharged and allowed to go home. Tom was still weak and had lost more weight but he badly wanted to be home with his family. Later in the summer, Tom spent another week at the VA hospital for shoulder pain and weakness in his arms. He complained that lifting his arms over his head or lifting even a small object was next to impossible. There really was no resolution for this problem other than physical therapy but the doctors wanted Tom to start making monthly trips to Omaha for checkups and tests to monitor his overall condition.

Bill and Natassa moved to Mildenhall, England, in July 1990 so Bill could work at the Royal Air Force (RAF) base after the base in Greece was closed.

Joyce's family came home for Christmas and Missy and Tom were able to have some quality time together during the holiday. Tom made good on his promise to Missy, ensuring she got lots of hugs from her Grandpa and Grandma.

Photo: Granddaughter Missy and Tom, Christmas 1990

1991

By May, Joan had completed her thesis and returned to Houston for the Baylor College of Medicine graduation ceremonies. She earned a PhD in microbiology and immunology. Dr. Michael DeBakey, the chancellor emeritus of Baylor College of Medicine and a world-renowned cardiac surgeon and innovator of numerous cardiovascular surgical procedures, handed Joan her diploma. Tom was feeling well enough for Anna to leave him home alone and she took a much needed vacation to see Joan graduate. Joan then returned to Washington, D.C., to complete her post-doctoral work.

On July 24, Bill and Natassa had their first child, a little girl they named Chelsea Anne. Bill and Natassa agreed that Chelsea's middle name should be his mother's name, but since Tom had always called Anna "Anne," that was the name the Bill wanted.

1992

In December 1991, Tom contracted a respiratory infection. Hospital reports stated that when Tom arrived for his February appointment in the radiology department, he was practically ambulatory. Shortness of breath had become a way of life for Tom, but frequent chest infections took away all the strength he had left, making it hard for him to walk or get around. Tom was put back on what was becoming his usual medications and recovered in time to finally have prostate surgery in March.

On September 1, Missy gave birth to Tom and Anna's first great-grandchild, Taylor Michael, so she was unable to attend Tom and Anna's fiftieth wedding anniversary celebration on September 13, 1992. Other than Missy and Taylor, all of their children and grandchildren were there, as well as Tom's brother, Chuck, and his wife, Eunice, from New York; and Anna's sister, Eva, and her family from Wisconsin. Tom did not want a big party but consented to an afternoon reception at the church. Anna decided she and Tom would take care of ordering a cake for the party. When she asked Tom whom they should ask to bake it for them, he surprised her. Despite his initial resistance to having a party, he had already made arrangements with their 90-year-old friend, Elna Andersen, to provide the cake.

Photo: Tom and Anna's 50th Anniversary, September 13, 1992.

Marg had her third daughter, named Rebecca Marie, on October 20.

Tom posed for his last photo as Kimballton fire chief that same month.

Photo: Tom's last photo with Kimballton Fire Department, October 1992

BACK ROW (L to R): Chief Thomas J. (Doc) Flynn D.V.M., Mark Smith, Wayne Hansen, Ken Ericksen, Don Jensen, James Mortensen, Eric Juelsgaard, Clark Steen

SECOND ROW (L to R, kneeling): Paul Christensen, Howard Juel, and John Andersen

FRONT ROW (L to R): Tramp the fire dog, Mike Mortensen, Mike Jensen, Lynn Mortensen, Verner Hansen, Earl Christensen, Bruce Poldberg

NOT PICTURED: Allan Andersen, Milo Buckley, Todd Larsen, Randy Leete, Jim McClain, Lloyd Petersen, and Mark Petersen

1993

Tom once again picked up a flu virus during a December visit to the VA and was sick for five days. As had become the standard course, the virus was accompanied by yet another respiratory infection. He skipped his January appointment at the regular clinic after this experience because he didn't want to get sick again.

Tom's Retirement from the Kimballton Fire Department

After his most recent illness, Tom decided it was time for him to retire from the Kimballton Fire Department, and a new fire chief was appointed. Tom was finding it difficult just to make it through each day, and he all too frequently took out his frustrations on Anna by being grouchy, short-tempered, and irritable. He knew that he shouldn't smoke, but at that point, he felt that smoking was all he had left. He didn't have the strength or lung capacity to do much except sit and watch TV, play cards, work on the crossword puzzle, or read.

In March 1993, the Kimballton Fire Department sponsored a steak supper in honor of "Doc's" twenty-seven years of unselfish dedication as fire chief. All the firefighters who had served in the department since Tom's tenure began forty-one years earlier in 1965 were invited. The men did their best to keep the true reason for the dinner a surprise, but Tom managed to find out that it was a retirement party just for him. As usual, Tom was reluctant to have a fuss made over him. He committed only to making a short appearance of half an hour or so. When Tom got there, however, he seemed to enjoy himself and wound up staying for nearly two hours, catching up with old friends and acquaintances.

Photo: Anna and Tom at the Fire Department retirement party, March 1993

Tom and Anna's children continued to come home to visit even more frequently that year since they all knew their dad was not doing very well. Although Tom had turned into a grumpy old man over the last several years, he finally had managed to become comfortable saying, "I love you" to his wife and children, the words he had always had such difficulty saying all these years.

On April 7, Tom was admitted to the VA hospital once again for pneumonia. At the end of the month, the Outpatient Clinic referred him to the hospital again when his shortness of breath worsened. Tom's lung capacity had continued to deteriorate, causing a marked increase in his shortness of breath compared to six months earlier. Hospital notes stated that Tom had walked only two blocks to Admitting, but once there he was too exhausted and winded to walk across the room. Since September, he had lost even more weight and now only weighed 115 pounds.

Based on Tom's symptoms, doctors initially suspected tuberculosis again and admitted him to isolation. However, after a thorough review of his records, they realized that he had been on anti-tuberculosis medications for over two years, so he was moved out of isolation. By this time, the radiologist had also begun to suspect Tom had a tumor in his lungs but again, Tom refused a bronchoscopy to determine if that was true. Tom was discharged on May 7 in deference to his strong preference to recuperate at home.

Marg came home in June to visit Tom, bringing all three of her little girls with her. It was hard to see her father so weak and thin.

In July, Tom was back in the hospital with another round of pneumonia. The COPD and emphysema were now in both lungs. Tom was still smoking a pack a day. The admitting nurses reported that Tom was very irritable, frustrated, and tired, and refused to be fully examined or to give any medical history. The notes stated, "Mr. Flynn is quite agitated and fatigued. He seems angry and perhaps a bit depressed as he stated, "I'm not any use anymore. It couldn't get any worse."

Tom was put on oxygen and antibiotics via IVs and prednisone. After about a week, Tom started to feel better and his mood improved. He made plans to go home after Anna got air-conditioning installed in their house. Tom was again discharged on July 19 and was to continue on antibiotics and steroids as well as use an inhaler. He was also to continue his monthly checkups.

Whoever Believes in Him Shall Not Perish

On November 18, 1993, Tom began to feel much worse, if that was possible, and he decided that Anna should take him to the hospital the next day. Missy called to check on him when Joyce told her Grandpa was going back to the hospital the next day. Missy had a horrible feeling that something wasn't right and she wanted to talk to him before he went to bed. She knew that her Grandpa had been especially weak lately and that he typically would only talk to his children on the phone. She called, hoping he would agree to take her call. Missy felt very lucky when he told Anna he wanted to talk to her. She told him that she was just checking up on him and that she loved him. They only spoke briefly but he ended the conversation by telling her that he loved her, too.

When Tom and Anna went to bed that night, Anna could feel that Tom's skin was cold and clammy. His legs were extremely swollen and she could hear the fluid in his chest as he labored to breath. She wondered if he would even make it through the night. Tom got up again sometime after midnight and walked into the bathroom, never to return. Anna awoke at 2:45 a.m. on November 19, 1993, to discover Tom was not in bed. Not knowing how long Tom had been up, she waited a few minutes before she got up to check on him. Anna found his lifeless body in the bathroom.

Anna called Mike Jensen, one of the young firefighters who also worked with the rescue unit, and then went back and sat with Tom until Mike arrived. Even after all Tom had been through in last five years, no amount of preparation could have readied Anna for that moment and the realization that after fifty-one years of marriage, she was alone. Mike came up to the house right away. He took care of everything and stayed with Anna until 6:30 a.m. By midmorning, the house was full of friends and food, and Anna was a little overwhelmed with it all. She called all the children, and Joyce and Gary made it to Kimballton by early afternoon. The rest of the children and most of their grandchildren planned to arrive throughout the weekend. Anna was thankful that Tom had died at home and that she had been able to take care of him.

Over 200 friends and family came to be with Anna and the family while Tom's body was at the funeral home. Her brother, Ole, and sister, Eva, came to the service, as well as several friends of the family from around the state.

Tom's funeral was on Monday, November 22 at 2 p.m. For late November, the weather wasn't terribly cold for Iowa but the sky was overcast and the gloomy darkness seemed to reflect the mood of the day. As Anna and her family drove up to the church for the funeral service, they were surprised to see so many cars surrounding the church and filling the adjacent streets. The Kimballton fire truck was parked out in front of the main entrance and was surrounded by Tom's friends and fellow firefighters. Inside, the church was packed with a standing-room-only crowd, including the rarely used balcony. The family estimated that well over 300 people came to pay their last respects that day—as many people as lived in the town.

Anna chose to break with what she felt was tradition, and even though Tom looked nice, she chose to have a closed casket for the church service and greeted their friends at the main entrance. Anna had asked six of the younger firefighters to be his pallbearers but encouraged their wives to sit with them during the service. The rest of the Kimballton firefighters were there in their dress firemen jackets, as were the AMVETS and the Elk Horn Fire Department. Anna had also requested no flowers; however, each of her children's employers had sent a beautiful bouquet.

Anna felt that Tom had a beautiful funeral service. It was very clear how much everyone loved and respected her husband, and this meant a great deal to the entire family.

Mike Jensen, with the Fire Department, gave a warm, heartfelt eulogy as he spoke about what a friendly man and leader Doc had been, citing his unselfish dedication of time and energy to the Kimballton Fire Department. Several other speakers also related how Tom had touched their lives; one individual reflecting on how Tom, either on his way to or from a fishing trip, had stopped to help a woman on the side of the road, performing CPR on her husband's lifeless body until an ambulance arrived forty-five minutes later.

Anna had requested that the Rev. Riggle not read Tom's obituary, so he instead spoke from his heart about conversations he had had with Tom. The Rev. Riggle was new to the community but as Tom's health had deteriorated, he had made it a point to try to get to know him as best he could, even though Tom never made it to church with Anna. Tom had assured the pastor that he still believed in God, but used vivid descriptions of his experiences as a POW to explain why he didn't attend church. It was clear to the pastor that Tom had never really made it out of that boxcar on Christmas Eve 1944. As the pastor repeated the story of the

Christmas Eve air raid to the congregation, Anna's brother, Ole, sat in horror, thinking that he had been one of the pilots who bombed the train yard where his brother-in-law, Tom, had been held. After all those years as friends, the two had never talked in detail about what they had been through during the war. It would not be until Alice's research of historical records for this book in 2009 that she could finally confirm that Ole's assumption had been incorrect. Ole's mission had been to bomb the airfield and train yard in Gross Ostheim, not Frankfurt, where Tom had been.

At the end of the service, pallbearers and firefighters Clark Steen, Jim McClain, Mike Jensen, Mike Mortensen, James Mortensen, and Allan Andersen escorted Tom's coffin to the hearse waiting just outside the church. The new Kimballton fire truck led the funeral procession to the cemetery on the western edge of town. On a clear day, the view from the cemetery was beautiful, overlooking the lush green Kimballton valley and the community that Tom had loved for almost fifty years. Anna had Tom buried next to her parents and sister. At the end of the brief, graveside service, the Harry Albertsen AMVET Post 51 provided full military graveside rites, ending with a twenty-one-gun salute. When the service ended, ten-year-old grandson Bradley walked over to where the AMVETS had just stood, picked up one of the discharged shells from the guns, and slipped it in his pocket as his remembrance of the day.

As the crowd started to break apart and head for their cars, Alice walked over to thank the pallbearers and fellow firefighters for what they had done for the funeral service and to let them know how much their contribution had meant to the family. She also wanted to make sure they knew how deeply Tom cared for each one of them and thank them for what they had done for her dad when he was still part of the department. She'd had few conversations with Tom over the last fifteen years in which he had not mentioned what the fire department was doing or told an anecdote about one of the firefighters. She knew these friendships had filled the void in Tom's life when she and her siblings had grown up and moved away. Clearly, these men had made him laugh and had brought him happiness, pride, and a feeling of self-worth. The Flynn family would be forever grateful.

Photo: Kimballton Fire Department escort to cemetery at Tom's funeral, November 23, 1993

CHAPTER 12

In Retrospect

At the time of Tom's death, his family did not know the full story of Tom's service and heroism during World War II, and couldn't imagine the detailed memories of battles, deaths, and imprisonment that seemed to have haunted him since returning home from the war. Even though Tom chose to share very little about those times with his family and friends, it is clear that Tom was no ordinary man and his path through life left a lasting footprint in the memories of those who knew him. Tom was a devoted husband of fifty-one years to Anna, the proud father of eight children, a veterinarian to the many farmers in the Kimballton community, a devoted firefighter, Town Council member and public servant, and a World War II veteran. He was a friend, a mentor, a leader, and a hero.

This final chapter provides details of the recognitions of Tom's contributions and legacy, many of which he never would know.

Reflection on World War II

Battle of the Bulge

The Battle of the Bulge lasted from December 16, 1944, through January 28, 1945, and has become known as the greatest battle ever fought by the United States Army. It involved more than a million men between the German and Allied forces (600,000 Germans, 500,000 Americans, and 55,000 British).

It is estimated that over 19,000 Americans soldiers died during the Battle of the Bulge and another 23,000 were captured. However, due to the significant destruction of records following the German attacks, exact numbers will never be known. Approximately 100,000 German soldiers were killed, wounded, or captured during the six-week period.

The National Archives WWII POW database (http://aad. archives.gov/aad/) on the 110th Infantry Regiment lists 1,570 men who were reported to have MIA/POW status from Dec. 20-25, 1944. Twenty-six of these men died while prisoners.

Two noteworthy comments about the importance of the 110th in the Battle of the Bulge are below:

In February 1945, Col. Hurley E. Fuller sent a letter to Maj. Gen. Norman D. Cota of 28th Infantry Division after his POW camp in Poland had been liberated by the advancing Russians, recommending his unit (the 110th) for a War Department Citation for its critical defense of the Ardennes region against the German assault from December 16-18, 1944. General Cota did not act on this recommendation but it reflects Colonel Fuller's highest regards for the men in his unit:

http://history.amedd.army.mil/booksdocs/wwii/ bulge/110thInfRegt/110thIRIntro.htm

General, I want you to know that Regimental Combat Team 110 fought a magnificent fight in trying to halt the German Advance. We went down and carried out your orders to the letter to "hold at all cost." For that reason, I feel that the following units of Regimental Combat Team 110 are deserving of a War Department Citation, and I so recommend it to you:

- *110th Infantry, Commanded by Col. Hurley E. Fuller, Inf.*
- *109th FA Bn, Commanded by Lt. Col. Robert E. Ewing, FA.*
- *Co B 103rd Engr Bn, Commanded by Captain Jarrett.*

For your information, in preparing a citation for these units, the following facts are submitted. These units were holding approximately 15 miles of front opposite the Siegfried Line in Luxemburg when the German offensive started on December 16, 1944. Although attacked by two panzer divisions, and one Infantry division these units blocked the advance of this superior hostile force for three days along its main axis of advance, thus affording time for the movement of reserves to prevent a disastrous breakthrough by the enemy.

After the first two days of fighting, all elements of the 110th Infantry and Company B, 103d Engr

Combat Battalion were completely surrounded. These units continued to fight stubbornly in place, until their ammunition was exhausted, and they were virtually annihilated before they were completely overwhelmed by superior forces of tanks and armored infantry.

In the preface of *Alamo in the Ardennes: The Untold Story of the American Soldiers Who Made the Defense of Bastogne Possible,* John C. McManus, a University of Missouri history professor, makes a similar conclusion that the defense by the 28th Infantry Division, especially the 110th and 112th regiment, were particularly critical to the successful defense of Bastogne.

The Germans' failure to occupy this strategic location (Bastogne) was the work of two distinct groups of American soldiers. History has largely focused on the group that endured the siege from the evening of December 20 through December 26. Most of the siege defenders were members of the 101st Airborne Division, and they fought with tenacity and resolve. But I would argue that the contribution of another group—those who fought east of Bastogne and in its outskirts from December 16 through December 20—were every bit as vital and noteworthy. Some of these men were from the 101st Airborne Division, but the vast majority were not. Most were members of the 28th Division, CCR of the 9th Armored or CCB of the 10th Armored. These soldiers fought a desperate delaying action. They were outnumbered and outgunned. In some cases, the odds were ten-to-one against them. They absorbed the brunt of Hitler's last-ditch gamble in the west.

They fought in what I term the Bastogne corridor, the area roughly along the 25-mile front that the 28th Infantry Division held when the battle began. This front stretched from Lutzkampen in the north all along the Luxembourg side of the Our River, through such towns as Heinerscheid, Marnach, and Hosingen, down the Bettendorf and Reisdorf. The most vital objectives were in the sectors held by the 110th and 112th Infantry Regiments.

Many more stories have been written and tributes paid to the men of the 110th Infantry Regiment for their role in the Battle of the Bulge, but excerpts from several that specifically acknowledge the role of K Company are highlighted below.

"Even the commander of the XLVII Panzer Corps, General von Lüttwitz, paid grudging respect to the Hosingen defenders. After the war, he wrote:

The first resistance of the U.S. 28th Infantry Division was broken in a surprisingly short time, but then, after having overcome the first shock, they fought excellently. Again and again, at points well chosen, they put themselves in front of our advancing columns. A special mention must be made of the defenders of Hosingen. We were able to break the resistance in Hosingen only after the 78th Grenadier Regt of the 26th VGD had arrived on December 17. After Hosingen was taken, the enemy resistance paralyzed considerably. Summing up, I must point out that the resistance of the U.S. 28th Infantry Division was altogether more stubborn than I had expected.[15]

---

15 Vannoy, 214.

In the Epilogue to *Against the Panzers, United States Infantry versus German Tanks, 1944-1945*, authors Allyn R. Vannoy and Jay Karamales wrote:

> *The defense of Hosingen was a small part of the stand of the 28th Division in front of Bastogne. Other small units clung tenaciously to other small towns at places like Marnach, Heinerscheid, Weiler, Hoscheid, Holzthum, Consthum, Clervaux, and Wiltz. All of these towns fell to the German eventually, but one town the Americans did hold—Bastogne. The failure of the 5th Panzer Army to take this vital crossroads sealed the failure of the Ardennes offensive. And yet, the defense of Bastogne would never have happened had not small garrisons like Company K of the 110th Infantry Regiment and Company B of the 103rd Engineer Combat Battalion held on to towns like Hosingen.*

From *The FReeper Foxhole Remembers the 110th Infantry at the Bulge (12/16-19/1944)*, Dec 16, 2003. http://209.157.64.200/focus/f-vetscor/1041184/posts:

> *One of the great strongpoint actions which occurred is the town of Hosingen, Luxembourg, where "K" Company of the 110th Infantry Regiment and "B" company of the 103rd Engineer Battalion (Combat) fought for the better part of three days. This effort clearly helped save Bastogne, only eighteen miles to the west, and bought precious time for the Allies.*

Depicted in a Painting

There is a well-known painting, called "Hold to the Last Round," that depicts the town of Hosingen ablaze while K Company and B Company fight on. The description of the painting found at http://www.ozarkairfieldartworks.com/jamesdietz.htm, vividly describes the battle in Hosingen:

When the German offensive opened, however, the order was changed to "Hold at All Cost," and thus each of the strongpoints had to fight its own battle... This print was taken from the magnificent painting depicting one of the great strongpoint actions which occurred in the town of Hosingen, Luxembourg, where "K" Company of the 110th Infantry Regiment and "B" Company of the 103rd Engineer Battalion (Combat) fought for the better part of three days. Although surrounded and greatly outnumbered, the soldiers of these two units held their ground with only a reinforcement of five tanks from the 707th Tank Battalion reaching their position. In this defense, these brave men inflicted an estimated 2,000 casualties upon their attackers and totally upset the German timetable. The 28th Division soldiers fought to the last round and were then authorized to break into small groups and escape as best they could.

The gallant defense of Hosingen, which is depicted in this painting, like the action at the other strongpoints of the 28th Division, sacrificed men for time. This effort clearly helped save Bastogne, only eighteen miles to the west, and bought precious time for the Allies. The painting and the limited edition prints are dedicated to all the brave men of the 28th Division whose courage and sacrifice delayed the German advance and contributed greatly to the final outcome of the "Battle of the Bulge."

Memorial to the American Liberators in Hosingen, Luxembourg

http://www.ww2museums.com/article/5719/Memorial-American-Liberators-Hosingen.htm

The large memorial consists of two plaques on a stone monument in the town. On each side of this monument, there are two flagstones in the grass on which plaques have been mounted. The text on the red plaque at the monument reads:

"WWII American first army Defenders of Hosingen, Luxembourg "k" Company, 110th Infantry Regiment, 28th Division, Captured by German Forces December 18, 1944. Roll on 110."

and on the second plaque:

"Paratus In honor to the valiant men of B Company, 103rd Engineer Combat Battalion, 28th US Infantry Division who gallantly defended Hosingen from December 16 to 18, 1944."

Reference Books

Tom's account of the events in Hosingen, Luxembourg, during the Battle of the Bulge, part of the National Archives WWII Records Group 407, are used extensively in portraying K Company's role in the battle. Three of these well-known books on the battle are:

- *A Time for Trumpets—The Untold Story of the Battle of the Bulge* by Charles B. MacDonald
- *Hitler's Last Offensive—The Full Story of the Battle of the Ardennes* by Peter Elstob
- *Guard Wars: The 28th Infantry Division in World War II* by Michael E. Weaver

In addition, Tom is specifically mentioned and/or quoted in at least four books:

- *To Save Bastogne* by Robert F. Phillips
- *Alamo in the Ardennes—The Untold Story of the American Soldiers Who Made the Defense of Bastogne Possible* by John C. McManus
- *Against the Panzers, United States Infantry versus German Tanks, 1944-1945* by Allyn R. Vannoy and Jay Karamales
- *Hitler's Last Gamble—The Battle of the Bulge, December 1944-January 1945* by Trevor N. Dupuy, David L Bongard, and Richard C. Anderson, Jr.

Probably the most widely used narrative from Tom's interview is his description of the events at the beginning of the battle. He describes how his men from 1st Platoon in the water tower observation post called in to report seeing "pinpoints of light" to their commanding officer, Captain Feiker, just before 2,000 artillery shells fell on Hosingen and the surrounding area. You will note that even the keynote speech by Brigadier General Carlson, provided below, used the phrase in his description of the onset of battle.

Referenced or Quoted in Speeches

From the Battle of the Bulge Keynote Speech given by Brigadier Gen. William E. Carlson on April 1, 2003, (http://www.condonewsonline.com/carlson_speech.htm)

*A split-second after five thirty a.m., an American soldier in the 28th Division, manning an observation post high on top of a water tower in the village of Hosingen, frantically turned the crank on his field telephone. He reported to his Company Commander that in the distance on the German side he could see a strange phenomenon—countless flickering **pinpoints of light** piercing the darkness of the early morning fog and mist. Within a few seconds, both he and his Company Commander had an explanation. They were the muzzle flashes of over 2,000 German artillery pieces…The real story of the Battle of the Bulge is the story of these soldiers and the intense combat action of the small units—the squads, the platoons, and the companies, and the soldiers who filled their ranks…The battle was very personal for them. Concerned with the fearful and consuming task of fighting and staying alive, these men did not think of the battle in terms of the "Big Picture" represented on the situation maps at higher headquarters…For a brief moment in history, these men held our nation's destiny in their hands. They did not fail us. Theirs was the face of victory. Super heroes—super patriots. Their legacy—victory, victory in the greatest battle ever fought by the United States Army.*

Kimballton Fire Department Memorial

After Tom's death, the Kimballton Fire Department submitted the name of "Thomas J. Flynn" for placement on the granite memorial wall of the new Iowa Firefighters' Memorial that would be dedicated the following spring in Coralville, Iowa. After serving forty-one years with the fire department, twenty- seven years as fire chief, Tom had also earned the respect of many firefighters in the state. His name was accepted and engraved on the wall.

On April 10, 1994, Kimballton firefighter Mike Jensen and his wife drove Anna 200 miles to the dedication ceremony, where Joyce, John, and Pat joined them. It was a very touching sentiment and tribute to see Tom's name inscribed in the granite wall among hundreds of other fallen and departed Iowa firefighters. Notice of Tom's death and a brief biography were published in the original issue of the Iowa Firemen's Association newsletter in June 1994.

Photo: Iowa Firefighters' Memorial. Photo provided courtesy of Iowa Firefighters' Memorial.

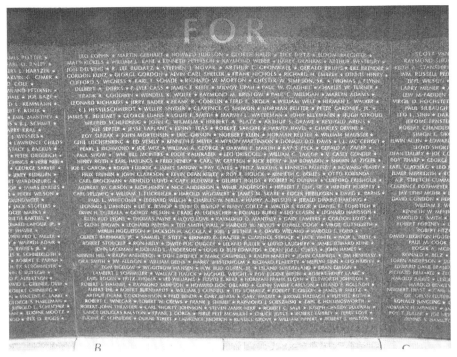

Photo: Iowa Firefighters' Memorial plaque. Tom's name is engraved at the far right of the 5th row. Photo provided courtesy of Iowa Firefighters' Memorial.

The Kimballton Fire Department has continued to serve Kimballton and the surrounding community, expanding and upgrading the department's equipment, facilities, and capabilities and is still considered one of the top volunteer fire departments in the state of Iowa.

The Volunteer firefighter roster is impressive, boasting over thirty members for the town of 300. There are still a handful of active members from Tom's tenure as chief. There is no doubt that Tom would be proud of them.

Reflections of Tom's Family

Education was very important to Tom and Anna and they expected their children to do well enough in high school to go on to college. Their attitude on the importance of education is evidenced by the fact that seven of Tom and Anna's children earned four-year college degrees. John went on to earn his law degree at the University of Iowa; Terry earned an M.B.A. at the University of Chicago; and Joan, a PhD in microbiology and immunology at Baylor College of Medicine. Bill spent four years in the United States Air Force in lieu of a four-year college education.

In addition, as of the writing of this book, all of Tom and Anna's adult grandchildren have completed a college education; ten earning four-year degrees and one earning a two-year degree at a technical college. Three are currently in college and one will start this fall as well as their eldest great-grandchild.

Grandchildren Missy and Brad both recognize their grandparents' influence on their career choices and their lives:

- Tom and Anna's close relationship with their oldest granddaughter, Missy, inspired her to complete both a B.A. in psychology and to become a registered nurse. She has also been a volunteer firefighter near Ames, Iowa, since 1997. Missy is proud to carry on the family traditions of both her maternal grandparents.
- Grandson Brad was ten years old at his grandfather Tom's funeral. Brad wrote about the experience in his medical school application:

While attending the funeral, I realized just how much of an impact one person can have on the lives of others. Kimballton has only about 300 residents, and nearly every one of them was in attendance that day, packing the small church. The reflective stories and anecdotes told at the service as well as the sheer number in attendance had a profound effect on me. One story recounted a fishing trip on which my grandfather came upon a woman huddled over her collapsed husband. My grandpa realized that the man had had a heart attack and was already dead. Nonetheless, concerned for the wife, he comforted her and performed CPR on the lifeless body for over forty-five minutes until paramedics could arrive. At the funeral, I realized that all those in attendance had been touched in a similar way at some point in their lives by my grandpa. This filled me with a sense of pride and admiration. I knew that I wanted to incorporate into my own life the qualities of his character that had permeated the lives of the people of Kimballton, such as compassion, selflessness, and dedication...

My grandpa's funeral made me realize how much I want to have an impact on the lives of other people. To this day, I keep a bullet casing from his twenty-one-gun salute in a special place in my room. My grandfather lived a life serving others as a father, soldier, veterinarian, and fireman. I want to have a similar effect, using my education, hard work, empathy, and compassion in the role of a physician. I get no greater fulfillment than knowing that someone appreciates what I have done for him or her. If I can improve the lives of even half as many people as my grandpa did, I will have lived a worthwhile life.

Brad is currently working on his anesthesiology residency in Kentucky.

* * *

In writing this book, I asked my brothers and sisters to share their memories of and thoughts about our father. It soon became apparent that Tom had developed a very special and unique relationship with each one of us, and I hope I have captured this in Part II of the book. I believe a summary of what my sister, Marg, shared with me sums up all of our perspectives:

With eight children, Dad and Mom may not have had much extra money but they provided their children everything they needed to grow to be successful in life. They set high expectations for earning good grades and pursuing a college education but at the same time, they respected each child's individuality and in their own way, let them pursue their own path in life without comparing them to their siblings (well, most of the time, anyway). And just as Dad and Mom both had done growing up, each child was expected to work when they could to help pay for the things they wanted and needed. Dad and Mom also felt giving back to the community was very important and they were dedicated to the selfless service of others. They both chose to lead by example and they exemplified what being a dedicated, patriotic, and community-minded citizen is all about.

I think this description applies to how both Dad and Mom raised us. They always encouraged us to try hard, to do our best, not to quit, and taught us that if we lived up to those ideals we had the potential to achieve many wonderful things. They lived a life based on hard work, strong principles, and service to others, while at the same time demonstrating the strength that arises from the deep love within a family. They instilled a strong sense of character in all of us, and for that I will be forever grateful and proud of both of them and of who I am!

Most importantly, I will always be thankful for the appreciation of nature that both Dad and Mom instilled in me. I love the beauty of flowers and the changing colors of the leaves. However, my deepest fondness comes when I hear the honks of the ducks or geese which frequently fly overhead. I never fail to think of Dad whenever I hear them and rush to see if I can spot where they are flying. Then I smile with a tear in my eyes, knowing how much he would love to see them, too.

* * *

Reflections of Tom's Friends

For most people, Kimballton is just a dot on the map in the southwest corner of a state that many people confuse with Ohio. Don't ask me why. But those who have a reason to know where Kimballton is on the IOWA map, or who have family there, will recognize the Flynn name. Some say Kimballton has never been the same since Tom passed away, and to this day, friends and acquaintances still stop the Flynn kids on the street to reminisce and share stories about their father when they come home to visit. There are always smiles on their faces and laughter in their hearts and voices, and they often say they can remember the conversation or story as if it were yesterday.

In recognition of what Tom meant to his family and friends, and of the numerous stories about who Tom was and what he meant to the people of Kimballton, how can this book be titled anything else but *Unforgettable*—an unforgettable story about an unforgettable man.

Capt. Thomas J. Flynn's Army Medals & Badges

Photo: Tom's Army medal display

Description of Medals and Badges and Inscriptions, Front and Back

Badges and medals earned by Capt. Thomas J. Flynn during his military service:

Top Row:
- **27ᵗʰ Infantry Division patch** (New York National Guard) at Fort McClellan in Alabama
- **28ᵗʰ Infantry Division (Pennsylvania National Guard), European Theater patch**
- **Army Ground Forces Replacement and Training Centers patch** at Weatherford, Texas

2ⁿᵈ Row:
- **Bronze Star**: "Heroic or Meritorious Achievement," *"Thomas J. Flynn"* is engraved on the back, in the center.
- **Combat Infantry Badge** (center cluster, top center)
- **Lapel Insignia** (center cluster, bottom left)
- **Captain bars** (center cluster, bottom center)
- **Crossed Rifle Infantry Insignia** (center cluster, bottom right)
- **Purple Heart with Oakleaf Cluster**: "For Military Merit"
  - The **Purple Heart** was awarded for a knee injury sustained as a result of being under direct enemy fire in the Battle of Hürtgen Forest.
  - The **Oakleaf Cluster** was awarded for a second injury during the course of direct contact with the German Army. (Not shown in the medal display above.)

3ʳᵈ Row:
- **MIA-POW Service Medal**: "For Honorable Service While a Prisoner of War"; "United States of America"
- **American Defense Service Medal**: "For Service during the limited emergency proclaimed by the President on May 27, 1941"
- **American Campaign Service Medal**

- **European-African-Middle Eastern Campaign Service Medal**: "United States of America 1941-1945"
- **WWII Victory Medal**: "World War II United States of America 1941-1945"; "Freedom from Fear and Want"; "Freedom of Speech and Religion"

4th Row:

- **Officer Candidate School—Infantry patch** at Fort Benning, Georgia
- **89th Infantry Division patch** at Camp Carson, Colorado Springs, Colorado
- **10th Mountain Infantry Division patch** at Camp Hale, Colorado

APPENDIX A

German Prisoner of War Experience, Route and Timeline as per 1st Lt. Thomas J. Flynn

28th Infantry Division, 110th Infantry Regiment, K Company was stationed in the town of Hosingen, Luxembourg, just four miles from the Siegfried Line. Bastogne, Belgium was eighteen miles to the rear.

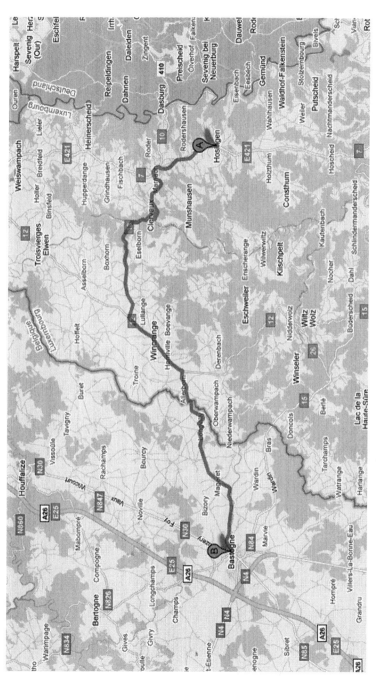

Map source: http://maps.google.com/maps

Hosingen, Luxembourg, to Eisenbach, Luxembourg (6.1 kilometers/3.8 miles)

On December 18, 1944, after 2½ days of battle, K Company and B Company Engineers surrendered to the German Army. That evening the POWs were marched to **Eisenbach, Luxembourg,** along the west bank of the Our River, where they were held overnight in a church.

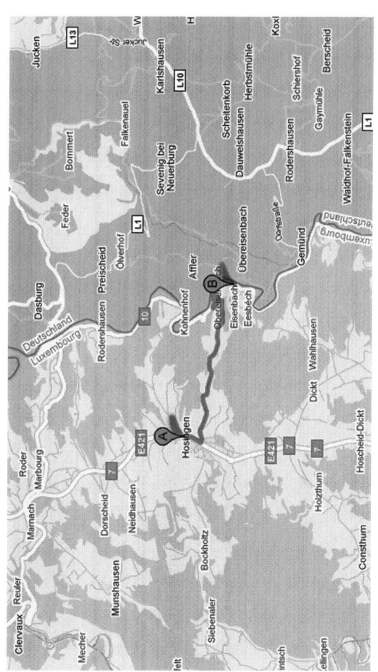

Map source: http://maps.google.com/maps

Eisenbach, Luxembourg, to Prum, Germany (39.9 kilometers/24.7 miles)

Starting on December 19, 1944, the POWs were marched from **Eisenbach, Luxembourg,** to **Prum, Germany**.

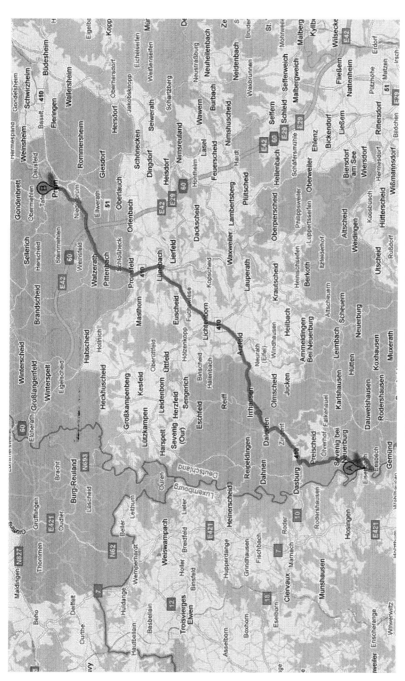

Map source: http://maps.google.com/maps

Prum, Germany, to Gerolstein, Germany (20.1 kilometers/12.5 miles)

Once they arrived at **Prum, Germany**, they were told the march would continue to **Gerolstein, Germany**. They were locked in an icehouse overnight in Prum, where they were joined by other POWs from the 110th Infantry Regiment who had been captured at other locations.

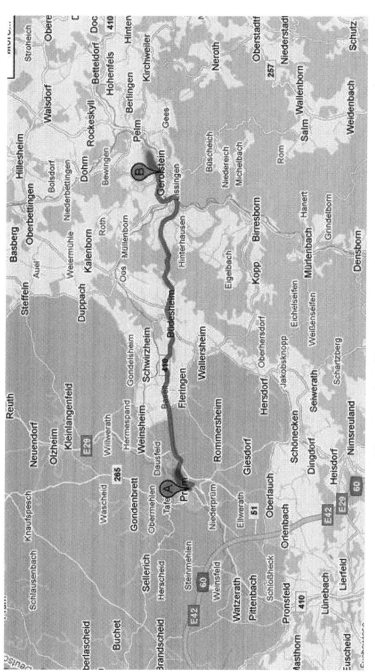

Map source: http://maps.google.com/maps

Gerolstein, Germany, to Frankfurt, Germany (237 kilometers/147 miles)

Once the prisoners reached **Gerolstein, Germany,** they were loaded into boxcars and shipped to **Frankfurt, Germany,** over the course of two days.

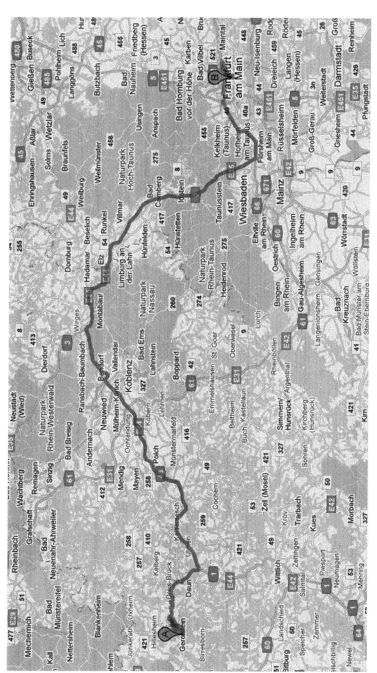

Map source: http://maps.google.com/maps

Frankfurt, Germany, to Stalag IXB at Bad Orb, Germany (57.4 kilometers/35.6 miles)

The Frankfurt marshalling yard was bombed by RAF on December 24, 1944. On December 26, the train left the marshalling yard for **Stalag IXB at Bad Orb, Germany**. Once all the POWs were processed, the officers were separated from the enlisted men.

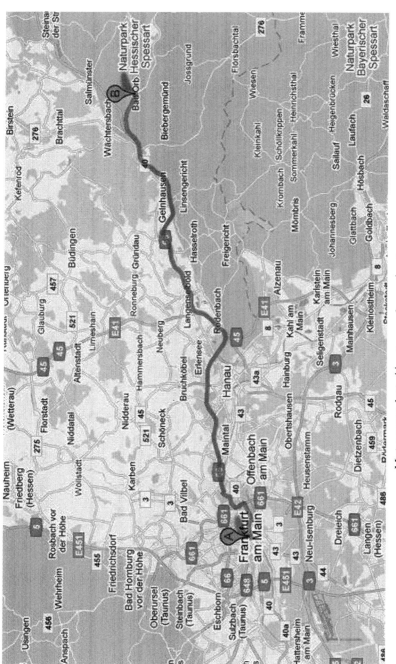

Map source: http://maps.google.com/maps

Bad Orb (Stalag IXB) to Hammelburg, Germany (Oflag 13B) (54.2 kilometers/33.7 miles)

Approximately two weeks after arriving at Stalag IXB, all officers in the camp were moved by train to Stalag 13B at Hammelburg on January 11 and 12, 1945.

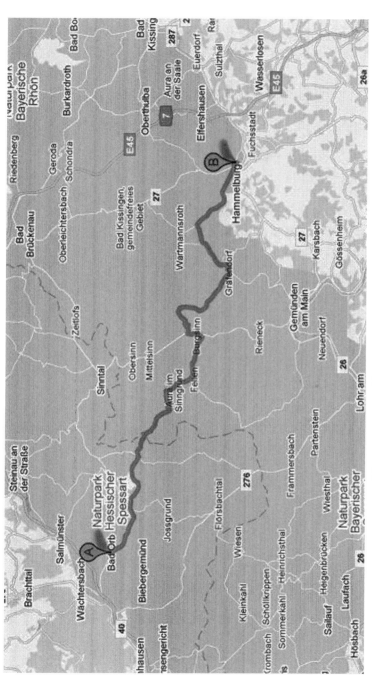

Map source: http://maps.google.com/maps

Hammelburg, Germany (Oflag 13B) to Gemunden, Germany (21.6 kilometers/13.4 miles)

Tom and the other officers remained at Stalag 13B for 2 1/2 months, until U.S. tanks broke through the German lines in an attempt to liberate the camp on March 27, 1945. Tom and several other officers left on their own to try to find their own way back to the American forces, as they knew from a number of sources that the Americans were moving deep into Germany by this time. They were recaptured on March 30, Good Friday, near Gemunden, Germany, and taken back to the Hammelburg POW camp.

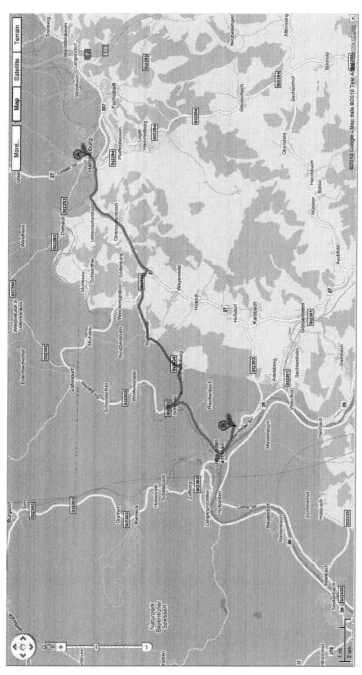

Map source: http://maps.google.com/maps

Hammelburg, Germany (Oflag 13B) to Nuremberg, Germany (Stalag Luft III) (155 kilometers/96 miles)

After their return to the Hammelburg camp, the POWs learned the camp was being evacuated and POWs were once again put on a train, this time headed for Nuremberg. Approximately 10 kilometers (6.2 miles) outside of Hammelburg, the unmarked train was strafed by an American P-51 and the men convinced the German soldiers that they would prefer to walk the rest of the way to Nuremberg (ninety miles) instead of taking their chances riding in an unmarked train. Once they finally arrived at Nuremberg, they were only there a few days when once again they were relocated by the Germans in an attempt to keep the POWs from being liberated by the advancing American Army.

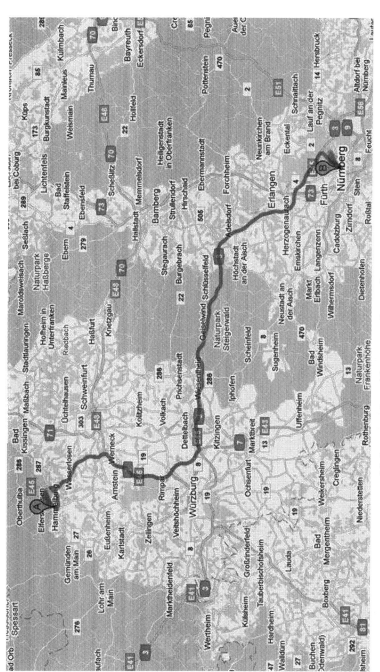

Map source: http://maps.google.com/maps

Nuremberg, Germany (Stalag Luft III) to Moosburg, Germany (Stalag VIIA) (152 kilometers /94.4 miles)

Tom and the other POWs were marched to Moosburg. They reached Moosburg around April 15, 1945. On April 29, 1945, at 1230 hours, US forces liberated the camp. At 1300 hours, the American flag was run up the flagpole. The following day, U.S. newspapers reported the number of POWs liberated from the Moosburg camp was 27,000 but retracted their report the next day after the army determined the number was closer to 110,000. There were men, women and children POWs from every nation that had been fighting the Germans. Stalag Luft III was the last Nazi POW camp to be liberated in Europe.

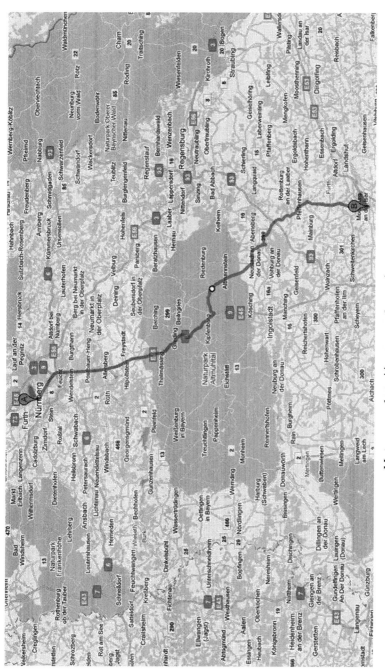

Map source: http://maps.google.com/maps

APPENDIX B

What Happened to the Men Mentioned in Chapter 5 Who Fought in Hosingen

Name & POW	Unit	Notes	Camp 1	Camp 2
Devlin, Charles F. * 25351	103	2nd Lt. Charles Devlin, 103B Eng., 3rd Platoon Died as Prisoner of War	Stalag 9B Bad Orb	Oflag 13B Hammelburg*
Feiker, Frederick C. * 25132	110	Capt. Frederick Feiker, CO, K Company Died as Prisoner of War outside Nuremberg	Stalag 9B Bad Orb	Oflag 13B Hammelburg*
Flynn, Thomas J. 25139	110	1st Lt. Thomas J. Flynn, executive officer, K Co.	Stalag 9B Bad Orb	Oflag 13B Hammelburg**
Hutter, Cary A. 25415	103	1st Lt. Cary Hutter, 103B Eng, 1st Platoon	Stalag 9B Bad Orb	Oflag 13B Hammelburg**
Morse, James D. 25550	110	1st Lt. James D. Morse, M Co, mortar section leader	Stalag 9B Bad Orb	Oflag 13B Hammelburg**
Payne, Robert A. 25515	707	Lt. Robert A. Payne, 707th Tank Battalion, A Co. Platoon leader	Stalag 9B Bad Orb	Oflag 13B Hammelburg**
Pickering, John A. 25352	103	2nd Lt. John Pickering, 103B Eng., 2nd Platoon	Stalag 9B Bad Orb	Oflag 13B Hammelburg**
Porter, Bernard U. 25324	110	1st Lt. Bernie Porter, K Company	Stalag 9B Bad Orb	Oflag 13B Hammelburg**
Arbella, James S.	110	Sgt. James Arbella, mortar section leader; K Company	Stalag 9B Bad Orb	
Cornell, Edwin H. J.	110	Pfc. Edwin Cornell, rifleman, K Company	Stalag 9B Bad Orb	
Epstein, Melvin	110	Pvt. Epstein, K Company, 1st Platoon gunner	Stalag 9B Bad Orb	
Gasper, Edward J.	110	Pfc. Edward Gasper, rifleman, K Co., 1st Platoon	Stalag 9B Bad Orb	

Name	No.	Description	Camp	
Williams, Donald K.	110	1st Sgt. Donald William, K Company, in room when decision was made to surrender	Stalag 9B Bad Orb	
Erickson, Wayne V	110	T/4, medic	Stalag 8A Gorlitz	Moosburg Murenberg) - Silesia 51-15
Forsell, John F.	110	Sgt. John F. Forsell, squad leader, K Company, 1st Platoon	Stalag 3B Furstenberg	
Jarrett, William H.	103	Capt. William H. Jarrett, CO, 103B Eng.	Stalag 4B Muhlberg	
Putz, John M.	103	T/5, John Putz, medic, captured when he went for medical supplies	Stalag 4B Muhlberg	
Smith, Franks S.	103	Pfc. Frank Smith, 103rd, captured when he went for medical supplies	Not Available	
Stevenson, George G.	103	Cpl. George G. Stevenson, 103B Eng.	Stalag 4B Muhlberg	
Tucker, Robert	110	T/4 Robert Tucker, medic, K Company	Stalag 4B Muhlberg	

Source: National Archives WWII POW database, Stalag 9B and Oflag 13B POW records

*Captain Feiker was killed by Allied bombing en route to Nuremberg Oflag Luft III POW camp

*Lt. Charles Devlin, who had been with the 103B Engineers in Hosingen, died while a prisoner of war.

**Tom and all but seventy-five POWs in Hammelburg were moved to Nuremberg Stalag Luft III and then Moosburg Stalag VIIA after the Americans temporarily liberated the Hammelburg Stalag XIIIB camp.

APPENDIX C

Getting Started on Your Own Research Project

During my quest to retrace my father's footsteps during WWII, I discovered that there are many others out there searching for the same thing: answers. All too often, these brave veterans who so proudly served our country had a very difficult time speaking about what happened during the war when they came home. As friends and family members, we just didn't think to ask what happened until it was too late and they were no longer with us.

While I am not a historian and I certainly could learn a lot from the professionals who do this every day, I believe the information that I present in this appendix will be helpful to people like me who are willing to invest a little time to understand the story behind that special veteran in their life.

Many people may not have the luck to discover as much detail as I was able to uncover on my father's story, but I believe that with some basic information on the veteran, with all the information posted on the internet, the willingness to commit some time to this worthwhile project, and most importantly, patience, researchers will find many resources that can help uncover at least the basic story to share with their families.

If you have access to and know how to use a computer, I would suggest creating a Word document to start documenting your research, as you will find it easier to edit an electronic file than to rewrite the story each time you uncover more information. The internet will be a critical, cost-effective tool in your research process and will allow you to work on your project when it fits your schedule and from the convenience of your own home.

Step 1: What You Know

Write down what you already know. Critical elements on this list may include:
- Complete full name
- Military rank
- Date of birth
- Time of service
- War or conflict, if applicable
- Unit(s) served in
- Countries and towns to which the unit was sent
- Battles fought in
- Time of captivity, if applicable
- State in which veteran lived at the time of enlistment or draft
- Significant details, events, names of friends or men in his unit, or stories that took place during time of enlistment

Step 2: What Do Others Know?

Now that you have identified what you already know, your next step is to reach out to other family members and friends for additional details, facts, and stories that your veteran may have shared with them. No detail is too frivolous to note, as it may be the piece that really ties a story together. An example of this was when I wrote about the officers of K Company in Hosingen trying to decide whether to try to escape or surrender on December 19, 1944, and my oldest sister, in just a general conversation about my work on this book, said, "I remember Dad told me it was his decision to surrender." To me, that provided an insightful, critical element to his story and that of the 300 men in Hosingen that possibly only she knew besides the men that were in the room.

Next, find out if there are any old letters, photos, or documents that anyone in the family may have saved. These things have a tendency to be spread out between family members with the death of a loved one as family members often want to have something physical they can look at or tuck away in a drawer to remember them by. You'd be surprised what may have been tucked away and forgotten about that may be a valuable piece of the puzzle or spark an interesting story. Don't be shy about reaching out to aunts, uncles, and cousins, and don't be shy about asking for copies of what you uncover. With all the computer technology available now, there isn't any reason why your family can't consolidate and share everything you collectively have, utilizing high-quality electronic files. Then no one has to feel left out.

If there are any medals, unit patches, or memorabilia from war that belongs or belonged to the veteran, ask if you can color copy or take close-up photos of them. Write down any inscriptions, front and back. You can look up many of these medals online to understand their significance. You also can order duplicate medals, if you are so inclined. The National Archives is one source that provides this service. They may not be the originals but you could have them to show and help tell the story you uncover.

If you are one of the lucky ones whose veteran is still alive, ask questions NOW. If your veteran is an older person who has trouble remembering details, discuss the facts that you have already uncovered to jog his memory on specific stories, rather than asking him to tell you about what happened. Be specific in your questions and get as many details as you can, including his thoughts and feelings as different events happened. Ask if he remembers the names of any commanding officers and buddies, and from when and where he remembers them. These names may prove helpful in your search because if you find these other names in books or online stories, the odds are that your veteran's situation was similar at that particular point in time.

Try to get the name of your veteran's regiment and company, as well has division. In my father's case, just knowing that he was with the 28th Infantry Division really didn't help me refine his story, since the three regiments that made up the 28th were scattered over a twenty-five-mile frontline during the Battle of the Bulge. Even breaking the 28th down to the regiment level, the 110th still covered thirteen miles of the frontline. Company-specific information will be very valuable in truly understanding exactly where he was and learning the stories that more closely reflect his situation. Please keep in mind that companies are typically denoted by a letter between A and M, so as you read the stories you will find many writers use nicknames for the company names, such as "Easy" Company for E Company.

I can't emphasize enough that knowing the division, regiment, and company to which your veteran was assigned will greatly increase your success in finding the level of detail I believe you are seeking. If you are having difficulty finding out this information from family members, all his military assignments and associated dates will be in his military files, which I discuss in Step 5.

Step 3: Write It Down

Now go back and write down the additional information you have uncovered and organize and label all the documents, photos, and records you have collected. It wouldn't hurt to ask the people who told you stories to read the draft of those passages to make sure you remembered and wrote them accurately. Sometimes, too, reading your account will remind them of more details. Try to keep the story in chronological order and provide dates or a general period to reference and refine throughout the research process.

Don't make the mistake of thinking you don't need to write the details down as you find them or note where you found them because "you know you won't forget." Odds are, you will forget or you won't remember details accurately and you will spend a lot of time trying to retrace your steps. Remember to utilize "Internet

Favorites" when you find a good Web site to which you may want to return later. Simple details will make the difference between an accurate account and an important, personal record of your veteran's experience. If you are going to go to all this effort, you might as well make sure your story will pass the scrutiny test of all the relatives who will be anxious to read what you've found.

Step 4: National Archives Military Records

Now that you have compiled some of the basic information, I suggest searching the National Archives Web site, which is a fairly comprehensive database of all military personnel and prisoner-of-war records from the Civil War to the present. The most critical information this site will provide is the serial number of the veteran, which will be important in requesting the veteran's files. (See Step 5.) The general link where you can browse by category is http://aad.archives.gov/aad/. The National Archives Web site address and format I discuss below may change over time, but the information they have made available should remain consistent and accessible.

Unfortunately, the level of detail on this site about each individual is minimal and there are frequent typos in the database. So if you don't find your veteran's name as you think it should be listed, try to broaden your search parameters by being less specific. For example, using a first initial only with the last name or just the initials and the state in which the veteran lived at the time of enlistment in the military.

Under the *Browse by Category* tab, you also can select the *Prisoner of War* option, if that is applicable to your veteran's story. Then select the specific database that you believe would be applicable. These records usually show the regiment to which an individual was assigned and typically one POW camp in which he was confined. In my father's case, the only POW camp listed was the first camp in which he was held—for ten days out of the 4½ months he was imprisoned. He was moved to three additional camps as the Germans tried to keep the American forces from liberating their officers.

Step 5: Accessing Your Veteran's Military Records

Due to the *Freedom of Information Act* (FOIA), spouses and next of kin have the legal right to receive copies of their veteran's personnel files. The serial number of the veteran that you obtained from the National Archives Web site will be important to use in your request for records. If you are diligent and patient, I'd recommend requesting the personnel files from both the National Personnel Center and your VA Regional Office. A number of items are identical in the two files, but there are enough differences that I would suggest requesting both. I found that each file also contained slightly different information that helped me build a detailed, accurate story.

For example, the National Personnel Center file had copies of the telegrams that were sent to my mother to notify her of my father's POW status as identified by the International Red Cross in two different POW camps and the notice of his liberation from the POW camp. The VA Regional Office file had all correspondence between my father and the VA, including a copy of his application for medical benefits, which provided detailed information on the POW camps at which he was held and details of his experience. Both files contained multiple forms that detailed all units with which he was associated (division, regiment, and company), all associated ranks with each unit, dates, places, and all military awards received. Any documents of relevance that I felt were important, I also scanned to easily share with my family, who were eager for information as well.

National Personnel Center

Spouses and next of kin may request records from the National Personnel Center, either through its Web site at http://www.archives.gov/veterans/evetrecs/index.html or by writing to the address below.

If you chose not to file your request electronically through the Web site, you can mail or fax your signed and dated request to the National Archives' National Personnel Record Center (NPRC). Most, but not all records, are stored at the NPRC.

Individuals not related to the veteran may also request records through the National Archives Web site. Instructions on this process and the SF-180 Form to complete are provided at the link referenced above.

Be sure to use the address specified by eVetRecs or the instructions on the SF-180.

National Personnel Records Center contact information:
National Personnel Records Center
Military Personnel Records
9700 Page Ave.
St Louis, MO, 63132-5100
Phone: 314-801-0800
Fax: 314-801-9195

Your request must contain certain basic information for staff to locate the requested service records. This information includes:

•The veteran's complete name used while in the service
•Service number (recommended but not required)
•Social security number
•Branch of service
•Dates of service
•Date and place of birth (especially if the service number is not known).
•All requests must be signed and dated by the veteran or next-of-kin.
•If you are the next of kin of a deceased veteran, you must provide proof of death of the veteran, such as a copy of death certificate, a letter from funeral home, or a published obituary.

To fulfill this last requirement, I was able to pull the copy of the Social Security Death Record for my dad on http://www.ancestry.com/ and I attached a copy of my birth certificate.

This is where the patience part comes in: It took seven months to receive this file. There is an e-mail address on the Web site that you can use to check on the status of your request after a reasonable period. I used it twice.

VA Regional Office

To request the Veteran Full "C" File, you will need to find your Regional VA Office and contact it directly. This request is based on where you live, not where the veteran may live or was living at the time of death.

Make sure the second line in the mailing address is "Attention: FOIA" and note you are requesting a "Veteran Full "C" File for {insert veteran's name}." Include in your letter identifying information so the staff can be sure they are accessing the correct individual's records.

> Example:
> {insert office name} Regional Office
> Attention: FOIA
> {insert Address}
> {insert Address}
> {insert City, State, Zip Code}
>
> Re: Request for Veteran Full "C" File for {insert veteran's name}
>
> Rank at discharge:
> Last unit served under:
> SSN:
> DOB:
> Deceased:

It only took three months to get this file.

Please note that these processes and the contact information for both organizations may change over time so I'd recommend you confirm the information before submitting your request. I have provided the above details so you will understand the general process at this time.

Step 6: Internet Research

While you are waiting to receive the veteran records, you can start your initial search with a more refined approach. Go back to the detailed information you have put together so far and start searching on the internet, utilizing key words that you know apply to your veteran's story; war, units, towns, names, battles, etc. I'd suggest trying all sorts of combinations of keyword searches, as different articles and Web sites will appear, depending on whether you spell out a word or phrase or abbreviate, and depending on the combination and order of keywords used. For example, try both "WWII" and "World War II." Again, more information will show up for broader keywords, such as using "28" rather than "28th" or "Inf" versus "Infantry." Company names are listed both ways, depending on the writer. I found references to both "K Company" and "Company K" and Company was often abbreviated as "Co".

The more you read and the more details you find, the more you can refine your search and with luck, discover the basic story of the unit to which your veteran belonged. Groups and individuals have created extensive Web sites dedicated to documenting and recognizing the contributions of our veterans in almost every scenario you can imagine. In addition, some people have accessed records from the National Archives and posted them on the internet for others to use, which I thought was very considerate and useful in my own research.

Google.com is my preferred search engine, and Google books http://books.google.com/ also was extremely helpful. This site allows you to search electronically the books that Google has scanned and will show you the pages that contain the key words in your search. This helps you identify whether a book is relevant to your research. That is how I found my dad's name in two of the books that were critical to my research. You can then read the selected pages and determine if the book is one you should buy. You can order the book directly from that site or go to another Web site that may ship to a large bookstore near your house where you can pick up the order, eliminating the delivery charge.

It also was interesting to incorporate Google maps http:// maps.google.com/maps?hl=en&tab=pl into my research. This Web site allowed me to determine distances between various locations, such as when my dad was forced to march from POW camp to POW camp, and the satellite feature helped me visualize the terrain discussed in the different stories I read.

Step 7: Source Material

Once you have found the relevant online resources and books, make sure you read all the reference materials the authors used in writing their books. There is nothing better than going back to original records or reports and reading them yourself. I caught several errors in other authors' writings and I believe they either misquoted or misinterpreted the original data, reports, or story to which they referred.

To read original records that are part of the National Archives records, you can send them a specific request. Once they find materials that they believe fit your search criteria, they will contact you and let you know what they have found and the cost to copy and mail it to you. The more specific you are, the more quickly they can respond and the less it will typically cost you. As records are archived at multiple locations, it would be advisable to call the phone number on the Web site and find out which specific location you need to contact for the records you are requesting.

After I received my father's VA files, I had the details I needed to request additional materials from the National Archives. An example of my request is below to assist you in your research process:

To National Archives Reference Branch Staff:

Records Request

Name:	*1ˢᵗ Lt. Thomas Joseph Flynn (Executive Officer)*
Unit:	*K Company, 110ᵗʰ Infantry Regiment, 28ᵗʰ Infantry Division*
Time Period:	*November 8-16, 1944*
WWII Battle:	*Hürtgen Forest Campaign*
Service Number:	*0 1285031*
Date of Birth:	*August 21, 1919*
Place of Birth:	*New York, New York*
Last unit served:	*28ᵗʰ Infantry Division*
Left the Service:	*Jan. 2, 1946*
Deceased:	*November 1993*

I am searching for any interviews that were conducted by Capt. John S. Howe and other 2ⁿᵈ Information and Historical Services staff from mid-November to mid-December 1944, covering the Hürtgen Forest Campaign and specific to or covering the period of November 8-16, 1944.

My father was in charge of K Company during that week as a new replacement officer, so stories specific to K Company, 110ᵗʰ Infantry Regiment, 28ᵗʰ Infantry Division, or stories that reference other 3ʳᵈ Battalion units may also be appropriate (Companies I, K, L, and M).

I have found references to these interviews as sourced below:

SOURCE: *National Archives and Records Administration, Record Group 407, Records of The Adjutant General, U.S. Army, Combat*

Interviews (CI-76), 28th Infantry Division, **Hürtgen Forest Campaign,** *Box 24032.*

SOURCE: *Exhibit B, History of the 110th Infantry APPENDIX, in National Archives and Records Administration, Record Group 407, Records of U.S. Army Adjutant General, World War II Records, 110th Infantry Regiment, 28th Infantry Division, History of the 110th Infantry Regiment, Box 8596.*

Please let me know a cost estimate and an estimate of how long it will take to provide what you find.

What I received with this request was the 3rd battalion report on this battle written by Capt. Howdy Rumbaugh. At $0.75 per page, this document cost less the $20 and took less a month to receive.

Step 8: Writing Your Story

Once you have received the National Personnel Center file and VA Regional Office file, you should be able to use the information and create an accurate timeline of dates, places, and events. It then is much easier to combine the stories, photos, and records shared by the veteran, family, and friends with the relevant material you found both online and in books, to write a unique, personalized version of the war that brings your veteran's story to life.

It won't be an easy or fast process. This book is the culmination of a year and a half of evenings and weekends spent researching and writing. It has also been an emotional and exciting journey for myself and my family and many a tear was shed as I uncovered the gruesome details of what my father went through during the war.

Whatever form your research project ultimately takes, I hope that you enjoy the process and feel a sense of fulfillment and accomplishment when you are done. I guarantee your family will appreciate your efforts and you will find satisfaction and pride knowing that your veteran's story will not be forgotten.

Bibliography

Books

Currey, Cecil B. *Follow Me and Die: The Destruction of an American Division in World War II. New York: Stein and Day, 1984.*

Goolrick, William K., and Ogden Tanner, *The Battle of the Bulge, World War II.* New York:Time-Life Books Inc., 1979.

McManus, John C. *Alamo in the Ardennes: The Untold Story of the American Soldiers Who Made the Defense of Bastogne Possible. New York: NAL Caliber, 2008.*

Phillips, Robert F. *To Save Bastogne,* Virginia: Borodino Books, 1996.

Vannoy, Robert F. and Jay Karamales, *Against the Panzers, United States Infantry versus German Tanks, 1944-1945.* North Carolina: McFarland & Company, Inc., 1996.

Whiting, Robert F. *The Battle of Hürtgen Forest. New York: Orion Books, 1989.*

Reports and Interviews

1st Lt. Thomas J. Flynn interview, K Company, 110th Infantry Regiment, 28th Infantry Division, National Archives, Record Group 407; May 1-2, 1945.

Col. Hurley E. Fuller *Unit Report No. 5–110th Infantry Regiment, 28th Infantry Division; 01Nov44-30Nov44,* Consthum, Luxembourg.

Capt. John S. Howe, interview with 3rd Battalion commander, Col. George H. Rumbaugh, 110th Infantry Regiment, 28th Infantry Division, December 15-16, 1944 at 3rd Battalion command post in

Consthum, Luxembourg. Part of National Archives and Records Administration, Record Group 407, Records of The Adjutant General, U.S. Army, Combat Interviews (CI-76), 28th Infantry Division, Hürtgen Forest Campaign.

International Red Cross Reports, Bad Orb-Stalag 9B and Hammelburg-Oflag XIIIB, prisoner of war camps, World War II, 1942-1945. Part of National Archives and Records Administration, Record Group 389.

Web sites

Army.com, *Enlist: Officer Candidate School*, http://www.army.com/enlist/officer-candidate-school.html (Dec. 29, 2009).

Axis History Forum, Hürtgen Forest, Factory of death, http://forum.axishistory.com/viewtopic.php?f=54&t=66893&start=30, (Dec. 29, 2009).

Battle of Hürtgen Forest, http://en.wikipedia.org/wiki/battle_of_h%C%BCrtgen_Forest, (Dec. 29, 2009).

Bradbeer, Thomas G. *Major General Cota and the Battle of the Hürtgen Forest: A Failure of Battle Command? http://usacac.army.mil/cac2/cgsc/repository/dcl_MGCota.pdf (Dec. 29, 2009).*

Ambrose, Stephen E. "Citizen Solders," http://members.aeroinc.net/breners/buckswar/forest.html, (Dec. 29, 2009).

Ethridge, Bill. *Time Out. A Remembrance of World War II*, http://www.moosburg.org/info/stalag/bilder/eth5.jpg (Jan. 12, 2010).

Christianson, Lt. Col. Thomas E., *The Destruction of the 28th Inf. Div. in the Huertgen Forest, Nov. 1944*, Scorpio's Web site, The Battle of the Hürtgen Forest, http://www.huertgenforest.be/ScoWeb.php (Dec. 29, 2009).

Department of the Navy, Naval Historical Center, *Online Library of Selected Images: Events, World War II in Europe Normandy Invasion, June 1944, Overview and Special Image Selection*, http://www.history.navy.mil/photos/events/wwii-eur/normandy/normandy.htm (Dec. 29, 2009).

Fact Sheet of the 28th Infantry Division, http://www.battleofthebulge.org/fact/fact_sheet_of_the_28th_infantry.html (Dec. 29, 2009).

Free Republic, LLC, *The FReeper Foxhole Remembers the 110th Infantry at the Bulge (12/16-19/1944) Dec 16, 2003*, http://209.157.64.200/focus/f-vetscor/1041184/posts (Dec. 29, 2009).

Google, *WWII German Panther tank footage*, http://video.google.com/videoplay?docid=3400216787641857936&ei=FPA_S4iQCZ WUqAPAtdnmDg&q=WWII+German+Panther+tank&hl=endoc id=7186358934547442029 (Jan. 2, 2010).

Holt, Major Jeffrey P. *Abstract of Thesis: The 28th Infantry Division in the 'Green Hell'*, Scorpio's Web site, The Battle of the Hürtgen Forest, http://www.huertgenforest.be/ScoWeb.php (Dec. 29, 2009).

LoneSentry.com, http://www.google.com/imgres?imgurl=http://www.lonesentry.com/articles/armoredforces/ (Jan. 2, 2010).

Lone Sentry.com, *Photographs of Stalag IX-B in Bad Orb, Germany*, http://www.lonesentry.com/badorb/index.html (Jan. 8, 2010).

Moosburg On-line, http://www.moosburg.org/info/stalag/bilder/ (Jan. 12, 2010).

Nideggen railroad siding, http://www.restlesswings.com/Documents/missioncals/TRs/December44/TR122444.pdf (Dec. 29, 2009).

Olive-Drab, *SCR-300 Backpack Radio*, http://www.olive-drab.com/od_electronics_scr300.php (Dec. 19, 2009).

Ozark Airfield Artworks, *Hold to the Last Round; The 28th Division in the Defense of Hosingen, Luxembourg, during the Battle of the Bulge*, http://www.ozarkairfieldartworks.com/jamesdietz.html (Jan. 2, 2010).

Popik, Barry. *The Big Apple: German Broadway or German Boulevard (East 86th Street in Yorkville)*, http://www.barrypopik.com/index.php/new_york_city/entry/german_broadway_or_german_boulevard_east_86th_street_in_yorkville/ (Dec. 29, 2009).

Scorpio's Web site, *The Battle of the Hürtgen Forest*, http://www.huertgenforest.be/ScoWeb.php (Dec. 29, 2009).

Strickler, Col. Daniel B. *110th Infantry Action Report of the German Ardennes Breakthrough, as I Saw It from 16 Dec. 1944 to 2 Jan. 1945,* http:// history.amedd.army.mil/booksdocs/wwii/bulge/110thInfRegt/ Strickler%20AAR%20Bulge.html (Dec. 29, 2009).

The Space Review: Lunar rovers past and future (page 1), http:// www.thespacereview.com/article/127/1, (Dec. 29, 2009).

United States Army Garrison, Fort McClellan, Alabama, *History of Fort McClellan 1917-1999,* http://www.mcclellan.army.mil/Info. asp (Dec. 29, 2009).

U.S. Army Medical Department Office of Medical History, *The Fight for the Hürtgen Forest,* http://history.amedd.army.mil/booksdocs/ wwii/HuertgenForest/HF.htm (Dec. 29, 2009).

U.S. Army photo. http://members.aeroinc.net/breners/buckswar/forest. html, (Dec. 29, 2009).

U.S. Army photo; http://members.aeroinc.net/breners/buckswar/kall. html, (Dec. 29, 2009).

Wikipedia, the free encyclopedia, *Post-WWII Sherman tanks,* http:// en.wikipedia.org/wiki/Post-WWII_Sherman_tanks (Jan. 2, 2010).

Wikipedia, the free encyclopedia, *World War II,* http:// en.wikipedia.org/wiki/World_War_II (Dec. 29, 2009).

Index

27317699R00193

Made in the USA
Lexington, KY
04 November 2013